Advanced Linux Programming

Conte

Advanced Linux Programming

Mark Mitchell, Jeffrey Oldham,
and Alex Samuel

www.newriders.com

201 West 103rd Street, Indianapolis, Indiana 46290
An Imprint of Pearson Education
Boston • Indianapolis • London • Munich • New York • San Francisco

Advanced Linux Programming

International Standard Book Number: 0-7357-1043-0

Library of Congress Catalog Card Number: *00-105343*

05 04 03 02 01   7 6 5 4 3 2 1

Interpretation of the printing code: The rightmost double-digit number is the year of the book's printing; the right-most single-digit number is the number of the book's printing. For example, the printing code 01-1 shows that the first printing of the book occurred in 2001.

Composed in Bembo and MCPdigital by New Riders Publishing.

Printed in the United States of America.

Trademarks

Warning and Disclaimer

Publisher
David Dwyer

Associate Publisher
Al Valvano

Executive Editor
Stephanie Wall

Managing Editor
Gina Brown

Acquisitions Editor
Ann Quinn

Development Editor
Laura Loveall

Product Marketing Manager
Stephanie Layton

Publicity Manager
Susan Petro

Project Editor
Caroline Wise

Copy Editor
Krista Hansing

Senior Indexer
Cheryl Lenser

Manufacturing Coordinator
Jim Conway

Book Designer
Louisa Klucznik

Cover Designer
Brainstorm Design, Inc.

Cover Production
Aren Howell

Proofreader
Debra Neel

Composition
Amy Parker

Table of Contents

Table of Program Listings

About the Authors

Mark Mitchell received a bachelor of arts degree in computer science from Harvard in 1994 and a master of science degree from Stanford in 1999. His research interests centered on computational complexity and computer security. Mark has participated substantially in the development of the GNU Compiler Collection, and he has a strong interest in developing quality software.

Jeffrey Oldham received a bachelor of arts degree in computer science from Rice University in 1991. After working at the Center for Research on Parallel Computation, he obtained a doctor of philosophy degree from Stanford in 2000. His research interests center on algorithm engineering, concentrating on flow and other combinatorial algorithms. He works on GCC and scientific computing software.

Alex Samuel graduated from Harvard in 1995 with a degree in physics. He worked as a software engineer at BBN before returning to study physics at Caltech and the Stanford Linear Accelerator Center. Alex administers the Software Carpentry project and works on various other projects, such as optimizations in GCC.

Mark and Alex founded **CodeSourcery LLC** together in 1999. Jeffrey joined the company in 2000. CodeSourcery's mission is to provide development tools for GNU/Linux and other operating systems; to make the GNU tool chain a commercial-quality, standards-conforming development tool set; and to provide general consulting and engineering services. CodeSourcery's Web site is http://www.codesourcery.com.

About the Technical Reviewers

These reviewers contributed their considerable hands-on expertise to the entire development process for *Advanced Linux Programming*. As the book was being written, these dedicated professionals reviewed all the material for technical content, organization, and flow. Their feedback was critical to ensuring that *Advanced Linux Programming* fits our reader's need for the highest quality technical information.

Glenn Becker has many degrees, all in theatre. He presently works as an online producer for SCIFI.COM, the online component of the SCI FI channel, in New York City. At home he runs Debian GNU/Linux and obsesses about such topics as system administration, security, software internationalization, and XML.

John Dean received a BSc(Hons) from the University of Sheffield in 1974, in pure science. As an undergraduate at Sheffield, John developed his interest in computing. In 1986 he received a MSc from Cranfield Institute of Science and Technology in Control Engineering. While working for Roll Royce and Associates, John became involved in developing control software for computer-aided inspection equipment of nuclear steam-raising plants. Since leaving RR&A in 1978, he has worked in the petrochemical industry developing and maintaining process control software. John worked a volunteer software developer for MySQL from 1996 until May 2000, when he joined MySQL as a full-time employee. John's area of responsibility is MySQL on MS Windows and developing a new MySQL GUI client using Trolltech's Qt GUI application toolkit on both Windows and platforms that run X-11.

Acknowledgments

We greatly appreciate the pioneering work of Richard Stallman, without whom there would never have been the GNU Project, and of Linus Torvalds, without whom there would never have been the Linux kernel. Countless others have worked on parts of the GNU/Linux operating system, and we thank them all.

We thank the faculties of Harvard and Rice for our undergraduate educations, and Caltech and Stanford for our graduate training. Without all who taught us, we would never have dared to teach others!

W. Richard Stevens wrote three excellent books on UNIX programming, and we have consulted them extensively. Roland McGrath, Ulrich Drepper, and many others wrote the GNU C library and its outstanding documentation.

Robert Brazile and Sam Kendall reviewed early outlines of this book and made wonderful suggestions about tone and content. Our technical editors and reviewers (especially Glenn Becker and John Dean) pointed out errors, made suggestions, and provided continuous encouragement. Of course, any errors that remain are no fault of theirs!

Thanks to Ann Quinn, of New Riders, for handling all the details involved in publishing a book; Laura Loveall, also of New Riders, for not letting us fall too far behind on our deadlines; and Stephanie Wall, also of New Riders, for encouraging us to write this book in the first place!

Tell Us What You Think

As the reader of this book, you are the most important critic and commentator. We value your opinion and want to know what we're doing right, what we could do better, what areas you'd like to see us publish in, and any other words of wisdom you're willing to pass our way.

As the Executive Editor for the Web Development team at New Riders Publishing, I welcome your comments. You can fax, email, or write me directly to let me know what you did or didn't like about this book—as well as what we can do to make our books stronger.

Please note that I cannot help you with technical problems related to the topic of this book, and that due to the high volume of mail I receive, I might not be able to reply to every message.

When you write, please be sure to include this book's title and author, as well as your name and phone or fax number. I will carefully review your comments and share them with the author and editors who worked on the book.

Fax:	317-581-4663
Email:	Stephanie.Wall@newriders.com
Mail:	Stephanie Wall
	Executive Editor
	New Riders Publishing
	201 West 103rd Street
	Indianapolis, IN 46290 USA

Introduction

GNU/Linux has taken the world of computers by storm. At one time, personal computer users were forced to choose among proprietary operating environments and applications. Users had no way of fixing or improving these programs, could not look "under the hood," and were often forced to accept restrictive licenses. GNU/Linux and other open source systems have changed that—now PC users, administrators, and developers can choose a free operating environment complete with tools, applications, and full source code.

A great deal of the success of GNU/Linux is owed to its open source nature. Because the source code for programs is publicly available, everyone can take part in development, whether by fixing a small bug or by developing and distributing a complete major application. This opportunity has enticed thousands of capable developers worldwide to contribute new components and improvements to GNU/Linux, to the point that modern GNU/Linux systems rival the features of any proprietary system, and distributions include thousands of programs and applications spanning many CD-ROMs or DVDs.

The success of GNU/Linux has also validated much of the UNIX philosophy. Many of the application programming interfaces (APIs) introduced in AT&T and BSD UNIX variants survive in Linux and form the foundation on which programs are built. The UNIX philosophy of many small command line-oriented programs working together is the organizational principle that makes GNU/Linux so powerful. Even when these programs are wrapped in easy-to-use graphical user interfaces, the underlying commands are still available for power users and automated scripts.

A powerful GNU/Linux application harnesses the power of these APIs and commands in its inner workings. GNU/Linux's APIs provide access to sophisticated features such as interprocess communication, multithreading, and high-performance networking. And many problems can be solved simply by assembling existing commands and programs using simple scripts.

GNU and Linux

Where did the name GNU/Liux come from? You've certainly heard of Linux before, and you may have heard of the GNU Project. You may not have heard the name GNU/Linux, although you're probably familiar with the system it refers to.

Linux is named after Linus Torvalds, the creator and original author of the *kernel* that runs a GNU/Linux system. The kernel is the program that performs the most basic functions of an operating system: It controls and interfaces with the computer's hardware, handles allocation of memory and other resources, allows multiple programs to run at the same time, manages the file system, and so on.

The kernel by itself doesn't provide features that are useful to users. It can't even provide a simple prompt for users to enter basic commands. It provides no way for users to manage or edit files, communicate with other computers, or write other programs. These tasks require the use of a wide array of other programs, including command shells, file utilities, editors, and compilers. Many of these programs, in turn, use libraries of general-purpose functions, such as the library containing standard C library functions, which are not included in the kernel.

On GNU/Linux systems, many of these other programs and libraries are software developed as part of the GNU Project.[1] A great deal of this software predates the Linux kernel. The aim of the GNU Project is "to develop a complete UNIX-like operating system which is free software" (from the GNU Project Web site, `http://www.gnu.org`).

The Linux kernel and software from the GNU Project has proven to be a powerful combination. Although the combination is often called "Linux" for short, the complete system couldn't work without GNU software, any more than it could operate without the kernel. For this reason, throughout this book we'll refer to the complete system as GNU/Linux, except when we are specifically talking about the Linux kernel.

The GNU General Public License

The source code contained in this book is covered by the GNU *General Public License* (*GPL*), which is listed in Appendix F, "GNU General Public License." A great deal of free software, especially GNU/Linux software, is licensed under it. For instance, the Linux kernel itself is licensed under the GPL, as are many other GNU programs and libraries you'll find in GNU/Linux distributions. If you use the source code in this book, be sure to read and understand the terms of the GPL.

The GNU Project Web site includes an extensive discussion of the GPL (`http://www.gnu.org/copyleft/`) and other free software licenses. You can find information about open source software licenses at `http://www.opensource.org/licenses/index.html`.

Who Should Read This Book?

This book is intended for three types of readers:

- You might be a developer already experienced with programming for the GNU/Linux system, and you want to learn about some of its advanced features and capabilities. You might be interested in writing more sophisticated programs with features such as multiprocessing, multithreading, interprocess communication, and interaction with hardware devices. You might want to improve your programs by making them run faster, more reliably, and more securely, or by designing them to interact better with the rest of the GNU/Linux system.

---

1. GNU is a recursive acronym: It stands for "GNU's Not UNIX."

- You might be a developer experienced with another UNIX-like system who's interested in developing GNU/Linux software, too. You might already be familiar with standard APIs such as those in the POSIX specification. To develop GNU/Linux software, you need to know the peculiarities of the system, its limitations, additional capabilities, and conventions.

- You might be a developer making the transition from a non-UNIX environment, such as Microsoft's Win32 platform. You might already be familiar with the general principles of writing good software, but you need to know the specific techniques that GNU/Linux programs use to interact with the system and with each other. And you want to make sure your programs fit naturally into the GNU/Linux system and behave as users expect them to.

This book is not intended to be a comprehensive guide or reference to all aspects of GNU/Linux programming. Instead, we'll take a tutorial approach, introducing the most important concepts and techniques, and giving examples of how to use them. Section 1.5, "Finding More Information," in Chapter 1, "Getting Started," contains references to additional documentation, where you can obtain complete details about these and other aspects of GNU/Linux programming.

Because this is a book about advanced topics, we'll assume that you are already familiar with the C programming language and that you know how to use the standard C library functions in your programs. The C language is the most widely used language for developing GNU/Linux software; most of the commands and libraries that we discuss in this book, and most of the Linux kernel itself, are written in C.

The information in this book is equally applicable to C++ programs because that language is roughly a superset of C. Even if you program in another language, you'll find this information useful because C language APIs and conventions are the *lingua franca* of GNU/Linux.

If you've programmed on another UNIX-like system platform before, chances are good that you already know your way around Linux's low-level I/O functions (open, read, stat, and so on). These are different from the standard C library's I/O functions (fopen, fprintf, fscanf, and so on). Both are useful in GNU/Linux programming, and we use both sets of I/O functions throughout this book. If you're not familiar with the low-level I/O functions, jump to the end of the book and read Appendix B, "Low-Level I/O," before you start Chapter 2, "Writing Good GNU/Linux Software."

This book does not provide a general introduction to GNU/Linux systems. We assume that you already have a basic knowledge of how to interact with a GNU/Linux system and perform basic operations in graphical and command-line environments. If you're new to GNU/Linux, start with one of the many excellent introductory books, such as Michael Tolber's *Inside Linux* (New Riders Publishing, 2001).

Conventions

This book follows a few typographical conventions:

- A new term is set in *italics* the first time it is introduced.

- Program text, functions, variables, and other "computer language" are set in a fixed-pitch font—for example, `printf ("Hello, world!\bksl n")`.

- Names of commands, files, and directories are also set in a fixed-pitch font—for example, `cd /`.

- When we show interactions with a command shell, we use `%` as the shell prompt (your shell is probably configured to use a different prompt). Everything after the prompt is what you type, while other lines of text are the system's response.

  For example, in this interaction

  ```
  % uname
  Linux
  ```

  the system prompted you with `%`. You entered the `uname` command. The system responded by printing `Linux`.

- The title of each source code listing includes a filename in parentheses. If you type in the listing, save it to a file by this name. You can also download the source code listings from the *Advanced Linux Programming* Web site (`http://www.newriders.com` or `http://www.advancedlinuxprogramming.com`).

We wrote this book and developed the programs listed in it using the Red Hat 6.2 distribution of GNU/Linux. This distribution incorporates release 2.2.14 of the Linux kernel, release 2.1.3 of the GNU C library, and the EGCS 1.1.2 release of the GNU C compiler. The information and programs in this book should generally be applicable to other versions and distributions of GNU/Linux as well, including 2.4 releases of the Linux kernel and 2.2 releases of the GNU C library.

I

Advanced UNIX Programming with Linux

1

Getting Started

THIS CHAPTER SHOWS YOU HOW TO PERFORM THE BASIC steps required to create a
C or C++ Linux program. In particular, this chapter shows you how to create and
modify C and C++ source code, compile that code, and debug the result. If you're
already accustomed to programming under Linux, you can skip ahead to Chapter 2,
"Writing Good GNU/Linux Software;" pay careful attention to Section 2.3, "Writing
and Using Libraries," for information about static versus dynamic linking that you
might not already know.

Throughout this book, we'll assume that you're familiar with the C or C++ programming languages and the most common functions in the standard C library. The
source code examples in this book are in C, except when demonstrating a particular
feature or complication of C++ programming. We also assume that you know how to
perform basic operations in the Linux command shell, such as creating directories and
copying files. Because many Linux programmers got started programming in the
Windows environment, we'll occasionally point out similarities and contrasts between
Windows and Linux.

1.1   Editing with Emacs

An *editor* is the program that you use to edit source code. Lots of different editors are available for Linux, but the most popular and full-featured editor is probably GNU Emacs.

> **About Emacs**
>
> Emacs is much more than an editor. It is an incredibly powerful program, so much so that at CodeSourcery, it is affectionately known as the One True Program, or just the OTP for short. You can read and send email from within Emacs, and you can customize and extend Emacs in ways far too numerous to discuss here. You can even browse the Web from within Emacs!

If you're familiar with another editor, you can certainly use it instead. Nothing in the rest of this book depends on using Emacs. If you don't already have a favorite Linux editor, then you should follow along with the mini-tutorial given here.

If you like Emacs and want to learn about its advanced features, you might consider reading one of the many Emacs books available. One excellent tutorial, *Learning GNU Emacs*, is written by Debra Cameron, Bill Rosenblatt, and Eric S. Raymond (O'Reilly, 1996).

1.1.1   Opening a C or C++ Source File

You can start Emacs by typing `emacs` in your terminal window and pressing the Return key. When Emacs has been started, you can use the menus at the top to create a new source file. Click the Files menu, choose Open Files, and then type the name of the file that you want to open in the "minibuffer" at the bottom of the screen.[1] If you want to create a C source file, use a filename that ends in `.c` or `.h`. If you want to create a C++ source file, use a filename that ends in `.cpp`, `.hpp`, `.cxx`, `.hxx`, `.C`, or `.H`. When the file is open, you can type as you would in any ordinary word-processing program. To save the file, choose the Save Buffer entry on the Files menu. When you're finished using Emacs, you can choose the Exit Emacs option on the Files menu.

If you don't like to point and click, you can use keyboard shortcuts to automatically open files, save files, and exit Emacs. To open a file, type `C-x C-f`. (The `C-x` means to hold down the Control key and then press the x key.) To save a file, type `C-x C-s`. To exit Emacs, just type `C-x C-c`. If you want to get a little better acquainted with Emacs, choose the Emacs Tutorial entry on the Help menu. The tutorial provides you with lots of tips on how to use Emacs effectively.

---

1. If you're not running in an X Window system, you'll have to press F10 to access the menus.

1.1.2   Automatic Formatting

If you're accustomed to programming in an *Integrated Development Environment (IDE)*, you'll also be accustomed to having the editor help you format your code. Emacs can provide the same kind of functionality. If you open a C or C++ source file, Emacs automatically figures out that the file contains source code, not just ordinary text. If you hit the Tab key on a blank line, Emacs moves the cursor to an appropriately indented point. If you hit the Tab key on a line that already contains some text, Emacs indents the text. So, for example, suppose that you have typed in the following:

```
int main ()
{
printf ("Hello, world\n");
}
```

If you press the Tab key on the line with the call to `printf`, Emacs will reformat your code to look like this:

```
int main ()
{
  printf ("Hello, world\n");
}
```

Notice how the line has been appropriately indented.

As you use Emacs more, you'll see how it can help you perform all kinds of complicated formatting tasks. If you're ambitious, you can program Emacs to perform literally any kind of automatic formatting you can imagine. People have used this facility to implement Emacs modes for editing just about every kind of document, to implement games[2], and to implement database front ends.

1.1.3   Syntax Highlighting

In addition to formatting your code, Emacs can make it easier to read C and C++ code by coloring different syntax elements. For example, Emacs can turn keywords one color, built-in types such as `int` another color, and comments another color. Using color makes it a lot easier to spot some common syntax errors.

The easiest way to turn on colorization is to edit the file `~/.emacs` and insert the following string:

```
(global-font-lock-mode t)
```

Save the file, exit Emacs, and restart. Now open a C or C++ source file and enjoy!

You might have noticed that the string you inserted into your `.emacs` looks like code from the LISP programming language. That's because it *is* LISP code! Much of Emacs is actually written in LISP. You can add functionality to Emacs by writing more LISP code.

---

2. Try running the command `M-x dunnet` if you want to play an old-fashioned text adventure game.

1.2   Compiling with GCC

A *compiler* turns human-readable source code into machine-readable object code that can actually run. The compilers of choice on Linux systems are all part of the GNU Compiler Collection, usually known as GCC.[3] GCC also include compilers for C, C++, Java, Objective-C, Fortran, and Chill. This book focuses mostly on C and C++ programming.

Suppose that you have a project like the one in Listing 1.2 with one C++ source file (reciprocal.cpp) and one C source file (main.c) like in Listing 1.1. These two files are supposed to be compiled and then linked together to produce a program called reciprocal.[4] This program will compute the reciprocal of an integer.

Listing 1.1   (*main.c*) **C source file—***main.c*

```
#include <stdio.h>
#include "reciprocal.hpp"

int main (int argc, char **argv)
{
  int i;

  i = atoi (argv[1]);
  printf ("The reciprocal of %d is %g\n", i, reciprocal (i));
  return 0;
}
```

Listing 1.2   (*reciprocal.cpp*) **C++ source file—***reciprocal.cpp*

```
#include <cassert>
#include "reciprocal.hpp"

double reciprocal (int i) {
  // I should be non-zero.
  assert (i != 0);
  return 1.0/i;
}
```

3. For more information about GCC, visit http://gcc.gnu.org.

4. In Windows, executables usually have names that end in .exe. Linux programs, on the other hand, usually have no extension. So, the Windows equivalent of this program would probably be called reciprocal.exe; the Linux version is just plain reciprocal.

There's also one header file called reciprocal.hpp (see Listing 1.3).

Listing 1.3   (*reciprocal.hpp*) **Header file—***reciprocal.hpp*

```
#ifdef __cplusplus
extern "C" {
#endif

extern  double reciprocal (int i);

#ifdef __cplusplus
}
#endif
```

The first step is to turn the C and C++ source code into object code.

1.2.1   Compiling a Single Source File

The name of the C compiler is gcc. To compile a C source file, you use the -c
option. So, for example, entering this at the command prompt compiles the main.c
source file:

```
% gcc -c main.c
```

The resulting object file is named main.o.

The C++ compiler is called g++. Its operation is very similar to gcc; compiling
reciprocal.cpp is accomplished by entering the following:

```
% g++ -c reciprocal.cpp
```

The -c option tells g++ to compile the program to an object file only; without it, g++
will attempt to link the program to produce an executable. After you've typed this
command, you'll have an object file called reciprocal.o.

You'll probably need a couple other options to build any reasonably large program.
The -I option is used to tell GCC where to search for header files. By default, GCC
looks in the current directory and in the directories where headers for the standard
libraries are installed. If you need to include header files from somewhere else, you'll
need the -I option. For example, suppose that your project has one directory called
src, for source files, and another called include. You would compile reciprocal.cpp
like this to indicate that g++ should use the ../include directory in addition to find
reciprocal.hpp:

```
% g++ -c -I ../include reciprocal.cpp
```

Sometimes you'll want to define macros on the command line. For example, in production code, you don't want the overhead of the assertion check present in reciprocal.cpp; that's only there to help you debug the program. You turn off the check by defining the macro NDEBUG. You could add an explicit #define to reciprocal.cpp, but that would require changing the source itself. It's easier to simply define NDEBUG on the command line, like this:

```
% g++ -c -D NDEBUG reciprocal.cpp
```

If you had wanted to define NDEBUG to some particular value, you could have done something like this:

```
% g++ -c -D NDEBUG=3 reciprocal.cpp
```

If you're really building production code, you probably want to have GCC optimize the code so that it runs as quickly as possible. You can do this by using the -O2 command-line option. (GCC has several different levels of optimization; the second level is appropriate for most programs.) For example, the following compiles reciprocal.cpp with optimization turned on:

```
% g++ -c -O2 reciprocal.cpp
```

Note that compiling with optimization can make your program more difficult to debug with a debugger (see Section 1.4, "Debugging with GDB"). Also, in certain instances, compiling with optimization can uncover bugs in your program that did not manifest themselves previously.

You can pass lots of other options to gcc and g++. The best way to get a complete list is to view the online documentation. You can do this by typing the following at your command prompt:

```
% info gcc
```

1.2.2   Linking Object Files

Now that you've compiled main.c and utilities.cpp, you'll want to link them. You should always use g++ to link a program that contains C++ code, even if it also contains C code. If your program contains only C code, you should use gcc instead. Because this program contains both C and C++, you should use g++, like this:

```
% g++ -o reciprocal main.o reciprocal.o
```

The -o option gives the name of the file to generate as output from the link step. Now you can run reciprocal like this:

```
% ./reciprocal 7
The reciprocal of 7 is 0.142857
```

As you can see, g++ has automatically linked in the standard C runtime library containing the implementation of printf. If you had needed to link in another library (such as a graphical user interface toolkit), you would have specified the library with the -l option. In Linux, library names almost always start with lib. For example, the Pluggable Authentication Module (PAM) library is called libpam.a. To link in libpam.a, you use a command like this:

```
% g++ -o reciprocal main.o reciprocal.o -lpam
```

The compiler automatically adds the lib prefix and the .a suffix.

As with header files, the linker looks for libraries in some standard places, including the /lib and /usr/lib directories that contain the standard system libraries. If you want the linker to search other directories as well, you should use the -L option, which is the parallel of the -I option discussed earlier. You can use this line to instruct the linker to look for libraries in the /usr/local/lib/pam directory before looking in the usual places:

```
% g++ -o reciprocal main.o reciprocal.o -L/usr/local/lib/pam -lpam
```

Although you don't have to use the -I option to get the preprocessor to search the current directory, you do have to use the -L option to get the linker to search the current directory. In particular, you could use the following to instruct the linker to find the test library in the current directory:

```
% gcc -o app app.o -L. -ltest
```

1.3   Automating the Process with GNU Make

If you're accustomed to programming for the Windows operating system, you're probably accustomed to working with an Integrated Development Environment (IDE). You add sources files to your project, and then the IDE builds your project automatically. Although IDEs are available for Linux, this book doesn't discuss them. Instead, this book shows you how to use GNU Make to automatically recompile your code, which is what most Linux programmers actually do.

The basic idea behind make is simple. You tell make what *targets* you want to build and then give *rules* explaining how to build them. You also specify *dependencies* that indicate when a particular target should be rebuilt.

In our sample reciprocal project, there are three obvious targets: reciprocal.o, main.o, and the reciprocal itself. You already have rules in mind for building these targets in the form of the command lines given previously. The dependencies require a little bit of thought. Clearly, reciprocal depends on reciprocal.o and main.o because you can't link the complete program until you have built each of the object files. The object files should be rebuilt whenever the corresponding source files change. There's one more twist in that a change to reciprocal.hpp also should cause both of the object files to be rebuilt because both source files include that header file.

In addition to the obvious targets, there should always be a clean target. This target removes all the generated object files and programs so that you can start fresh. The rule for this target uses the rm command to remove the files.

You can convey all that information to make by putting the information in a file named Makefile. Here's what Makefile contains:

```
reciprocal: main.o reciprocal.o
        g++ $(CFLAGS) -o reciprocal main.o reciprocal.o

main.o: main.c reciprocal.hpp
        gcc $(CFLAGS) -c main.c

reciprocal.o: reciprocal.cpp reciprocal.hpp
        g++ $(CFLAGS) -c reciprocal.cpp

clean:
        rm -f *.o reciprocal
```

You can see that targets are listed on the left, followed by a colon and then any dependencies. The rule to build that target is on the next line. (Ignore the $(CFLAGS) bit for the moment.) The line with the rule on it must start with a Tab character, or make will get confused. If you edit your Makefile in Emacs, Emacs will help you with the formatting.

If you remove the object files that you've already built, and just type

```
% make
```

on the command-line, you'll see the following:

```
% make
gcc -c main.c
g++ -c reciprocal.cpp
g++ -o reciprocal main.o reciprocal.o
```

You can see that make has automatically built the object files and then linked them. If you now change main.c in some trivial way and type make again, you'll see the following:

```
% make
gcc -c main.c
g++ -o reciprocal main.o reciprocal.o
```

You can see that make knew to rebuild main.o and to re-link the program, but it didn't bother to recompile reciprocal.cpp because none of the dependencies for reciprocal.o had changed.

The $(CFLAGS) is a make variable. You can define this variable either in the Makefile itself or on the command line. GNU make will substitute the value of the variable when it executes the rule. So, for example, to recompile with optimization enabled, you would do this:

```
% make clean
rm -f *.o reciprocal
% make CFLAGS=-O2
gcc -O2 -c main.c
g++ -O2 -c reciprocal.cpp
g++ -O2 -o reciprocal main.o reciprocal.o
```

Note that the -O2 flag was inserted in place of $(CFLAGS) in the rules.

In this section, you've seen only the most basic capabilities of make. You can find out more by typing this:

```
% info make
```

In that manual, you'll find information about how to make maintaining a Makefile easier, how to reduce the number of rules that you need to write, and how to automatically compute dependencies. You can also find more information in *GNU, Autoconf, Automake, and Libtool* by Gary V. Vaughan, Ben Elliston, Tom Tromey, and Ian Lance Taylor (New Riders Publishing, 2000).

1.4   Debugging with GNU Debugger (GDB)

The *debugger* is the program that you use to figure out why your program isn't behaving the way you think it should. You'll be doing this a lot.[5] The GNU Debugger (GDB) is the debugger used by most Linux programmers. You can use GDB to step through your code, set breakpoints, and examine the value of local variables.

1.4.1   Compiling with Debugging Information

To use GDB, you'll have to compile with debugging information enabled. Do this by adding the -g switch on the compilation command line. If you're using a Makefile as described previously, you can just set CFLAGS equal to -g when you run make, as shown here:

```
% make CFLAGS=-g
gcc -g -c main.c
g++ -g -c reciprocal.cpp
g++ -g -o reciprocal main.o reciprocal.o
```

When you compile with -g, the compiler includes extra information in the object files and executables. The debugger uses this information to figure out which addresses correspond to which lines in which source files, how to print out local variables, and so forth.

1.4.2   Running GDB

You can start up gdb by typing:

```
% gdb reciprocal
```

When gdb starts up, you should see the GDB prompt:

```
(gdb)
```

---

5. ...unless your programs always work the first time.

The first step is to run your program inside the debugger. Just enter the command run and any program arguments. Try running the program without any arguments, like this:

```
(gdb) run
Starting program: reciprocal

Program received signal SIGSEGV, Segmentation fault.
__strtol_internal (nptr=0x0, endptr=0x0, base=10, group=0)
at strtol.c:287
287      strtol.c: No such file or directory.
(gdb)
```

The problem is that there is no error-checking code in main. The program expects one argument, but in this case the program was run with no arguments. The SIGSEGV message indicates a program crash. GDB knows that the actual crash happened in a function called __strtol_internal. That function is in the standard library, and the source isn't installed, which explains the "No such file or directory" message. You can see the stack by using the where command:

```
(gdb) where
#0  __strtol_internal (nptr=0x0, endptr=0x0, base=10, group=0)
    at strtol.c:287
#1  0x40096fb6 in atoi (nptr=0x0) at ../stdlib/stdlib.h:251
#2  0x804863e in main (argc=1, argv=0xbffff5e4) at main.c:8
```

You can see from this display that main called the atoi function with a NULL pointer, which is the source of the trouble.

You can go up two levels in the stack until you reach main by using the up command:

```
(gdb) up 2
#2  0x804863e in main (argc=1, argv=0xbffff5e4) at main.c:8
8            i = atoi (argv[1]);
```

Note that gdb is capable of finding the source for main.c, and it shows the line where the erroneous function call occurred. You can view the value of variables using the print command:

```
(gdb) print argv[1]
$2 = 0x0
```

That confirms that the problem is indeed a NULL pointer passed into atoi.

You can set a breakpoint by using the break command:

```
(gdb) break main
Breakpoint 1 at 0x804862e: file main.c, line 8.
```

This command sets a breakpoint on the first line of main.[6] Now try rerunning the program with an argument, like this:

```
(gdb) run 7
Starting program: reciprocal 7

Breakpoint 1, main (argc=2, argv=0xbffff5e4) at main.c:8
8            i = atoi (argv[1]);
```

You can see that the debugger has stopped at the breakpoint.

You can step over the call to atoi using the next command:

```
(gdb) next
9                printf ("The reciprocal of %d is %g\n", i, reciprocal (i));
```

If you want to see what's going on inside reciprocal, use the step command like this:

```
(gdb) step
reciprocal (i=7) at reciprocal.cpp:6
6                assert (i != 0);
```

You're now in the body of the reciprocal function.

You might find it more convenient to run gdb from within Emacs rather than using gdb directly from the command line. Use the command M-x gdb to start up gdb in an Emacs window. If you are stopped at a breakpoint, Emacs automatically pulls up the appropriate source file. It's easier to figure out what's going on when you're looking at the whole file rather than just one line of text.

1.5   Finding More Information

Nearly every Linux distribution comes with a great deal of useful documentation. You could learn most of what we'll talk about in this book by reading documentation in your Linux distribution (although it would probably take you much longer). The documentation isn't always well-organized, though, so the tricky part is finding what you need. Documentation is also sometimes out-of-date, so take everything that you read with a grain of salt. If the system doesn't behave the way a *man page* (manual pages) says it should, for instance, it may be that the man page is outdated.

To help you navigate, here are the most useful sources of information about advanced Linux programming.

---

6. Some people have commented that saying break main is a little bit funny because usually you want to do this only when main is already broken.

1.5.1 Man Pages

Linux distributions include man pages for most standard commands, system calls, and standard library functions. The man pages are divided into numbered sections; for programmers, the most important are these:

(1) User commands

(2) System calls

(3) Standard library functions

(8) System/administrative commands

The numbers denote man page sections. Linux's man pages come installed on your system; use the man command to access them. To look up a man page, simply invoke man *name*, where *name* is a command or function name. In a few cases, the same name occurs in more than one section; you can specify the section explicitly by placing the section number before the name. For example, if you type the following, you'll get the man page for the sleep command (in section 1 of the Linux man pages):

```
% man sleep
```

To see the man page for the sleep library function, use this command:

```
% man 3 sleep
```

Each man page includes a one-line summary of the command or function. The whatis *name* command displays all man pages (in all sections) for a command or function matching *name*. If you're not sure which command or function you want, you can perform a keyword search on the summary lines, using man -k *keyword*.

Man pages include a lot of very useful information and should be the first place you turn for help. The man page for a command describes command-line options and arguments, input and output, error codes, configuration, and the like. The man page for a system call or library function describes parameters and return values, lists error codes and side effects, and specifies which include file to use if you call the function.

1.5.2 Info

The Info documentation system contains more detailed documentation for many core components of the GNU/Linux system, plus several other programs. Info pages are hypertext documents, similar to Web pages. To launch the text-based Info browser, just type info in a shell window. You'll be presented with a menu of Info documents installed on your system. (Press Control+H to display the keys for navigating an Info document.)

Among the most useful Info documents are these:

- gcc—The gcc compiler
- libc—The GNU C library, including many system calls
- gdb—The GNU debugger

- `emacs`—The Emacs text editor
- `info`—The Info system itself

Almost all the standard Linux programming tools (including `ld`, the linker; `as`, the assembler; and `gprof`, the profiler) come with useful Info pages. You can jump directly to a particular Info document by specifying the page name on the command line:

```
% info libc
```

If you do most of your programming in Emacs, you can access the built-in Info browser by typing `M-x info` or `C-h i`.

1.5.3 Header Files

You can learn a lot about the system functions that are available and how to use them by looking at the system header files. These reside in `/usr/include` and `/usr/include/sys`. If you are getting compile errors from using a system call, for instance, take a look in the corresponding header file to verify that the function's signature is the same as what's listed in the man page.

On Linux systems, a lot of the nitty-gritty details of how the system calls work are reflected in header files in the directories `/usr/include/bits`, `/usr/include/asm`, and `/usr/include/linux`. For instance, the numerical values of signals (described in Section 3.3, "Signals," in Chapter 3, "Processes") are defined in `/usr/include/bits/signum.h`. These header files make good reading for inquiring minds. Don't include them directly in your programs, though; always use the header files in `/usr/include` or as mentioned in the man page for the function you're using.

1.5.4 Source Code

This is Open Source, right? The final arbiter of how the system works is the system source code itself, and luckily for Linux programmers, that source code is freely available. Chances are, your Linux distribution includes full source code for the entire system and all programs included with it; if not, you're entitled under the terms of the GNU General Public License to request it from the distributor. (The source code might not be installed on your disk, though. See your distribution's documentation for instructions on installing it.)

The source code for the Linux kernel itself is usually stored under `/usr/src/linux`. If this book leaves you thirsting for details of how processes, shared memory, and system devices work, you can always learn straight from the source code. Most of the system functions described in this book are implemented in the GNU C library; check your distribution's documentation for the location of the C library source code.

2

Writing Good GNU/Linux Software

THIS CHAPTER COVERS SOME BASIC TECHNIQUES THAT MOST GNU/Linux programmers use. By following the guidelines presented, you'll be able to write programs that work well within the GNU/Linux environment and meet GNU/Linux users' expectations of how programs should operate.

2.1 Interaction With the Execution Environment

When you first studied C or C++, you learned that the special main function is the primary entry point for a program. When the operating system executes your program, it automatically provides certain facilities that help the program communicate with the operating system and the user. You probably learned about the two parameters to main, usually called argc and argv, which receive inputs to your program. You learned about the stdout and stdin (or the cout and cin streams in C++) that provide console input and output. These features are provided by the C and C++ languages, and they interact with the GNU/Linux system in certain ways. GNU/Linux provides other ways for interacting with the operating environment, too.

2.1.1   The Argument List

You run a program from a shell prompt by typing the name of the program.
Optionally, you can supply additional information to the program by typing one or
more words after the program name, separated by spaces. These are called *command-line
arguments*. (You can also include an argument that contains a space, by enclosing the
argument in quotes.) More generally, this is referred to as the program's *argument list*
because it need not originate from a shell command line. In Chapter 3, "Processes,"
you'll see another way of invoking a program, in which a program can specify the
argument list of another program directly.

When a program is invoked from the shell, the argument list contains the entire
command line, including the name of the program and any command-line arguments
that may have been provided. Suppose, for example, that you invoke the ls command
in your shell to display the contents of the root directory and corresponding file sizes
with this command line:

```
% ls -s /
```

The argument list that the ls program receives has three elements. The first one is the
name of the program itself, as specified on the command line, namely ls. The second
and third elements of the argument list are the two command-line arguments, -s and /.

The main function of your program can access the argument list via the argc and
argv parameters to main (if you don't use them, you may simply omit them). The first
parameter, argc, is an integer that is set to the number of items in the argument list.
The second parameter, argv, is an array of character pointers. The size of the array is
argc, and the array elements point to the elements of the argument list, as NUL-
terminated character strings.

Using command-line arguments is as easy as examining the contents of argc and
argv. If you're not interested in the name of the program itself, don't forget to skip the
first element.

Listing 2.1 demonstrates how to use argc and argv.

Listing 2.1   (*arglist.c*) Using *argc* and *argv*

```c
#include <stdio.h>

int main (int argc, char* argv[])
{
  printf ("The name of this program is '%s'.\n", argv[0]);
  printf ("This program was invoked with %d arguments.\n", argc - 1);

  /* Were any command-line arguments specified? */
  if (argc > 1) {
    /* Yes, print them. */
    int i;
    printf ("The arguments are:\n");
    for (i = 1; i < argc; ++i)
```

```
        printf (" %s\n", argv[i]);
    }

    return 0;
}
```

2.1.2 GNU/Linux Command-Line Conventions

Almost all GNU/Linux programs obey some conventions about how command-line arguments are interpreted. The arguments that programs expect fall into two categories: *options* (or *flags*) and other arguments. Options modify how the program behaves, while other arguments provide inputs (for instance, the names of input files).

Options come in two forms:

- *Short options* consist of a single hyphen and a single character (usually a lowercase or uppercase letter). Short options are quicker to type.

- *Long options* consist of two hyphens, followed by a name made of lowercase and uppercase letters and hyphens. Long options are easier to remember and easier to read (in shell scripts, for instance).

Usually, a program provides both a short form and a long form for most options it supports, the former for brevity and the latter for clarity. For example, most programs understand the options -h and --help, and treat them identically. Normally, when a program is invoked from the shell, any desired options follow the program name immediately. Some options expect an argument immediately following. Many programs, for example, interpret the option --output foo to specify that output of the program should be placed in a file named foo. After the options, there may follow other command-line arguments, typically input files or input data.

For example, the command ls -s / displays the contents of the root directory. The -s option modifies the default behavior of ls by instructing it to display the size (in kilobytes) of each entry. The / argument tells ls which directory to list. The --size option is synonymous with -s, so the same command could have been invoked as ls --size /.

The *GNU Coding Standards* list the names of some commonly used command-line options. If you plan to provide any options similar to these, it's a good idea to use the names specified in the coding standards. Your program will behave more like other programs and will be easier for users to learn. You can view the GNU Coding Standards' guidelines for command-line options by invoking the following from a shell prompt on most GNU/Linux systems:

```
% info "(standards)User Interfaces"
```

2.1.3   Using *getopt_long*

Parsing command-line options is a tedious chore. Luckily, the GNU C library provides a function that you can use in C and C++ programs to make this job somewhat easier (although still a bit annoying). This function, getopt_long, understands both short and long options. If you use this function, include the header file <getopt.h>.

Suppose, for example, that you are writing a program that is to accept the three options shown in Table 2.1.

Table 2.1   **Example Program Options**

Short Form	Long Form	Purpose
-h	--help	Display usage summary and exit
-o *filename*	--output *filename*	Specify output filename
-v	--verbose	Print verbose messages

In addition, the program is to accept zero or more additional command-line arguments, which are the names of input files.

To use getopt_long, you must provide two data structures. The first is a character string containing the valid short options, each a single letter. An option that requires an argument is followed by a colon. For your program, the string ho:v indicates that the valid options are -h, -o, and -v, with the second of these options followed by an argument.

To specify the available long options, you construct an array of struct option elements. Each element corresponds to one long option and has four fields. In normal circumstances, the first field is the name of the long option (as a character string, without the two hyphens); the second is 1 if the option takes an argument, or 0 otherwise; the third is NULL; and the fourth is a character constant specifying the short option synonym for that long option. The last element of the array should be all zeros. You could construct the array like this:

```
const struct option long_options[] = {
  { "help",    0, NULL, 'h' },
  { "output",  1, NULL, 'o' },
  { "verbose", 0, NULL, 'v' },
  { NULL,      0, NULL, 0   }
};
```

You invoke the getopt_long function, passing it the argc and argv arguments to main, the character string describing short options, and the array of struct option elements describing the long options.

- Each time you call getopt_long, it parses a single option, returning the short-option letter for that option, or −1 if no more options are found.

- Typically, you'll call getopt_long in a loop, to process all the options the user has specified, and you'll handle the specific options in a switch statement.

- If getopt_long encounters an invalid option (an option that you didn't specify as a valid short or long option), it prints an error message and returns the character ? (a question mark). Most programs will exit in response to this, possibly after displaying usage information.
- When handling an option that takes an argument, the global variable optarg points to the text of that argument.
- After getopt_long has finished parsing all the options, the global variable optind contains the index (into argv) of the first nonoption argument.

Listing 2.2 shows an example of how you might use getopt_long to process your arguments.

Listing 2.2   (*getopt_long.c*) **Using** *getopt_long*

```
#include <getopt.h>
#include <stdio.h>
#include <stdlib.h>

/* The name of this program.  */
const char* program_name;

/* Prints usage information for this program to STREAM (typically
   stdout or stderr), and exit the program with EXIT_CODE.  Does not
   return.  */

void print_usage (FILE* stream, int exit_code)
{
  fprintf (stream, "Usage:  %s options [ inputfile ... ]\n", program_name);
  fprintf (stream,
           "  -h  --help             Display this usage information.\n"
           "  -o  --output filename  Write output to file.\n"
           "  -v  --verbose          Print verbose messages.\n");
  exit (exit_code);
}

/* Main program entry point.  ARGC contains number of argument list
   elements; ARGV is an array of pointers to them.  */

int main (int argc, char* argv[])
{
  int next_option;

  /* A string listing valid short options letters.  */
  const char* const short_options = "ho:v";
  /* An array describing valid long options.  */
  const struct option long_options[] = {
    { "help",    0, NULL, 'h' },
    { "output",  1, NULL, 'o' },
    { "verbose", 0, NULL, 'v' },
```

continues

Listing 2.2 **Continued**

```
  { NULL,       0, NULL, 0   }   /* Required at end of array.  */
};

/* The name of the file to receive program output, or NULL for
   standard output.  */
const char* output_filename = NULL;
/* Whether to display verbose messages.  */
int verbose = 0;

/* Remember the name of the program, to incorporate in messages.
   The name is stored in argv[0].  */
program_name = argv[0];

do {
  next_option = getopt_long (argc, argv, short_options,
                             long_options, NULL);
  switch (next_option)
  {
  case 'h':   /* -h or --help */
    /* User has requested usage information.  Print it to standard
       output, and exit with exit code zero (normal termination).  */
    print_usage (stdout, 0);

  case 'o':   /* -o or --output */
    /* This option takes an argument, the name of the output file.  */
    output_filename = optarg;
    break;

  case 'v':   /* -v or  --verbose */
    verbose = 1;
    break;

  case '?':   /* The user specified an invalid option.  */
    /* Print usage information to standard error, and exit with exit
       code one (indicating abnormal termination).  */
    print_usage (stderr, 1);

  case -1:    /* Done with options.  */
    break;

  default:    /* Something else: unexpected.  */
    abort ();
  }
}
while (next_option != -1);

/* Done with options.  OPTIND points to first nonoption argument.
   For demonstration purposes, print them if the verbose option was
   specified.  */
```

```
    if (verbose) {
      int i;
      for (i = optind; i < argc; ++i)
        printf ("Argument: %s\n", argv[i]);
    }

    /* The main program goes here.  */

    return 0;
  }
```

Using `getopt_long` may seem like a lot of work, but writing code to parse the command-line options yourself would take even longer. The `getopt_long` function is very sophisticated and allows great flexibility in specifying what kind of options to accept. However, it's a good idea to stay away from the more advanced features and stick with the basic option structure described.

2.1.4 Standard I/O

The standard C library provides standard input and output streams (`stdin` and `stdout`, respectively). These are used by `scanf`, `printf`, and other library functions. In the UNIX tradition, use of standard input and output is customary for GNU/Linux programs. This allows the chaining of multiple programs using shell pipes and input and output redirection. (See the man page for your shell to learn its syntax.)

The C library also provides `stderr`, the standard error stream. Programs should print warning and error messages to standard error instead of standard output. This allows users to separate normal output and error messages, for instance, by redirecting standard output to a file while allowing standard error to print on the console. The `fprintf` function can be used to print to `stderr`, for example:

```
fprintf (stderr, ("Error: ..."));
```

These three streams are also accessible with the underlying UNIX I/O commands (`read`, `write`, and so on) via file descriptors. These are file descriptors 0 for `stdin`, 1 for `stdout`, and 2 for `stderr`.

When invoking a program, it is sometimes useful to redirect both standard output and standard error to a file or pipe. The syntax for doing this varies among shells; for Bourne-style shells (including `bash`, the default shell on most GNU/Linux distributions), the syntax is this:

```
% program > output_file.txt 2>&1
% program 2>&1 | filter
```

The 2>&1 syntax indicates that file descriptor 2 (`stderr`) should be merged into file descriptor 1 (`stdout`). Note that 2>&1 must follow a file redirection (the first example) but must precede a pipe redirection (the second example).

Note that stdout is buffered. Data written to stdout is not sent to the console (or other device, if it's redirected) until the buffer fills, the program exits normally, or stdout is closed. You can explicitly flush the buffer by calling the following:

```
fflush (stdout);
```

In contrast, stderr is not buffered; data written to stderr goes directly to the console.[1]

This can produce some surprising results. For example, this loop does not print one period every second; instead, the periods are buffered, and a bunch of them are printed together when the buffer fills.

```
while (1) {
  printf (".");
  sleep (1);
}
```

In this loop, however, the periods do appear once a second:

```
while (1) {
  fprintf (stderr, ".");
  sleep (1);
}
```

2.1.5   Program Exit Codes

When a program ends, it indicates its status with an exit code. The exit code is a small integer; by convention, an exit code of zero denotes successful execution, while nonzero exit codes indicate that an error occurred. Some programs use different nonzero exit code values to distinguish specific errors.

With most shells, it's possible to obtain the exit code of the most recently executed program using the special $? variable. Here's an example in which the ls command is invoked twice and its exit code is printed after each invocation. In the first case, ls executes correctly and returns the exit code zero. In the second case, ls encounters an error (because the filename specified on the command line does not exist) and thus returns a nonzero exit code.

```
% ls /
bin   coda  etc   lib          misc  nfs  proc  sbin  usr
boot  dev   home  lost+found   mnt   opt  root  tmp   var
% echo $?
0
% ls bogusfile
ls: bogusfile: No such file or directory
% echo $?
1
```

1. In C++, the same distinction holds for cout and cerr, respectively. Note that the endl token flushes a stream in addition to printing a newline character; if you don't want to flush the stream (for performance reasons, for example), use a newline constant, '\n', instead.

A C or C++ program specifies its exit code by returning that value from the `main` function. There are other methods of providing exit codes, and special exit codes are assigned to programs that terminate abnormally (by a signal). These are discussed further in Chapter 3.

2.1.6   The Environment

GNU/Linux provides each running program with an *environment*. The environment is a collection of variable/value pairs. Both environment variable names and their values are character strings. By convention, environment variable names are spelled in all capital letters.

You're probably familiar with several common environment variables already. For instance:

- `USER` contains your username.
- `HOME` contains the path to your home directory.
- `PATH` contains a colon-separated list of directories through which Linux searches for commands you invoke.
- `DISPLAY` contains the name and display number of the X Window server on which windows from graphical X Window programs will appear.

Your shell, like any other program, has an environment. Shells provide methods for examining and modifying the environment directly. To print the current environment in your shell, invoke the `printenv` program. Various shells have different built-in syntax for using environment variables; the following is the syntax for Bourne-style shells.

- The shell automatically creates a shell variable for each environment variable that it finds, so you can access environment variable values using the `$varname` syntax. For instance:

  ```
  % echo $USER
  samuel
  % echo $HOME
  /home/samuel
  ```

- You can use the `export` command to export a shell variable into the environment. For example, to set the `EDITOR` environment variable, you would use this:

  ```
  % EDITOR=emacs
  % export EDITOR
  ```

  Or, for short:

  ```
  % export EDITOR=emacs
  ```

In a program, you access an environment variable with the `getenv` function in `<stdlib.h>`. That function takes a variable name and returns the corresponding value as a character string, or `NULL` if that variable is not defined in the environment. To set or clear environment variables, use the `setenv` and `unsetenv` functions, respectively.

Enumerating all the variables in the environment is a little trickier. To do this, you must access a special global variable named `environ`, which is defined in the GNU C library. This variable, of type `char**`, is a `NULL`-terminated array of pointers to character strings. Each string contains one environment variable, in the form `VARIABLE=value`.

The program in Listing 2.3, for instance, simply prints the entire environment by looping through the `environ` array.

Listing 2.3 (*print-env.c*) **Printing the Execution Environment**

```
#include <stdio.h>

/* The ENVIRON variable contains the environment.  */
extern char** environ;

int main ()
{
  char** var;
  for (var = environ; *var != NULL; ++var)
    printf ("%s\n", *var);
  return 0;
}
```

Don't modify `environ` yourself; use the `setenv` and `unsetenv` functions instead.

Usually, when a new program is started, it inherits a copy of the environment of the program that invoked it (the shell program, if it was invoked interactively). So, for instance, programs that you run from the shell may examine the values of environment variables that you set in the shell.

Environment variables are commonly used to communicate configuration information to programs. Suppose, for example, that you are writing a program that connects to an Internet server to obtain some information. You could write the program so that the server name is specified on the command line. However, suppose that the server name is not something that users will change very often. You can use a special environment variable—say `SERVER_NAME`—to specify the server name; if that variable doesn't exist, a default value is used. Part of your program might look as shown in Listing 2.4.

Listing 2.4 (*client.c*) **Part of a Network Client Program**

```
#include <stdio.h>
#include <stdlib.h>

int main ()
{
```

```
    char* server_name = getenv ("SERVER_NAME");
    if (server_name == NULL)
      /* The SERVER_NAME environment variable was not set.  Use the
         default.  */
      server_name = "server.my-company.com";

    printf ("accessing server %s\n", server_name);
    /* Access the server here...  */

    return 0;
  }
```

Suppose that this program is named `client`. Assuming that you haven't set the `SERVER_NAME` variable, the default value for the server name is used:

```
% client
accessing server server.my-company.com
```

But it's easy to specify a different server:

```
% export SERVER_NAME=backup-server.elsewhere.net
% client
accessing server backup-server.elsewhere.net
```

2.1.7 Using Temporary Files

Sometimes a program needs to make a temporary file, to store large data for a while or to pass data to another program. On GNU/Linux systems, temporary files are stored in the `/tmp` directory. When using temporary files, you should be aware of the following pitfalls:

- More than one instance of your program may be run simultaneously (by the same user or by different users). The instances should use different temporary filenames so that they don't collide.

- The file permissions of the temporary file should be set in such a way that unauthorized users cannot alter the program's execution by modifying or replacing the temporary file.

- Temporary filenames should be generated in a way that cannot be predicted externally; otherwise, an attacker can exploit the delay between testing whether a given name is already in use and opening a new temporary file.

GNU/Linux provides functions, `mkstemp` and `tmpfile`, that take care of these issues for you (in addition to several functions that don't). Which you use depends on whether you plan to hand the temporary file to another program, and whether you want to use UNIX I/O (`open`, `write`, and so on) or the C library's stream I/O functions (`fopen`, `fprintf`, and so on).

Using *mkstemp*

The `mkstemp` function creates a unique temporary filename from a filename template, creates the file with permissions so that only the current user can access it, and opens the file for read/write. The filename template is a character string ending with "XXXXXX" (six capital X's); `mkstemp` replaces the X's with characters so that the filename is unique. The return value is a file descriptor; use the `write` family of functions to write to the temporary file.

Temporary files created with `mkstemp` are not deleted automatically. It's up to you to remove the temporary file when it's no longer needed. (Programmers should be very careful to clean up temporary files; otherwise, the /tmp file system will fill up eventually, rendering the system inoperable.) If the temporary file is for internal use only and won't be handed to another program, it's a good idea to call `unlink` on the temporary file immediately. The `unlink` function removes the directory entry corresponding to a file, but because files in a file system are reference-counted, the file itself is not removed until there are no open file descriptors for that file, either. This way, your program may continue to use the temporary file, and the file goes away automatically as soon as you close the file descriptor. Because Linux closes file descriptors when a program ends, the temporary file will be removed even if your program terminates abnormally.

The pair of functions in Listing 2.5 demonstrates `mkstemp`. Used together, these functions make it easy to write a memory buffer to a temporary file (so that memory can be freed or reused) and then read it back later.

Listing 2.5   (*temp_file.c*) Using *mkstemp*

```c
#include <stdlib.h>
#include <unistd.h>

/* A handle for a temporary file created with write_temp_file.  In
   this implementation, it's just a file descriptor.  */
typedef int temp_file_handle;

/* Writes LENGTH bytes from BUFFER into a temporary file.  The
   temporary file is immediately unlinked.  Returns a handle to the
   temporary file.  */

temp_file_handle write_temp_file (char* buffer, size_t length)
{
  /* Create the filename and file.  The XXXXXX will be replaced with
     characters that make the filename unique.  */
  char temp_filename[] = "/tmp/temp_file.XXXXXX";
  int fd = mkstemp (temp_filename);
  /* Unlink the file immediately, so that it will be removed when the
     file descriptor is closed.  */
  unlink (temp_filename);
  /* Write the number of bytes to the file first.  */
  write (fd, &length, sizeof (length));
```

```
  /* Now write the data itself.  */
  write (fd, buffer, length);
  /* Use the file descriptor as the handle for the temporary file.  */
  return fd;
}
```

```
/* Reads the contents of a temporary file TEMP_FILE created with
   write_temp_file.  The return value is a newly allocated buffer of
   those contents, which the caller must deallocate with free.
   *LENGTH is set to the size of the contents, in bytes.  The
   temporary file is removed.  */

char* read_temp_file (temp_file_handle temp_file, size_t* length)
{
  char* buffer;
  /* The TEMP_FILE handle is a file descriptor to the temporary file.  */
  int fd = temp_file;
  /* Rewind to the beginning of the file.  */
  lseek (fd, 0, SEEK_SET);
  /* Read the size of the data in the temporary file.  */
  read (fd, length, sizeof (*length));
  /* Allocate a buffer and read the data.  */
  buffer = (char*) malloc (*length);
  read (fd, buffer, *length);
  /* Close the file descriptor, which will cause the temporary file to
     go away.  */
  close (fd);
  return buffer;
}
```

Using *tmpfile*

If you are using the C library I/O functions and don't need to pass the temporary file to another program, you can use the `tmpfile` function. This creates and opens a temporary file, and returns a file pointer to it. The temporary file is already unlinked, as in the previous example, so it is deleted automatically when the file pointer is closed (with `fclose`) or when the program terminates.

GNU/Linux provides several other functions for generating temporary files and temporary filenames, including `mktemp`, `tmpnam`, and `tempnam`. Don't use these functions, though, because they suffer from the reliability and security problems already mentioned.

2.2   Coding Defensively

Writing programs that run correctly under "normal" use is hard; writing programs that behave gracefully in failure situations is harder. This section demonstrates some coding techniques for finding bugs early and for detecting and recovering from problems in a running program.

The code samples presented later in this book deliberately skip extensive error checking and recovery code because this would obscure the basic functionality being presented. However, the final example in Chapter 11, "A Sample GNU/Linux Application," comes back to demonstrating how to use these techniques to write robust programs.

2.2.1   Using *assert*

A good objective to keep in mind when coding application programs is that bugs or unexpected errors should cause the program to fail dramatically, as early as possible. This will help you find bugs earlier in the development and testing cycles. Failures that don't exhibit themselves dramatically are often missed and don't show up until the application is in users' hands.

One of the simplest methods to check for unexpected conditions is the standard C assert macro. The argument to this macro is a Boolean expression. The program is terminated if the expression evaluates to false, after printing an error message containing the source file and line number and the text of the expression. The assert macro is very useful for a wide variety of consistency checks internal to a program. For instance, use assert to test the validity of function arguments, to test preconditions and postconditions of function calls (and method calls, in C++), and to test for unexpected return values.

Each use of assert serves not only as a runtime check of a condition, but also as documentation about the program's operation within the source code. If your program contains an assert (*condition*) that says to someone reading your source code that *condition* should always be true at that point in the program, and if *condition* is not true, it's probably a bug in the program.

For performance-critical code, runtime checks such as uses of assert can impose a significant performance penalty. In these cases, you can compile your code with the NDEBUG macro defined, by using the -DNDEBUG flag on your compiler command line. With NDEBUG set, appearances of the assert macro will be preprocessed away. It's a good idea to do this only when necessary for performance reasons, though, and only with performance-critical source files.

Because it is possible to preprocess assert macros away, be careful that any expression you use with assert has no side effects. Specifically, you shouldn't call functions inside assert expressions, assign variables, or use modifying operators such as ++.

Suppose, for example, that you call a function, `do_something`, repeatedly in a loop. The `do_something` function returns zero on success and nonzero on failure, but you don't expect it ever to fail in your program. You might be tempted to write:

```
for (i = 0; i < 100; ++i)
  assert (do_something () == 0);
```

However, you might find that this runtime check imposes too large a performance penalty and decide later to recompile with `NDEBUG` defined. This will remove the `assert` call entirely, so the expression will never be evaluated and `do_something` will never be called. You should write this instead:

```
for (i = 0; i < 100; ++i) {
  int status = do_something ();
  assert (status == 0);
}
```

Another thing to bear in mind is that you should not use `assert` to test for invalid user input. Users don't like it when applications simply crash with a cryptic error message, even in response to invalid input. You should still always check for invalid input and produce sensible error messages in response input. Use `assert` for internal runtime checks only.

Some good places to use `assert` are these:

- Check against null pointers, for instance, as invalid function arguments. The error message generated by {`assert (pointer != NULL)`},

  ```
  Assertion 'pointer != ((void *)0)' failed.
  ```

  is more informative than the error message that would result if your program dereferenced a null pointer:

  ```
  Segmentation fault (core dumped)
  ```

- Check conditions on function parameter values. For instance, if a function should be called only with a positive value for parameter `foo`, use this at the beginning of the function body:

  ```
  assert (foo > 0);
  ```

  This will help you detect misuses of the function, and it also makes it very clear to someone reading the function's source code that there is a restriction on the parameter's value.

Don't hold back; use `assert` liberally throughout your programs.

2.2.2   System Call Failures

Most of us were originally taught how to write programs that execute to completion along a well-defined path. We divide the program into tasks and subtasks, and each function completes a task by invoking other functions to perform corresponding subtasks. Given appropriate inputs, we expect a function to produce the correct output and side effects.

The realities of computer hardware and software intrude into this idealized dream. Computers have limited resources; hardware fails; many programs execute at the same time; users and programmers make mistakes. It's often at the boundary between the application and the operating system that these realities exhibit themselves. Therefore, when using system calls to access system resources, to perform I/O, or for other purposes, it's important to understand not only what happens when the call succeeds, but also how and when the call can fail.

System calls can fail in many ways. For example:

- The system can run out of resources (or the program can exceed the resource limits enforced by the system of a single program). For example, the program might try to allocate too much memory, to write too much to a disk, or to open too many files at the same time.

- Linux may block a certain system call when a program attempts to perform an operation for which it does not have permission. For example, a program might attempt to write to a file marked read-only, to access the memory of another process, or to kill another user's program.

- The arguments to a system call might be invalid, either because the user provided invalid input or because of a program bug. For instance, the program might pass an invalid memory address or an invalid file descriptor to a system call. Or, a program might attempt to open a directory as an ordinary file, or might pass the name of an ordinary file to a system call that expects a directory.

- A system call can fail for reasons external to a program. This happens most often when a system call accesses a hardware device. The device might be faulty or might not support a particular operation, or perhaps a disk is not inserted in the drive.

- A system call can sometimes be interrupted by an external event, such as the delivery of a signal. This might not indicate outright failure, but it is the responsibility of the calling program to restart the system call, if desired.

In a well-written program that makes extensive use of system calls, it is often the case that more code is devoted to detecting and handling errors and other exceptional circumstances than to the main work of the program.

2.2.3 Error Codes from System Calls

A majority of system calls return zero if the operation succeeds, or a nonzero value if the operation fails. (Many, though, have different return value conventions; for instance, malloc returns a null pointer to indicate failure. Always read the man page carefully when using a system call.) Although this information may be enough to determine whether the program should continue execution as usual, it probably does not provide enough information for a sensible recovery from errors.

Most system calls use a special variable named errno to store additional information in case of failure.[2] When a call fails, the system sets errno to a value indicating what went wrong. Because all system calls use the same errno variable to store error information, you should copy the value into another variable immediately after the failed call. The value of errno will be overwritten the next time you make a system call.

Error values are integers; possible values are given by preprocessor macros, by convention named in all capitals and starting with "E"—for example, EACCES and EINVAL. Always use these macros to refer to errno values rather than integer values. Include the <errno.h> header if you use errno values.

GNU/Linux provides a convenient function, strerror, that returns a character string description of an errno error code, suitable for use in error messages. Include <string.h> if you use strerror.

GNU/Linux also provides perror, which prints the error description directly to the stderr stream. Pass to perror a character string prefix to print before the error description, which should usually include the name of the function that failed. Include <stdio.h> if you use perror.

This code fragment attempts to open a file; if the open fails, it prints an error message and exits the program. Note that the open call returns an open file descriptor if the open operation succeeds, or −1 if the operation fails.

```
fd = open ("inputfile.txt", O_RDONLY);
if (fd == -1) {
  /* The open failed.  Print an error message and exit.  */
  fprintf (stderr, "error opening file: %s\n", strerror (errno));
  exit (1);
}
```

Depending on your program and the nature of the system call, the appropriate action in case of failure might be to print an error message, to cancel an operation, to abort the program, to try again, or even to ignore the error. It's important, though, to include logic that handles all possible failure modes in some way or another.

---

2. Actually, for reasons of thread safety, errno is implemented as a macro, but it is used like a global variable.

One possible error code that you should be on the watch for, especially with I/O functions, is `EINTR`. Some functions, such as `read`, `select`, and `sleep`, can take significant time to execute. These are considered *blocking* functions because program execution is blocked until the call is completed. However, if the program receives a signal while blocked in one of these calls, the call will return without completing the operation. In this case, errno is set to `EINTR`. Usually, you'll want to retry the system call in this case.

Here's a code fragment that uses the `chown` call to change the owner of a file given by `path` to the user by `user_id`. If the call fails, the program takes action depending on the value of errno. Notice that when we detect what's probably a bug in the program, we exit using `abort` or `assert`, which cause a core file to be generated. This can be useful for post-mortem debugging. For other unrecoverable errors, such as out-of-memory conditions, we exit using `exit` and a nonzero exit value instead because a core file wouldn't be very useful.

```
rval = chown (path, user_id, -1);
if (rval != 0) {
  /* Save errno because it's clobbered by the next system call. */
  int error_code = errno;
  /* The operation didn't succeed; chown should return -1 on error. */
  assert (rval == -1);
  /* Check the value of errno, and take appropriate action. */
  switch (error_code) {
  case EPERM:         /* Permission denied. */
  case EROFS:         /* PATH is on a read-only file system. */
  case ENAMETOOLONG:  /* PATH is too long. */
  case ENOENT:        /* PATH does not exit. */
  case ENOTDIR:       /* A component of PATH is not a directory. */
  case EACCES:        /* A component of PATH is not accessible. */
    /* Something's wrong with the file.  Print an error message. */
    fprintf (stderr, "error changing ownership of %s: %s\n",
             path, strerror (error_code));
    /* Don't end the program; perhaps give the user a chance to
       choose another file... */
    break;

  case EFAULT:
    /* PATH contains an invalid memory address.  This is probably a bug. */
    abort ();

  case ENOMEM:
    /* Ran out of kernel memory. */
    fprintf (stderr, "%s\n", strerror (error_code));
    exit (1);

  default:
    /* Some other, unexpected, error code.  We've tried to handle all
       possible error codes; if we've missed one, that's a bug! */
    abort ();
  };
}
```

You could simply have used this code, which behaves the same way if the call succeeds:

```
rval = chown (path, user_id, -1);
assert (rval == 0);
```

But if the call fails, this alternative makes no effort to report, handle, or recover from errors.

Whether you use the first form, the second form, or something in between depends on the error detection and recovery requirements for your program.

2.2.4   Errors and Resource Allocation

Often, when a system call fails, it's appropriate to cancel the current operation but not to terminate the program because it may be possible to recover from the error. One way to do this is to return from the current function, passing a return code to the caller indicating the error.

If you decide to return from the middle of a function, it's important to make sure that any resources successfully allocated previously in the function are first deallocated. These resources can include memory, file descriptors, file pointers, temporary files, synchronization objects, and so on. Otherwise, if your program continues running, the resources allocated before the failure occurred will be leaked.

Consider, for example, a function that reads from a file into a buffer. The function might follow these steps:

1. Allocate the buffer.
2. Open the file.
3. Read from the file into the buffer.
4. Close the file.
5. Return the buffer.

If the file doesn't exist, Step 2 will fail. An appropriate course of action might be to return NULL from the function. However, if the buffer has already been allocated in Step 1, there is a risk of leaking that memory. You must remember to deallocate the buffer somewhere along any flow of control from which you don't return. If Step 3 fails, not only must you deallocate the buffer before returning, but you also must close the file.

Listing 2.6 shows an example of how you might write this function.

Listing 2.6   (*readfile.c*) **Freeing Resources During Abnormal Conditions**

```
#include <fcntl.h>
#include <stdlib.h>
#include <sys/stat.h>
#include <sys/types.h>
#include <unistd.h>
```

continues

Listing 2.6 **Continued**

```
char* read_from_file (const char* filename, size_t length)
{
  char* buffer;
  int fd;
  ssize_t bytes_read;

  /* Allocate the buffer.  */
  buffer = (char*) malloc (length);
  if (buffer == NULL)
    return NULL;
  /* Open the file.  */
  fd = open (filename, O_RDONLY);
  if (fd == -1) {
    /* open failed.  Deallocate buffer before returning.  */
    free (buffer);
    return NULL;
  }
  /* Read the data.  */
  bytes_read = read (fd, buffer, length);
  if (bytes_read != length) {
    /* read failed.  Deallocate buffer and close fd before returning.  */
    free (buffer);
    close (fd);
    return NULL;
  }
  /* Everything's fine.  Close the file and return the buffer.  */
  close (fd);
  return buffer;
}
```

Linux cleans up allocated memory, open files, and most other resources when a program terminates, so it's not necessary to deallocate buffers and close files before calling exit. You might need to manually free other shared resources, however, such as temporary files and shared memory, which can potentially outlive a program.

2.3 Writing and Using Libraries

Virtually all programs are linked against one or more libraries. Any program that uses a C function (such as printf or malloc) will be linked against the C runtime library. If your program has a graphical user interface (GUI), it will be linked against windowing libraries. If your program uses a database, the database provider will give you libraries that you can use to access the database conveniently.

In each of these cases, you must decide whether to link the library *statically* or *dynamically*. If you choose to link statically, your programs will be bigger and harder to upgrade, but probably easier to deploy. If you link dynamically, your programs will be smaller, easier to upgrade, but harder to deploy. This section explains how to link both statically and dynamically, examines the trade-offs in more detail, and gives some "rules of thumb" for deciding which kind of linking is better for you.

2.3.1   Archives

An *archive* (or static library) is simply a collection of object files stored as a single file. (An archive is roughly the equivalent of a Windows .LIB file.) When you provide an archive to the linker, the linker searches the archive for the object files it needs, extracts them, and links them into your program much as if you had provided those object files directly.

You can create an archive using the ar command. Archive files traditionally use a .a extension rather than the .o extension used by ordinary object files. Here's how you would combine test1.o and test2.o into a single libtest.a archive:

```
% ar cr libtest.a test1.o test2.o
```

The cr flags tell ar to create the archive.[3] Now you can link with this archive using the -ltest option with gcc or g++, as described in Section 1.2.2, "Linking Object Files," in Chapter 1, "Getting Started."

When the linker encounters an archive on the command line, it searches the archive for all definitions of symbols (functions or variables) that are referenced from the object files that it has already processed but not yet defined. The object files that define those symbols are extracted from the archive and included in the final executable. Because the linker searches the archive when it is encountered on the command line, it usually makes sense to put archives at the end of the command line. For example, suppose that test.c contains the code in Listing 2.7 and app.c contains the code in Listing 2.8.

Listing 2.7   (*test.c*) **Library Contents**

```
int f ()
{
  return 3;
}
```

Listing 2.8   (*app.c*) **A Program That Uses Library Functions**

```
int main ()
{
  return f ();
}
```

3. You can use other flags to remove a file from an archive or to perform other operations on the archive. These operations are rarely used but are documented on the ar man page.

Now suppose that `test.o` is combined with some other object files to produce the `libtest.a` archive. The following command line will not work:

```
% gcc -o app -L. -ltest app.o
app.o: In function 'main':
app.o(.text+0x4): undefined reference to 'f'
collect2: ld returned 1 exit status
```

The error message indicates that even though `libtest.a` contains a definition of `f`, the linker did not find it. That's because `libtest.a` was searched when it was first encountered, and at that point the linker hadn't seen any references to `f`.

On the other hand, if we use this line, no error messages are issued:

```
% gcc -o app app.o -L. –ltest
```

The reason is that the reference to `f` in `app.o` causes the linker to include the `test.o` object file from the `libtest.a` archive.

2.3.2   Shared Libraries

A *shared library* (also known as a shared object, or as a dynamically linked library) is similar to a archive in that it is a grouping of object files. However, there are many important differences. The most fundamental difference is that when a shared library is linked into a program, the final executable does not actually contain the code that is present in the shared library. Instead, the executable merely contains a reference to the shared library. If several programs on the system are linked against the same shared library, they will all reference the library, but none will actually be included. Thus, the library is "shared" among all the programs that link with it.

A second important difference is that a shared library is not merely a collection of object files, out of which the linker chooses those that are needed to satisfy undefined references. Instead, the object files that compose the shared library are combined into a single object file so that a program that links against a shared library always includes all of the code in the library, rather than just those portions that are needed.

To create a shared library, you must compile the objects that will make up the library using the `-fPIC` option to the compiler, like this:

```
% gcc -c -fPIC test1.c
```

The `-fPIC` option tells the compiler that you are going to be using `test.o` as part of a shared object.

> **Position–Independent Code (PIC)**
>
> PIC stands for position-independent code. The functions in a shared library may be loaded at different addresses in different programs, so the code in the shared object must not depend on the address (or position) at which it is loaded. This consideration has no impact on you, as the programmer, except that you must remember to use the `-fPIC` flag when compiling code that will be used in a shared library.

Then you combine the object files into a shared library, like this:

```
% gcc -shared -fPIC -o libtest.so test1.o test2.o
```

The -shared option tells the linker to produce a shared library rather than an ordinary executable. Shared libraries use the extension .so, which stands for shared object. Like static archives, the name always begins with lib to indicate that the file is a library.

Linking with a shared library is just like linking with a static archive. For example, the following line will link with libtest.so if it is in the current directory, or one of the standard library search directories on the system:

```
% gcc -o app app.o -L. -ltest
```

Suppose that both libtest.a and libtest.so are available. Then the linker must choose one of the libraries and not the other. The linker searches each directory (first those specified with -L options, and then those in the standard directories). When the linker finds a directory that contains either libtest.a or libtest.so, the linker stops search directories. If only one of the two variants is present in the directory, the linker chooses that variant. Otherwise, the linker chooses the shared library version, unless you explicitly instruct it otherwise. You can use the -static option to demand static archives. For example, the following line will use the libtest.a archive, even if the libtest.so shared library is also available:

```
% gcc -static -o app app.o -L. -ltest
```

The ldd command displays the shared libraries that are linked into an executable. These libraries need to be available when the executable is run. Note that ldd will list an additional library called ld-linux.so, which is a part of GNU/Linux's dynamic linking mechanism.

Using *LD_LIBRARY_PATH*

When you link a program with a shared library, the linker does not put the full path to the shared library in the resulting executable. Instead, it places only the name of the shared library. When the program is actually run, the system searches for the shared library and loads it. The system searches only /lib and /usr/lib, by default. If a shared library that is linked into your program is installed outside those directories, it will not be found, and the system will refuse to run the program.

One solution to this problem is to use the -Wl,-rpath option when linking the program. Suppose that you use this:

```
% gcc -o app app.o -L. -ltest -Wl,-rpath,/usr/local/lib
```

Then, when app is run, the system will search /usr/local/lib for any required shared libraries.

Another solution to this problem is to set the LD_LIBRARY_PATH environment variable when running the program. Like the PATH environment variable, LD_LIBRARY_PATH is a colon-separated list of directories. For example, if LD_LIBRARY_PATH is /usr/local/lib:/opt/lib, then /usr/local/lib and /opt/lib will be searched before the standard /lib and /usr/lib directories. You should also note that if you have LD_LIBRARY_PATH, the linker will search the directories given there in addition to the directories given with the -L option when it is building an executable.[4]

2.3.3   Standard Libraries

Even if you didn't specify any libraries when you linked your program, it almost certainly uses a shared library. That's because GCC automatically links in the standard C library, libc, for you. The standard C library math functions are not included in libc; instead, they're in a separate library, libm, which you need to specify explicitly. For example, to compile and link a program compute.c which uses trigonometric functions such as sin and cos, you must invoke this code:

```
% gcc -o compute compute.c -lm
```

If you write a C++ program and link it using the c++ or g++ commands, you'll also get the standard C++ library, libstdc++, automatically.

2.3.4   Library Dependencies

One library will often depend on another library. For example, many GNU/Linux systems include libtiff, a library that contains functions for reading and writing image files in the TIFF format. This library, in turn, uses the libraries libjpeg (JPEG image routines) and libz (compression routines).

Listing 2.9 shows a very small program that uses libtiff to open a TIFF image file.

Listing 2.9   *(tifftest.c)* **Using** *libtiff*

```
#include <stdio.h>
#include <tiffio.h>

int main (int argc, char** argv)
{
  TIFF* tiff;
  tiff = TIFFOpen (argv[1], "r");
  TIFFClose (tiff);
  return 0;
}
```

4. You might see a reference to LD_RUN_PATH in some online documentation. Don't believe what you read; this variable does not actually do anything under GNU/Linux.

Save this source file as `tifftest.c`. To compile this program and link with `libtiff`, specify `-ltiff` on your link line:

```
% gcc -o tifftest tifftest.c -ltiff
```

By default, this will pick up the shared-library version of `libtiff`, found at `/usr/lib/libtiff.so`. Because `libtiff` uses `libjpeg` and `libz`, the shared-library versions of these two are also drawn in (a shared library can point to other shared libraries that it depends on). To verify this, use the `ldd` command:

```
% ldd tifftest
        libtiff.so.3 => /usr/lib/libtiff.so.3 (0x4001d000)
        libc.so.6 => /lib/libc.so.6 (0x40060000)
        libjpeg.so.62 => /usr/lib/libjpeg.so.62 (0x40155000)
        libz.so.1 => /usr/lib/libz.so.1 (0x40174000)
        /lib/ld-linux.so.2 => /lib/ld-linux.so.2 (0x40000000)
```

Static libraries, on the other hand, cannot point to other libraries. If decide to link with the static version of `libtiff` by specifying `-static` on your command line, you will encounter unresolved symbols:

```
% gcc -static -o tifftest tifftest.c -ltiff
/usr/bin/../lib/libtiff.a(tif_jpeg.o): In function 'TIFFjpeg_error_exit':
tif_jpeg.o(.text+0x2a): undefined reference to 'jpeg_abort'
/usr/bin/../lib/libtiff.a(tif_jpeg.o): In function 'TIFFjpeg_create_compress':
tif_jpeg.o(.text+0x8d): undefined reference to 'jpeg_std_error'
tif_jpeg.o(.text+0xcf): undefined reference to 'jpeg_CreateCompress'
...
```

To link this program statically, you must specify the other two libraries yourself:

```
% gcc -static -o tifftest tifftest.c -ltiff -ljpeg -lz
```

Occasionally, two libraries will be mutually dependent. In other words, the first archive will reference symbols defined in the second archive, and vice versa. This situation generally arises out of poor design, but it does occasionally arise. In this case, you can provide a single library multiple times on the command line. The linker will research the library each time it occurs. For example, this line will cause `libfoo.a` to be searched multiple times:

```
% gcc -o app app.o -lfoo -lbar -lfoo
```

So, even if `libfoo.a` references symbols in `libbar.a`, and vice versa, the program will link successfully.

2.3.5   Pros and Cons

Now that you know all about static archives and shared libraries, you're probably wondering which to use. There are a few major considerations to keep in mind.

One major advantage of a shared library is that it saves space on the system where the program is installed. If you are installing 10 programs, and they all make use of the same shared library, then you save a lot of space by using a shared library. If you used a static archive instead, the archive is included in all 10 programs. So, using shared libraries saves disk space. It also reduces download times if your program is being downloaded from the Web.

A related advantage to shared libraries is that users can upgrade the libraries without upgrading all the programs that depend on them. For example, suppose that you produce a shared library that manages HTTP connections. Many programs might depend on this library. If you find a bug in this library, you can upgrade the library. Instantly, all the programs that depend on the library will be fixed; you don't have to relink all the programs the way you do with a static archive.

Those advantages might make you think that you should always use shared libraries. However, substantial reasons exist to use static archives instead. The fact that an upgrade to a shared library affects all programs that depend on it can be a disadvantage. For example, if you're developing mission-critical software, you might rather link to a static archive so that an upgrade to shared libraries on the system won't affect your program. (Otherwise, users might upgrade the shared library, thereby breaking your program, and then call your customer support line, blaming you!)

If you're not going to be able to install your libraries in /lib or /usr/lib, you should definitely think twice about using a shared library. (You won't be able to install your libraries in those directories if you expect users to install your software without administrator privileges.) In particular, the -Wl,-rpath trick won't work if you don't know where the libraries are going to end up. And asking your users to set LD_LIBRARY_PATH means an extra step for them. Because each user has to do this individually, this is a substantial additional burden.

You'll have to weigh these advantages and disadvantages for every program you distribute.

2.3.6 Dynamic Loading and Unloading

Sometimes you might want to load some code at run time without explicitly linking in that code. For example, consider an application that supports "plug-in" modules, such as a Web browser. The browser allows third-party developers to create plug-ins to provide additional functionality. The third-party developers create shared libraries and place them in a known location. The Web browser then automatically loads the code in these libraries.

This functionality is available under Linux by using the dlopen function. You could open a shared library named libtest.so by calling dlopen like this:

```
dlopen ("libtest.so", RTLD_LAZY)
```

(The second parameter is a flag that indicates how to bind symbols in the shared library. You can consult the online man pages for `dlopen` if you want more information, but `RTLD_LAZY` is usually the setting that you want.) To use dynamic loading functions, include the `<dlfcn.h>` header file and link with the `-ldl` option to pick up the `libdl` library.

The return value from this function is a `void *` that is used as a handle for the shared library. You can pass this value to the `dlsym` function to obtain the address of a function that has been loaded with the shared library. For example, if `libtest.so` defines a function named `my_function`, you could call it like this:

```
void* handle = dlopen ("libtest.so", RTLD_LAZY);
void (*test)() = dlsym (handle, "my_function");
(*test)();
dlclose (handle);
```

The `dlsym` system call can also be used to obtain a pointer to a static variable in the shared library.

Both `dlopen` and `dlsym` return `NULL` if they do not succeed. In that event, you can call `dlerror` (with no parameters) to obtain a human-readable error message describing the problem.

The `dlclose` function unloads the shared library. Technically, `dlopen` actually loads the library only if it is not already loaded. If the library has already been loaded, `dlopen` simply increments the library reference count. Similarly, `dlclose` decrements the reference count and then unloads the library only if the reference count has reached zero.

If you're writing the code in your shared library in C++, you will probably want to declare those functions and variables that you plan to access elsewhere with the `extern "C"` linkage specifier. For instance, if the C++ function `my_function` is in a shared library and you want to access it with `dlsym`, you should declare it like this:

```
extern "C" void foo ();
```

This prevents the C++ compiler from mangling the function name, which would change the function's name from `foo` to a different, funny-looking name that encodes extra information about the function. A C compiler will not mangle names; it will use whichever name you give to your function or variable.

3

Processes

A RUNNING INSTANCE OF A PROGRAM IS CALLED A *PROCESS*. If you have two
terminal windows showing on your screen, then you are probably running the
same terminal program twice—you have two terminal processes. Each terminal
window is probably running a shell; each running shell is another process. When you
invoke a command from a shell, the corresponding program is executed in a new
process; the shell process resumes when that process completes.

Advanced programmers often use multiple cooperating processes in a single application to enable the application to do more than one thing at once, to increase
application robustness, and to make use of already-existing programs.

Most of the process manipulation functions described in this chapter are similar to
those on other UNIX systems. Most are declared in the header file <unistd.h>; check
the man page for each function to be sure.

3.1 Looking at Processes

Even as you sit down at your computer, there are processes running. Every executing
program uses one or more processes. Let's start by taking a look at the processes
already on your computer.

3.1.1 Process IDs

Each process in a Linux system is identified by its unique *process ID*, sometimes referred to as *pid*. Process IDs are 16-bit numbers that are assigned sequentially by Linux as new processes are created.

Every process also has a parent process (except the special `init` process, described in Section 3.4.3, "Zombie Processes"). Thus, you can think of the processes on a Linux system as arranged in a tree, with the `init` process at its root. The *parent process ID*, or *ppid*, is simply the process ID of the process's parent.

When referring to process IDs in a C or C++ program, always use the `pid_t` typedef, which is defined in `<sys/types.h>`. A program can obtain the process ID of the process it's running in with the `getpid()` system call, and it can obtain the process ID of its parent process with the `getppid()` system call. For instance, the program in Listing 3.1 prints its process ID and its parent's process ID.

Listing 3.1 (*print-pid.c*) **Printing the Process ID**

```
#include <stdio.h>
#include <unistd.h>

int main ()
{
  printf ("The process ID is %d\n", (int) getpid ());
  printf ("The parent process ID is %d\n", (int) getppid ());
  return 0;
}
```

Observe that if you invoke this program several times, a different process ID is reported because each invocation is in a new process. However, if you invoke it every time from the same shell, the parent process ID (that is, the process ID of the shell process) is the same.

3.1.2 Viewing Active Processes

The `ps` command displays the processes that are running on your system. The GNU/Linux version of `ps` has lots of options because it tries to be compatible with versions of `ps` on several other UNIX variants. These options control which processes are listed and what information about each is shown.

By default, invoking `ps` displays the processes controlled by the terminal or terminal window in which `ps` is invoked. For example:

```
% ps
  PID TTY          TIME CMD
21693 pts/8    00:00:00 bash
21694 pts/8    00:00:00 ps
```

This invocation of ps shows two processes. The first, bash, is the shell running on this terminal. The second is the running instance of the ps program itself. The first column, labeled PID, displays the process ID of each.

For a more detailed look at what's running on your GNU/Linux system, invoke this:

```
% ps -e -o pid,ppid,command
```

The -e option instructs ps to display all processes running on the system. The -o pid,ppid,command option tells ps what information to show about each process— in this case, the process ID, the parent process ID, and the command running in this process.

> **ps Output Formats**
>
> With the -o option to the ps command, you specify the information about processes that you want in the output as a comma-separated list. For example, ps -o pid,user,start_time,command displays the process ID, the name of the user owning the process, the wall clock time at which the process started, and the command running in the process. See the man page for ps for the full list of field codes. You can use the -f (full listing), -l (long listing), or -j (jobs listing) options instead to get three different preset listing formats.

Here are the first few lines and last few lines of output from this command on my system. You may see different output, depending on what's running on your system.

```
% ps -e -o pid,ppid,command
  PID  PPID COMMAND
    1     0 init [5]
    2     1 [kflushd]
    3     1 [kupdate]
...
21725 21693 xterm
21727 21725 bash
21728 21727 ps -e -o pid,ppid,command
```

Note that the parent process ID of the ps command, 21727, is the process ID of bash, the shell from which I invoked ps. The parent process ID of bash is in turn 21725, the process ID of the xterm program in which the shell is running.

3.1.3 Killing a Process

You can kill a running process with the kill command. Simply specify on the command line the process ID of the process to be killed.

The kill command works by sending the process a SIGTERM, or termination, signal.[1] This causes the process to terminate, unless the executing program explicitly handles or masks the SIGTERM signal. Signals are described in Section 3.3, "Signals."

---

1. You can also use the kill command to send other signals to a process. This is described in Section 3.4, "Process Termination."

3.2 Creating Processes

Two common techniques are used for creating a new process. The first is relatively simple but should be used sparingly because it is inefficient and has considerably security risks. The second technique is more complex but provides greater flexibility, speed, and security.

3.2.1 Using *system*

The system function in the standard C library provides an easy way to execute a command from within a program, much as if the command had been typed into a shell. In fact, system creates a subprocess running the standard Bourne shell (/bin/sh) and hands the command to that shell for execution. For example, this program in Listing 3.2 invokes the ls command to display the contents of the root directory, as if you typed ls -l / into a shell.

Listing 3.2 (*system.c*) Using the *system* Call

```
#include <stdlib.h>

int main ()
{
  int return_value;
  return_value = system ("ls -l /");
  return return_value;
}
```

The system function returns the exit status of the shell command. If the shell itself cannot be run, system returns 127; if another error occurs, system returns −1.

Because the system function uses a shell to invoke your command, it's subject to the features, limitations, and security flaws of the system's shell. You can't rely on the availability of any particular version of the Bourne shell. On many UNIX systems, /bin/sh is a symbolic link to another shell. For instance, on most GNU/Linux systems, /bin/sh points to bash (the Bourne-Again SHell), and different GNU/Linux distributions use different versions of bash. Invoking a program with root privilege with the system function, for instance, can have different results on different GNU/Linux systems. Therefore, it's preferable to use the fork and exec method for creating processes.

3.2.2 Using *fork* and *exec*

The DOS and Windows API contains the spawn family of functions. These functions take as an argument the name of a program to run and create a new process instance of that program. Linux doesn't contain a single function that does all this in one step. Instead, Linux provides one function, fork, that makes a child process that is an exact copy of its parent process. Linux provides another set of functions, the exec family, that causes a particular process to cease being an instance of one program and to instead become an instance of another program. To spawn a new process, you first use fork to make a copy of the current process. Then you use exec to transform one of these processes into an instance of the program you want to spawn.

Calling *fork*

When a program calls fork, a duplicate process, called the *child process*, is created. The parent process continues executing the program from the point that fork was called. The child process, too, executes the same program from the same place.

So how do the two processes differ? First, the child process is a new process and therefore has a new process ID, distinct from its parent's process ID. One way for a program to distinguish whether it's in the parent process or the child process is to call getpid. However, the fork function provides different return values to the parent and child processes—one process "goes in" to the fork call, and two processes "come out," with different return values. The return value in the parent process is the process ID of the child. The return value in the child process is zero. Because no process ever has a process ID of zero, this makes it easy for the program whether it is now running as the parent or the child process.

Listing 3.3 is an example of using fork to duplicate a program's process. Note that the first block of the if statement is executed only in the parent process, while the else clause is executed in the child process.

Listing 3.3   (*fork.c*) **Using** *fork* **to Duplicate a Program's Process**

```
#include <stdio.h>
#include <sys/types.h>
#include <unistd.h>

int main ()
{
  pid_t child_pid;

  printf ("the main program process ID is %d\n", (int) getpid ());

  child_pid = fork ();
  if (child_pid != 0) {
    printf ("this is the parent process, with id %d\n", (int) getpid ());
    printf ("the child's process ID is %d\n", (int) child_pid);
  }
  else
    printf ("this is the child process, with id %d\n", (int) getpid ());

  return 0;
}
```

Using the *exec* Family

The exec functions replace the program running in a process with another program. When a program calls an exec function, that process immediately ceases executing that program and begins executing a new program from the beginning, assuming that the exec call doesn't encounter an error.

Within the exec family, there are functions that vary slightly in their capabilities and how they are called.

- Functions that contain the letter *p* in their names (execvp and execlp) accept a program name and search for a program by that name in the current execution path; functions that don't contain the *p* must be given the full path of the program to be executed.

- Functions that contain the letter v in their names (execv, execvp, and execve) accept the argument list for the new program as a NULL-terminated array of pointers to strings. Functions that contain the letter *l* (execl, execlp, and execle) accept the argument list using the C language's varargs mechanism.

- Functions that contain the letter *e* in their names (execve and execle) accept an additional argument, an array of environment variables. The argument should be a NULL-terminated array of pointers to character strings. Each character string should be of the form "VARIABLE=value".

Because exec replaces the calling program with another one, it never returns unless an error occurs.

The argument list passed to the program is analogous to the command-line arguments that you specify to a program when you run it from the shell. They are available through the argc and argv parameters to main. Remember, when a program is invoked from the shell, the shell sets the first element of the argument list argv[0] to the name of the program, the second element of the argument list (argv[1]) to the first command-line argument, and so on. When you use an exec function in your programs, you, too, should pass the name of the function as the first element of the argument list.

Using *fork* and *exec* Together

A common pattern to run a subprogram within a program is first to fork the process and then exec the subprogram. This allows the calling program to continue execution in the parent process while the calling program is replaced by the subprogram in the child process.

The program in Listing 3.4, like Listing 3.2, lists the contents of the root directory using the ls command. Unlike the previous example, though, it invokes the ls command directly, passing it the command-line arguments -l and / rather than invoking it through a shell.

Listing 3.4   (*fork-exec.c*) **Using** *fork* **and** *exec* **Together**

```c
#include <stdio.h>
#include <stdlib.h>
#include <sys/types.h>
#include <unistd.h>

/* Spawn a child process running a new program. PROGRAM is the name
   of the program to run; the path will be searched for this program.
   ARG_LIST is a NULL-terminated list of character strings to be
   passed as the program's argument list. Returns the process ID of
   the spawned process.  */

int spawn (char* program, char** arg_list)
{
  pid_t child_pid;

  /* Duplicate this process.  */
  child_pid = fork ();
  if (child_pid != 0)
    /* This is the parent process.  */
    return child_pid;
  else {
    /* Now execute PROGRAM, searching for it in the path.  */
    execvp (program, arg_list);
    /* The execvp function returns only if an error occurs.  */
    fprintf (stderr, "an error occurred in execvp\n");
    abort ();
  }
}

int main ()
{
  /* The argument list to pass to the "ls" command.  */
  char* arg_list[] = {
    "ls",       /* argv[0], the name of the program.  */
    "-l",
    "/",
    NULL        /* The argument list must end with a NULL.  */
  };

  /* Spawn a child process running the "ls" command.  Ignore the
     returned child process ID.  */
  spawn ("ls", arg_list);

  printf ("done with main program\n");

  return 0;
}
```

3.2.3   Process Scheduling

Linux schedules the parent and child processes independently; there's no guarantee of which one will run first, or how long it will run before Linux interrupts it and lets the other process (or some other process on the system) run. In particular, none, part, or all of the ls command may run in the child process before the parent completes.[2] Linux promises that each process will run eventually—no process will be completely starved of execution resources.

You may specify that a process is less important—and should be given a lower priority—by assigning it a higher *niceness* value. By default, every process has a niceness of zero. A higher niceness value means that the process is given a lesser execution priority; conversely, a process with a lower (that is, negative) niceness gets more execution time.

To run a program with a nonzero niceness, use the nice command, specifying the niceness value with the -n option. For example, this is how you might invoke the command "sort input.txt > output.txt", a long sorting operation, with a reduced priority so that it doesn't slow down the system too much:

```
% nice -n 10 sort input.txt > output.txt
```

You can use the renice command to change the niceness of a running process from the command line.

To change the niceness of a running process programmatically, use the nice function. Its argument is an increment value, which is added to the niceness value of the process that calls it. Remember that a positive value raises the niceness value and thus reduces the process's execution priority.

Note that only a process with root privilege can run a process with a negative niceness value or reduce the niceness value of a running process. This means that you may specify negative values to the nice and renice commands only when logged in as root, and only a process running as root can pass a negative value to the nice function. This prevents ordinary users from grabbing execution priority away from others using the system.

3.3   Signals

Signals are mechanisms for communicating with and manipulating processes in Linux. The topic of signals is a large one; here we discuss some of the most important signals and techniques that are used for controlling processes.

A signal is a special message sent to a process. Signals are asynchronous; when a process receives a signal, it processes the signal immediately, without finishing the current function or even the current line of code. There are several dozen different signals, each with a different meaning. Each signal type is specified by its signal number, but in programs, you usually refer to a signal by its name. In Linux, these are defined in /usr/include/bits/signum.h. (You shouldn't include this header file directly in your programs; instead, use <signal.h>.)

---

2. A method for serializing the two processes is presented in Section 3.4.1, "Waiting for Process Termination."

When a process receives a signal, it may do one of several things, depending on the signal's *disposition*. For each signal, there is a *default disposition*, which determines what happens to the process if the program does not specify some other behavior. For most signal types, a program may specify some other behavior—either to ignore the signal or to call a special *signal-handler* function to respond to the signal. If a signal handler is used, the currently executing program is paused, the signal handler is executed, and, when the signal handler returns, the program resumes.

The Linux system sends signals to processes in response to specific conditions. For instance, SIGBUS (bus error), SIGSEGV (segmentation violation), and SIGFPE (floating point exception) may be sent to a process that attempts to perform an illegal operation. The default disposition for these signals it to terminate the process and produce a core file.

A process may also send a signal to another process. One common use of this mechanism is to end another process by sending it a SIGTERM or SIGKILL signal.[3] Another common use is to send a command to a running program. Two "user-defined" signals are reserved for this purpose: SIGUSR1 and SIGUSR2. The SIGHUP signal is sometimes used for this purpose as well, commonly to wake up an idling program or cause a program to reread its configuration files.

The sigaction function can be used to set a signal disposition. The first parameter is the signal number. The next two parameters are pointers to sigaction structures; the first of these contains the desired disposition for that signal number, while the second receives the previous disposition. The most important field in the first or second sigaction structure is sa_handler. It can take one of three values:

- SIG_DFL, which specifies the default disposition for the signal.
- SIG_IGN, which specifies that the signal should be ignored.
- A pointer to a signal-handler function. The function should take one parameter, the signal number, and return void.

Because signals are asynchronous, the main program may be in a very fragile state when a signal is processed and thus while a signal handler function executes. Therefore, you should avoid performing any I/O operations or calling most library and system functions from signal handlers.

A signal handler should perform the minimum work necessary to respond to the signal, and then return control to the main program (or terminate the program). In most cases, this consists simply of recording the fact that a signal occurred. The main program then checks periodically whether a signal has occurred and reacts accordingly.

It is possible for a signal handler to be interrupted by the delivery of another signal. While this may sound like a rare occurrence, if it does occur, it will be very difficult to diagnose and debug the problem. (This is an example of a race condition, discussed in Chapter 4, "Threads," Section 4.4, "Synchronization and Critical Sections.") Therefore, you should be very careful about what your program does in a signal handler.

---

3. What's the difference? The SIGTERM signal asks a process to terminate; the process may ignore the request by masking or ignoring the signal. The SIGKILL signal always kills the process immediately because the process may not mask or ignore SIGKILL.

Even assigning a value to a global variable can be dangerous because the assignment may actually be carried out in two or more machine instructions, and a second signal may occur between them, leaving the variable in a corrupted state. If you use a global variable to flag a signal from a signal-handler function, it should be of the special type `sig_atomic_t`. Linux guarantees that assignments to variables of this type are performed in a single instruction and therefore cannot be interrupted midway. In Linux, `sig_atomic_t` is an ordinary `int`; in fact, assignments to integer types the size of `int` or smaller, or to pointers, are atomic. If you want to write a program that's portable to any standard UNIX system, though, use `sig_atomic_t` for these global variables.

This program skeleton in Listing 3.5, for instance, uses a signal-handler function to count the number of times that the program receives `SIGUSR1`, one of the signals reserved for application use.

Listing 3.5   (*sigusr1.c*) **Using a Signal Handler**

```
#include <signal.h>
#include <stdio.h>
#include <string.h>
#include <sys/types.h>
#include <unistd.h>

sig_atomic_t sigusr1_count = 0;

void handler (int signal_number)
{
  ++sigusr1_count;
}

int main ()
{
  struct sigaction sa;
  memset (&sa, 0, sizeof (sa));
  sa.sa_handler = &handler;
  sigaction (SIGUSR1, &sa, NULL);

  /* Do some lengthy stuff here.  */
  /* ...  */

  printf ("SIGUSR1 was raised %d times\n", sigusr1_count);
  return 0;
}
```

3.4   Process Termination

Normally, a process terminates in one of two ways. Either the executing program calls the `exit` function, or the program's `main` function returns. Each process has an exit code: a number that the process returns to its parent. The exit code is the argument passed to the `exit` function, or the value returned from `main`.

A process may also terminate abnormally, in response to a signal. For instance, the `SIGBUS`, `SIGSEGV`, and `SIGFPE` signals mentioned previously cause the process to terminate. Other signals are used to terminate a process explicitly. The `SIGINT` signal is sent to a process when the user attempts to end it by typing Ctrl+C in its terminal. The `SIGTERM` signal is sent by the `kill` command. The default disposition for both of these is to terminate the process. By calling the `abort` function, a process sends itself the `SIGABRT` signal, which terminates the process and produces a core file. The most powerful termination signal is `SIGKILL`, which ends a process immediately and cannot be blocked or handled by a program.

Any of these signals can be sent using the `kill` command by specifying an extra command-line flag; for instance, to end a troublesome process by sending it a `SIGKILL`, invoke the following, where `pid` is its process ID:

```
% kill -KILL pid
```

To send a signal from a program, use the `kill` function. The first parameter is the target process ID. The second parameter is the signal number; use `SIGTERM` to simulate the default behavior of the `kill` command. For instance, where `child pid` contains the process ID of the child process, you can use the `kill` function to terminate a child process from the parent by calling it like this:

```
kill (child_pid, SIGTERM);
```

Include the `<sys/types.h>` and `<signal.h>` headers if you use the `kill` function.

By convention, the exit code is used to indicate whether the program executed correctly. An exit code of zero indicates correct execution, while a nonzero exit code indicates that an error occurred. In the latter case, the particular value returned may give some indication of the nature of the error. It's a good idea to stick with this convention in your programs because other components of the GNU/Linux system assume this behavior. For instance, shells assume this convention when you connect multiple programs with the `&&` (logical and) and `||` (logical or) operators. Therefore, you should explicitly return zero from your `main` function, unless an error occurs.

With most shells, it's possible to obtain the exit code of the most recently executed program using the special `$?` variable. Here's an example in which the `ls` command is invoked twice and its exit code is displayed after each invocation. In the first case, `ls` executes correctly and returns the exit code zero. In the second case, `ls` encounters an error (because the filename specified on the command line does not exist) and thus returns a nonzero exit code.

```
% ls /
bin   coda  etc   lib           misc  nfs  proc  sbin  usr
boot  dev   home  lost+found    mnt   opt  root  tmp   var
% echo $?
0
% ls bogusfile
ls: bogusfile: No such file or directory
% echo $?
1
```

Note that even though the parameter type of the `exit` function is `int` and the `main` function returns an `int`, Linux does not preserve the full 32 bits of the return code. In fact, you should use exit codes only between zero and 127. Exit codes above 128 have a special meaning—when a process is terminated by a signal, its exit code is 128 plus the signal number.

3.4.1   Waiting for Process Termination

If you typed in and ran the `fork` and `exec` example in Listing 3.4, you may have noticed that the output from the `ls` program often appears after the "main program" has already completed. That's because the child process, in which `ls` is run, is scheduled independently of the parent process. Because Linux is a multitasking operating system, both processes appear to execute simultaneously, and you can't predict whether the `ls` program will have a chance to run before or after the parent process runs.

In some situations, though, it is desirable for the parent process to wait until one or more child processes have completed. This can be done with the `wait` family of system calls. These functions allow you to wait for a process to finish executing, and enable the parent process to retrieve information about its child's termination. There are four different system calls in the `wait` family; you can choose to get a little or a lot of information about the process that exited, and you can choose whether you care about which child process terminated.

3.4.2   The *wait* System Calls

The simplest such function is called simply `wait`. It blocks the calling process until one of its child processes exits (or an error occurs). It returns a status code via an integer pointer argument, from which you can extract information about how the child process exited. For instance, the `WEXITSTATUS` macro extracts the child process's exit code.

You can use the WIFEXITED macro to determine from a child process's exit status whether that process exited normally (via the exit function or returning from main) or died from an unhandled signal. In the latter case, use the WTERMSIG macro to extract from its exit status the signal number by which it died.

Here is the main function from the fork and exec example again. This time, the parent process calls wait to wait until the child process, in which the ls command executes, is finished.

```
int main ()
{
  int child_status;

  /* The argument list to pass to the "ls" command.  */
  char* arg_list[] = {
    "ls",      /* argv[0], the name of the program.  */
    "-l",
    "/",
    NULL       /* The argument list must end with a NULL.  */
  };

  /* Spawn a child process running the "ls" command.  Ignore the
     returned child process ID.  */
  spawn ("ls", arg_list);

  /* Wait for the child process to complete.  */
  wait (&child_status);
  if (WIFEXITED (child_status))
    printf ("the child process exited normally, with exit code %d\n",
            WEXITSTATUS (child_status));
  else
    printf ("the child process exited abnormally\n");

  return 0;
}
```

Several similar system calls are available in Linux, which are more flexible or provide more information about the exiting child process. The waitpid function can be used to wait for a specific child process to exit instead of any child process. The wait3 function returns CPU usage statistics about the exiting child process, and the wait4 function allows you to specify additional options about which processes to wait for.

3.4.3 Zombie Processes

If a child process terminates while its parent is calling a wait function, the child process vanishes and its termination status is passed to its parent via the wait call. But what happens when a child process terminates and the parent is not calling wait? Does it simply vanish? No, because then information about its termination—such as whether it exited normally and, if so, what its exit status is—would be lost. Instead, when a child process terminates, is becomes a zombie process.

A *zombie process* is a process that has terminated but has not been cleaned up yet. It is the responsibility of the parent process to clean up its zombie children. The wait functions do this, too, so it's not necessary to track whether your child process is still executing before waiting for it. Suppose, for instance, that a program forks a child process, performs some other computations, and then calls wait. If the child process has not terminated at that point, the parent process will block in the wait call until the child process finishes. If the child process finishes before the parent process calls wait, the child process becomes a zombie. When the parent process calls wait, the zombie child's termination status is extracted, the child process is deleted, and the wait call returns immediately.

What happens if the parent does not clean up its children? They stay around in the system, as zombie processes. The program in Listing 3.6 forks a child process, which terminates immediately and then goes to sleep for a minute, without ever cleaning up the child process.

Listing 3.6   (*zombie.c*) **Making a Zombie Process**

```
#include <stdlib.h>
#include <sys/types.h>
#include <unistd.h>

int main ()
{
  pid_t child_pid;

  /* Create a child process.  */
  child_pid = fork ();
  if (child_pid > 0) {
    /* This is the parent process.  Sleep for a minute.  */
    sleep (60);
  }
  else {
    /* This is the child process.  Exit immediately.  */
    exit (0);
  }
  return 0;
}
```

Try compiling this file to an executable named make-zombie. Run it, and while it's still running, list the processes on the system by invoking the following command in another window:

```
% ps -e -o pid,ppid,stat,cmd
```

This lists the process ID, parent process ID, process status, and process command line. Observe that, in addition to the parent make-zombie process, there is another make-zombie process listed. It's the child process; note that its parent process ID is the process ID of the main make-zombie process. The child process is marked as <defunct>, and its status code is Z, for zombie.

What happens when the main make-zombie program ends when the parent process exits, without ever calling wait? Does the zombie process stay around? No—try running ps again, and note that both of the make-zombie processes are gone. When a program exits, its children are inherited by a special process, the init program, which always runs with process ID of 1 (it's the first process started when Linux boots). The init process automatically cleans up any zombie child processes that it inherits.

3.4.4 Cleaning Up Children Asynchronously

If you're using a child process simply to exec another program, it's fine to call wait immediately in the parent process, which will block until the child process completes. But often, you'll want the parent process to continue running, as one or more children execute synchronously. How can you be sure that you clean up child processes that have completed so that you don't leave zombie processes, which consume system resources, lying around?

One approach would be for the parent process to call wait3 or wait4 periodically, to clean up zombie children. Calling wait for this purpose doesn't work well because, if no children have terminated, the call will block until one does. However, wait3 and wait4 take an additional flag parameter, to which you can pass the flag value WNOHANG. With this flag, the function runs in *nonblocking mode*—it will clean up a terminated child process if there is one, or simply return if there isn't. The return value of the call is the process ID of the terminated child in the former case, or zero in the latter case.

A more elegant solution is to notify the parent process when a child terminates. There are several ways to do this using the methods discussed in Chapter 5, "Interprocess Communication," but fortunately Linux does this for you, using signals. When a child process terminates, Linux sends the parent process the SIGCHLD signal. The default disposition of this signal is to do nothing, which is why you might not have noticed it before.

Thus, an easy way to clean up child processes is by handling SIGCHLD. Of course, when cleaning up the child process, it's important to store its termination status if this information is needed, because once the process is cleaned up using wait, that information is no longer available. Listing 3.7 is what it looks like for a program to use a SIGCHLD handler to clean up its child processes.

Listing 3.7   *(sigchld.c)* **Cleaning Up Children by Handling** *SIGCHLD*

```
#include <signal.h>
#include <string.h>
#include <sys/types.h>
#include <sys/wait.h>

sig_atomic_t child_exit_status;

void clean_up_child_process (int signal_number)
{
  /* Clean up the child process.  */
  int status;
  wait (&status);
  /* Store its exit status in a global variable.  */
  child_exit_status = status;
}

int main ()
{
  /* Handle SIGCHLD by calling clean_up_child_process.  */
  struct sigaction sigchld_action;
  memset (&sigchld_action, 0, sizeof (sigchld_action));
  sigchld_action.sa_handler = &clean_up_child_process;
  sigaction (SIGCHLD, &sigchld_action, NULL);

  /* Now do things, including forking a child process.  */
  /* ...  */

  return 0;
}
```

Note how the signal handler stores the child process's exit status in a global variable, from which the main program can access it. Because the variable is assigned in a signal handler, its type is sig_atomic_t.

4

Threads

THREADS, LIKE PROCESSES, ARE A MECHANISM TO ALLOW A PROGRAM to do more than
one thing at a time. As with processes, threads appear to run concurrently; the Linux
kernel schedules them asynchronously, interrupting each thread from time to time to
give others a chance to execute.

Conceptually, a thread exists within a process. Threads are a finer-grained unit of
execution than processes. When you invoke a program, Linux creates a new process
and in that process creates a single thread, which runs the program sequentially. That
thread can create additional threads; all these threads run the same program in the
same process, but each thread may be executing a different part of the program at any
given time.

We've seen how a program can fork a child process. The child process is initially
running its parent's program, with its parent's virtual memory, file descriptors, and so
on copied. The child process can modify its memory, close file descriptors, and the like
without affecting its parent, and vice versa. When a program creates another thread,
though, nothing is copied. The creating and the created thread share the same memory
space, file descriptors, and other system resources as the original. If one thread changes
the value of a variable, for instance, the other thread subsequently will see the modified value. Similarly, if one thread closes a file descriptor, other threads may not read

from or write to that file descriptor. Because a process and all its threads can be executing only one program at a time, if any thread inside a process calls one of the exec functions, all the other threads are ended (the new program may, of course, create new threads).

GNU/Linux implements the POSIX standard thread API (known as *pthreads*). All thread functions and data types are declared in the header file <pthread.h>. The pthread functions are not included in the standard C library. Instead, they are in libpthread, so you should add -lpthread to the command line when you link your program.

4.1 Thread Creation

Each thread in a process is identified by a *thread ID*. When referring to thread IDs in C or C++ programs, use the type pthread_t.

Upon creation, each thread executes a *thread function*. This is just an ordinary function and contains the code that the thread should run. When the function returns, the thread exits. On GNU/Linux, thread functions take a single parameter, of type void*, and have a void* return type. The parameter is the *thread argument*: GNU/Linux passes the value along to the thread without looking at it. Your program can use this parameter to pass data to a new thread. Similarly, your program can use the return value to pass data from an exiting thread back to its creator.

The pthread_create function creates a new thread. You provide it with the following:

1. A pointer to a pthread_t variable, in which the thread ID of the new thread is stored.

2. A pointer to a *thread attribute* object. This object controls details of how the thread interacts with the rest of the program. If you pass NULL as the thread attribute, a thread will be created with the default thread attributes. Thread attributes are discussed in Section 4.1.5, "Thread Attributes."

3. A pointer to the thread function. This is an ordinary function pointer, of this type:

    ```
    void* (*) (void*)
    ```

4. A thread argument value of type void*. Whatever you pass is simply passed as the argument to the thread function when the thread begins executing.

A call to pthread_create returns immediately, and the original thread continues executing the instructions following the call. Meanwhile, the new thread begins executing the thread function. Linux schedules both threads asynchronously, and your program must not rely on the relative order in which instructions are executed in the two threads.

The program in Listing 4.1 creates a thread that prints x's continuously to standard error. After calling `pthread_create`, the main thread prints o's continuously to standard error.

Listing 4.1 (*thread–create.c*) **Create a Thread**

```
#include <pthread.h>
#include <stdio.h>

/* Prints x's to stderr.  The parameter is unused.  Does not return.  */

void* print_xs (void* unused)
{
  while (1)
    fputc ('x', stderr);
  return NULL;
}

/* The main program.  */

int main ()
{
  pthread_t thread_id;
  /* Create a new thread.  The new thread will run the print_xs
     function.  */
  pthread_create (&thread_id, NULL, &print_xs, NULL);
  /* Print o's continuously to stderr.  */
  while (1)
    fputc ('o', stderr);
  return 0;
}
```

Compile and link this program using the following code:

```
% cc -o thread-create thread-create.c -lpthread
```

Try running it to see what happens. Notice the unpredictable pattern of x's and o's as Linux alternately schedules the two threads.

Under normal circumstances, a thread exits in one of two ways. One way, as illustrated previously, is by returning from the thread function. The return value from the thread function is taken to be the return value of the thread. Alternately, a thread can exit explicitly by calling `pthread_exit`. This function may be called from within the thread function or from some other function called directly or indirectly by the thread function. The argument to `pthread_exit` is the thread's return value.

4.1.1 Passing Data to Threads

The thread argument provides a convenient method of passing data to threads. Because the type of the argument is void*, though, you can't pass a lot of data directly via the argument. Instead, use the thread argument to pass a pointer to some structure or array of data. One commonly used technique is to define a structure for each thread function, which contains the "parameters" that the thread function expects.

Using the thread argument, it's easy to reuse the same thread function for many threads. All these threads execute the same code, but on different data.

The program in Listing 4.2 is similar to the previous example. This one creates two new threads, one to print x's and the other to print o's. Instead of printing infinitely, though, each thread prints a fixed number of characters and then exits by returning from the thread function. The same thread function, char_print, is used by both threads, but each is configured differently using struct char_print_parms.

Listing 4.2 *(thread-create2)* **Create Two Threads**

```
#include <pthread.h>
#include <stdio.h>

/* Parameters to print_function.  */

struct char_print_parms
{
  /* The character to print.  */
  char character;
  /* The number of times to print it.  */
  int count;
};

/* Prints a number of characters to stderr, as given by PARAMETERS,
   which is a pointer to a struct char_print_parms.  */

void* char_print (void* parameters)
{
  /* Cast the cookie pointer to the right type.  */
  struct char_print_parms* p = (struct char_print_parms*) parameters;
  int i;

  for (i = 0; i < p->count; ++i)
    fputc (p->character, stderr);
  return NULL;
}

/* The main program.  */

int main ()
{
  pthread_t thread1_id;
```

```
  pthread_t thread2_id;
  struct char_print_parms thread1_args;
  struct char_print_parms thread2_args;

  /* Create a new thread to print 30,000 'x's.  */
  thread1_args.character = 'x';
  thread1_args.count = 30000;
  pthread_create (&thread1_id, NULL, &char_print, &thread1_args);

  /* Create a new thread to print 20,000 o's.  */
  thread2_args.character = 'o';
  thread2_args.count = 20000;
  pthread_create (&thread2_id, NULL, &char_print, &thread2_args);

  return 0;
}
```

But wait! The program in Listing 4.2 has a serious bug in it. The main thread (which runs the main function) creates the thread parameter structures (thread1_args and thread2_args) as local variables, and then passes pointers to these structures to the threads it creates. What's to prevent Linux from scheduling the three threads in such a way that main finishes executing before either of the other two threads are done? *Nothing!* But if this happens, the memory containing the thread parameter structures will be deallocated while the other two threads are still accessing it.

4.1.2 Joining Threads

One solution is to force main to wait until the other two threads are done. What we need is a function similar to wait that waits for a thread to finish instead of a process. That function is pthread_join, which takes two arguments: the thread ID of the thread to wait for, and a pointer to a void* variable that will receive the finished thread's return value. If you don't care about the thread return value, pass NULL as the second argument.

Listing 4.3 shows the corrected main function for the buggy example in Listing 4.2. In this version, main does not exit until both of the threads printing x's and o's have completed, so they are no longer using the argument structures.

Listing 4.3 **Revised *Main* Function for *thread-create2.c***

```
int main ()
{
  pthread_t thread1_id;
  pthread_t thread2_id;
  struct char_print_parms thread1_args;
  struct char_print_parms thread2_args;
```

continues

Listing 4.3   **Continued**

```
/* Create a new thread to print 30,000 x's.  */
thread1_args.character = 'x';
thread1_args.count = 30000;
pthread_create (&thread1_id, NULL, &char_print, &thread1_args);

/* Create a new thread to print 20,000 o's.  */
thread2_args.character = 'o';
thread2_args.count = 20000;
pthread_create (&thread2_id, NULL, &char_print, &thread2_args);

/* Make sure the first thread has finished.  */
pthread_join (thread1_id, NULL);
/* Make sure the second thread has finished.  */
pthread_join (thread2_id, NULL);

/* Now we can safely return.  */
return 0;
}
```

The moral of the story: Make sure that any data you pass to a thread by reference is not deallocated, *even by a different thread*, until you're sure that the thread is done with it. This is true both for local variables, which are deallocated when they go out of scope, and for heap-allocated variables, which you deallocate by calling `free` (or using `delete` in C++).

4.1.3   Thread Return Values

If the second argument you pass to `pthread_join` is non-null, the thread's return value will be placed in the location pointed to by that argument. The thread return value, like the thread argument, is of type `void*`. If you want to pass back a single `int` or other small number, you can do this easily by casting the value to `void*` and then casting back to the appropriate type after calling `pthread_join`.[1]

The program in Listing 4.4 computes the *n*th prime number in a separate thread. That thread returns the desired prime number as its thread return value. The main thread, meanwhile, is free to execute other code. Note that the successive division algorithm used in `compute_prime` is quite inefficient; consult a book on numerical algorithims if you need to compute many prime numbers in your programs.

---

1. Note that this is not portable, and it's up to you to make sure that your value can be cast safely to `void*` and back without losing bits.

Listing 4.4 (*primes.c*) **Compute Prime Numbers in a Thread**

```c
#include <pthread.h>
#include <stdio.h>

/* Compute successive prime numbers (very inefficiently).  Return the
   Nth prime number, where N is the value pointed to by *ARG.  */

void* compute_prime (void* arg)
{
  int candidate = 2;
  int n = *((int*) arg);

  while (1) {
    int factor;
    int is_prime = 1;

    /* Test primality by successive division.  */
    for (factor = 2; factor < candidate; ++factor)
      if (candidate % factor == 0) {
        is_prime = 0;
        break;
      }
    /* Is this the prime number we're looking for?  */
    if (is_prime) {
      if (--n == 0)
        /* Return the desired prime number as the thread return value.  */
        return (void*) candidate;
    }
    ++candidate;
  }
  return NULL;
}

int main ()
{
  pthread_t thread;
  int which_prime = 5000;
  int prime;

  /* Start the computing thread, up to the 5,000th prime number.  */
  pthread_create (&thread, NULL, &compute_prime, &which_prime);
  /* Do some other work here...  */
  /* Wait for the prime number thread to complete, and get the result.  */
  pthread_join (thread, (void*) &prime);
  /* Print the largest prime it computed.  */
  printf("The %dth prime number is %d.\n", which_prime, prime);
  return 0;
}
```

4.1.4 More on Thread IDs

Occasionally, it is useful for a sequence of code to determine which thread is executing it. The pthread_self function returns the thread ID of the thread in which it is called. This thread ID may be compared with another thread ID using the pthread_equal function.

These functions can be useful for determining whether a particular thread ID corresponds to the current thread. For instance, it is an error for a thread to call pthread_join to join itself. (In this case, pthread_join would return the error code EDEADLK.) To check for this beforehand, you might use code like this:

```
if (!pthread_equal (pthread_self (), other_thread))
  pthread_join (other_thread, NULL);
```

4.1.5 Thread Attributes

Thread attributes provide a mechanism for fine-tuning the behavior of individual threads. Recall that pthread_create accepts an argument that is a pointer to a thread attribute object. If you pass a null pointer, the default thread attributes are used to configure the new thread. However, you may create and customize a thread attribute object to specify other values for the attributes.

To specify customized thread attributes, you must follow these steps:

1. Create a pthread_attr_t object. The easiest way is simply to declare an automatic variable of this type.

2. Call pthread_attr_init, passing a pointer to this object. This initializes the attributes to their default values.

3. Modify the attribute object to contain the desired attribute values.

4. Pass a pointer to the attribute object when calling pthread_create.

5. Call pthread_attr_destroy to release the attribute object. The pthread_attr_t variable itself is not deallocated; it may be reinitialized with pthread_attr_init.

A single thread attribute object may be used to start several threads. It is not necessary to keep the thread attribute object around after the threads have been created.

For most GNU/Linux application programming tasks, only one thread attribute is typically of interest (the other available attributes are primarily for specialty real-time programming). This attribute is the thread's *detach state*. A thread may be created as a *joinable thread* (the default) or as a *detached thread*. A joinable thread, like a process, is not automatically cleaned up by GNU/Linux when it terminates. Instead, the thread's exit state hangs around in the system (kind of like a zombie process) until another thread calls pthread_join to obtain its return value. Only then are its resources released. A detached thread, in contrast, is cleaned up automatically when it terminates. Because a detached thread is immediately cleaned up, another thread may not synchronize on its completion by using pthread_join or obtain its return value.

To set the detach state in a thread attribute object, use `pthread_attr_setdetachstate`. The first argument is a pointer to the thread attribute object, and the second is the desired detach state. Because the joinable state is the default, it is necessary to call this only to create detached threads; pass `PTHREAD_CREATE_DETACHED` as the second argument.

The code in Listing 4.5 creates a detached thread by setting the detach state thread attribute for the thread.

Listing 4.5   (*detached.c*) **Skeleton Program That Creates a Detached Thread**

```
#include <pthread.h>

void* thread_function (void* thread_arg)
{
  /* Do work here... */
}

int main ()
{
  pthread_attr_t attr;
  pthread_t thread;

  pthread_attr_init (&attr);
  pthread_attr_setdetachstate (&attr, PTHREAD_CREATE_DETACHED);
  pthread_create (&thread, &attr, &thread_function, NULL);
  pthread_attr_destroy (&attr);

  /* Do work here... */

  /* No need to join the second thread. */
  return 0;
}
```

Even if a thread is created in a joinable state, it may later be turned into a detached thread. To do this, call `pthread_detach`. Once a thread is detached, it cannot be made joinable again.

4.2   Thread Cancellation

Under normal circumstances, a thread terminates when it exits normally, either by returning from its thread function or by calling `pthread_exit`. However, it is possible for a thread to request that another thread terminate. This is called *canceling* a thread.

To cancel a thread, call `pthread_cancel`, passing the thread ID of the thread to be canceled. A canceled thread may later be joined; in fact, you should join a canceled thread to free up its resources, unless the thread is detached (see Section 4.1.5, "Thread Attributes"). The return value of a canceled thread is the special value given by `PTHREAD_CANCELED`.

Often a thread may be in some code that must be executed in an all-or-nothing fashion. For instance, the thread may allocate some resources, use them, and then deallocate them. If the thread is canceled in the middle of this code, it may not have the opportunity to deallocate the resources, and thus the resources will be leaked. To counter this possibility, it is possible for a thread to control whether and when it can be canceled.

A thread may be in one of three states with regard to thread cancellation.

- The thread may be *asynchronously cancelable*. The thread may be canceled at any point in its execution.

- The thread may be *synchronously cancelable*. The thread may be canceled, but not at just any point in its execution. Instead, cancellation requests are queued, and the thread is canceled only when it reaches specific points in its execution.

- A thread may be *uncancelable*. Attempts to cancel the thread are quietly ignored.

When initially created, a thread is synchronously cancelable.

4.2.1 Synchronous and Asynchronous Threads

An asynchronously cancelable thread may be canceled at any point in its execution. A synchronously cancelable thread, in contrast, may be canceled only at particular places in its execution. These places are called *cancellation points*. The thread will queue a cancellation request until it reaches the next cancellation point.

To make a thread asynchronously cancelable, use `pthread_setcanceltype`. This affects the thread that actually calls the function. The first argument should be `PTHREAD_CANCEL_ASYNCHRONOUS` to make the thread asynchronously cancelable, or `PTHREAD_CANCEL_DEFERRED` to return it to the synchronously cancelable state. The second argument, if not null, is a pointer to a variable that will receive the previous cancellation type for the thread. This call, for example, makes the calling thread asynchronously cancelable.

```
pthread_setcanceltype (PTHREAD_CANCEL_ASYNCHRONOUS, NULL);
```

What constitutes a cancellation point, and where should these be placed? The most direct way to create a cancellation point is to call `pthread_testcancel`. This does nothing except process a pending cancellation in a synchronously cancelable thread. You should call `pthread_testcancel` periodically during lengthy computations in a thread function, at points where the thread can be canceled without leaking any resources or producing other ill effects.

Certain other functions are implicitly cancellation points as well. These are listed on the `pthread_cancel` man page. Note that other functions may use these functions internally and thus will indirectly be cancellation points.

4.2.2 Uncancelable Critical Sections

A thread may disable cancellation of itself altogether with the
`pthread_setcancelstate` function. Like `pthread_setcanceltype`, this affects the calling
thread. The first argument is `PTHREAD_CANCEL_DISABLE` to disable cancellation, or
`PTHREAD_CANCEL_ENABLE` to re-enable cancellation. The second argument, if not null,
points to a variable that will receive the previous cancellation state. This call, for
instance, disables thread cancellation in the calling thread.

```
pthread_setcancelstate (PTHREAD_CANCEL_DISABLE, NULL);
```

Using `pthread_setcancelstate` enables you to implement *critical sections*. A critical section is a sequence of code that must be executed either in its entirety or not at all; in other words, if a thread begins executing the critical section, it must continue until the end of the critical section without being canceled.

For example, suppose that you're writing a routine for a banking program that transfers money from one account to another. To do this, you must add value to the balance in one account and deduct the same value from the balance of another account. If the thread running your routine happened to be canceled at just the wrong time between these two operations, the program would have spuriously increased the bank's total deposits by failing to complete the transaction. To prevent this possibility, place the two operations in a critical section.

You might implement the transfer with a function such as `process_transaction`, shown in Listing 4.6. This function disables thread cancellation to start a critical section before it modifies either account balance.

Listing 4.6 (*critical-section.c*) **Protect a Bank Transaction with a Critical Section**

```c
#include <pthread.h>
#include <stdio.h>
#include <string.h>

/* An array of balances in accounts, indexed by account number.  */

float* account_balances;

/* Transfer DOLLARS from account FROM_ACCT to account TO_ACCT.  Return
   0 if the transaction succeeded, or 1 if the balance FROM_ACCT is
   too small.  */

int process_transaction (int from_acct, int to_acct, float dollars)
{
  int old_cancel_state;

  /* Check the balance in FROM_ACCT.  */
  if (account_balances[from_acct] < dollars)
    return 1;
```

continues

Listing 4.6   **Continued**

```
/* Begin critical section.  */
pthread_setcancelstate (PTHREAD_CANCEL_DISABLE, &old_cancel_state);
/* Move the money.  */
account_balances[to_acct] += dollars;
account_balances[from_acct] -= dollars;
/* End critical section.  */
pthread_setcancelstate (old_cancel_state, NULL);

return 0;
}
```

Note that it's important to restore the old cancel state at the end of the critical section rather than setting it unconditionally to PTHREAD_CANCEL_ENABLE. This enables you to call the process_transaction function safely from within another critical section—in that case, your function will leave the cancel state the same way it found it.

4.2.3   When to Use Thread Cancellation

In general, it's a good idea not to use thread cancellation to end the execution of a thread, except in unusual circumstances. During normal operation, a better strategy is to indicate to the thread that it should exit, and then to wait for the thread to exit on its own in an orderly fashion. We'll discuss techniques for communicating with the thread later in this chapter, and in Chapter 5, "Interprocess Communication."

4.3   Thread-Specific Data

Unlike processes, all threads in a single program share the same address space. This means that if one thread modifies a location in memory (for instance, a global variable), the change is visible to all other threads. This allows multiple threads to operate on the same data without the use interprocess communication mechanisms (which are described in Chapter 5).

Each thread has its own call stack, however. This allows each thread to execute different code and to call and return from subroutines in the usual way. As in a single-threaded program, each invocation of a subroutine in each thread has its own set of local variables, which are stored on the stack for that thread.

Sometimes, however, it is desirable to duplicate a certain variable so that each thread has a separate copy. GNU/Linux supports this by providing each thread with a *thread-specific data* area. The variables stored in this area are duplicated for each thread, and each thread may modify its copy of a variable without affecting other threads. Because all threads share the same memory space, thread-specific data may not be accessed using normal variable references. GNU/Linux provides special functions for setting and retrieving values from the thread-specific data area.

You may create as many thread-specific data items as you want, each of type void*. Each item is referenced by a key. To create a new key, and thus a new data item for each thread, use pthread_key_create. The first argument is a pointer to a pthread_key_t variable. That key value can be used by each thread to access its own copy of the corresponding data item. The second argument to pthread_key_t is a cleanup function. If you pass a function pointer here, GNU/Linux automatically calls that function when each thread exits, passing the thread-specific value corresponding to that key. This is particularly handy because the cleanup function is called even if the thread is canceled at some arbitrary point in its execution. If the thread-specific value is null, the thread cleanup function is not called. If you don't need a cleanup function, you may pass null instead of a function pointer.

After you've created a key, each thread can set its thread-specific value corresponding to that key by calling pthread_setspecific. The first argument is the key, and the second is the void* thread-specific value to store. To retrieve a thread-specific data item, call pthread_getspecific, passing the key as its argument.

Suppose, for instance, that your application divides a task among multiple threads. For audit purposes, each thread is to have a separate log file, in which progress messages for that thread's tasks are recorded. The thread-specific data area is a convenient place to store the file pointer for the log file for each individual thread.

Listing 4.7 shows how you might implement this. The main function in this sample program creates a key to store the thread-specific file pointer and then stores it in thread_log_key. Because this is a global variable, it is shared by all threads. When each thread starts executing its thread function, it opens a log file and stores the file pointer under that key. Later, any of these threads may call write_to_thread_log to write a message to the thread-specific log file. That function retrieves the file pointer for the thread's log file from thread-specific data and writes the message.

Listing 4.7   (*tsd.c*) **Per-Thread Log Files Implemented with Thread-Specific Data**

```
#include <malloc.h>
#include <pthread.h>
#include <stdio.h>

/* The key used to associate a log file pointer with each thread.  */
static pthread_key_t thread_log_key;

/* Write MESSAGE to the log file for the current thread.  */

void write_to_thread_log (const char* message)
{
  FILE* thread_log = (FILE*) pthread_getspecific (thread_log_key);
  fprintf (thread_log, "%s\n", message);
}

/* Close the log file pointer THREAD_LOG.  */

void close_thread_log (void* thread_log)
```

continues

Listing 4.7 **Continued**

```
{
  fclose ((FILE*) thread_log);
}

void* thread_function (void* args)
{
  char thread_log_filename[20];
  FILE* thread_log;

  /* Generate the filename for this thread's log file.  */
  sprintf (thread_log_filename, "thread%d.log", (int) pthread_self ());
  /* Open the log file.  */
  thread_log = fopen (thread_log_filename, "w");
  /* Store the file pointer in thread-specific data under thread_log_key.  */
  pthread_setspecific (thread_log_key, thread_log);

  write_to_thread_log ("Thread starting.");
  /* Do work here... */

  return NULL;
}

int main ()
{
  int i;
  pthread_t threads[5];

  /* Create a key to associate thread log file pointers in
     thread-specific data.  Use close_thread_log to clean up the file
     pointers.  */
  pthread_key_create (&thread_log_key, close_thread_log);
  /* Create threads to do the work.  */
  for (i = 0; i < 5; ++i)
    pthread_create (&(threads[i]), NULL, thread_function, NULL);
  /* Wait for all threads to finish.  */
  for (i = 0; i < 5; ++i)
    pthread_join (threads[i], NULL);
  return 0;
}
```

Observe that `thread_function` does not need to close the log file. That's because when the log file key was created, `close_thread_log` was specified as the cleanup function for that key. Whenever a thread exits, GNU/Linux calls that function, passing the thread-specific value for the thread log key. This function takes care of closing the log file.

4.3.1 Cleanup Handlers

The cleanup functions for thread-specific data keys can be very handy for ensuring that resources are not leaked when a thread exits or is canceled. Sometimes, though, it's useful to be able to specify cleanup functions without creating a new thread-specific data item that's duplicated for each thread. GNU/Linux provides *cleanup handlers* for this purpose.

A cleanup handler is simply a function that should be called when a thread exits. The handler takes a single `void*` parameter, and its argument value is provided when the handler is registered—this makes it easy to use the same handler function to deallocate multiple resource instances.

A cleanup handler is a temporary measure, used to deallocate a resource only if the thread exits or is canceled instead of finishing execution of a particular region of code. Under normal circumstances, when the thread does not exit and is not canceled, the resource should be deallocated explicitly and the cleanup handler should be removed.

To register a cleanup handler, call `pthread_cleanup_push`, passing a pointer to the cleanup function and the value of its `void*` argument. The call to `pthread_cleanup_push` must be balanced by a corresponding call to `pthread_cleanup_pop`, which unregisters the cleanup handler. As a convenience, `pthread_cleanup_pop` takes an `int` flag argument; if the flag is nonzero, the cleanup action is actually performed as it is unregistered.

The program fragment in Listing 4.8 shows how you might use a cleanup handler to make sure that a dynamically allocated buffer is cleaned up if the thread terminates.

Listing 4.8 **(*cleanup.c*) Program Fragment Demonstrating a Thread Cleanup Handler**

```
#include <malloc.h>
#include <pthread.h>

/* Allocate a temporary buffer.  */

void* allocate_buffer (size_t size)
{
  return malloc (size);
}

/* Deallocate a temporary buffer.  */

void deallocate_buffer (void* buffer)
{
  free (buffer);
}

void do_some_work ()
{
  /* Allocate a temporary buffer.  */
```

continues

Listing 4.8   **Continued**

```
    void* temp_buffer = allocate_buffer (1024);
    /* Register a cleanup handler for this buffer, to deallocate it in
       case the thread exits or is cancelled.  */
    pthread_cleanup_push (deallocate_buffer, temp_buffer);

    /* Do some work here that might call pthread_exit or might be
       cancelled...  */

    /* Unregister the cleanup handler.  Because we pass a nonzero value,
       this actually performs the cleanup by calling
       deallocate_buffer.  */
    pthread_cleanup_pop (1);
}
```

Because the argument to `pthread_cleanup_pop` is nonzero in this case, the cleanup function `deallocate_buffer` is called automatically here and does not need to be called explicitly. In this simple case, we could have used the standard library function `free` directly as our cleanup handler function instead of `deallocate_buffer`.

4.3.2   Thread Cleanup in C++

C++ programmers are accustomed to getting cleanup "for free" by wrapping cleanup actions in object destructors. When the objects go out of scope, either because a block is executed to completion or because an exception is thrown, C++ makes sure that destructors are called for those automatic variables that have them. This provides a handy mechanism to make sure that cleanup code is called no matter how the block is exited.

If a thread calls `pthread_exit`, though, C++ doesn't guarantee that destructors are called for all automatic variables on the thread's stack. A clever way to recover this functionality is to invoke `pthread_exit` at the top level of the thread function by throwing a special exception.

The program in Listing 4.9 demonstrates this. Using this technique, a function indicates its intention to exit the thread by throwing a `ThreadExitException` instead of calling `pthread_exit` directly. Because the exception is caught in the top-level thread function, all local variables on the thread's stack will be destroyed properly as the exception percolates up.

Listing 4.9   (*cxx-exit.cpp*) **Implementing Safe Thread Exit with C++ Exceptions**

```
#include <pthread.h>

class ThreadExitException
{
public:
    /* Create an exception-signaling thread exit with RETURN_VALUE.  */
    ThreadExitException (void* return_value)
      : thread_return_value_ (return_value)
```

```
  {
  }

  /* Actually exit the thread, using the return value provided in the
     constructor.  */
  void* DoThreadExit ()
  {
    pthread_exit (thread_return_value_);
  }

private:
  /* The return value that will be used when exiting the thread.  */
  void* thread_return_value_;
};

void do_some_work ()
{
  while (1) {
    /* Do some useful things here...  */

    if (should_exit_thread_immediately ())
      throw ThreadExitException (/* thread's return value = */ NULL);
  }
}

void* thread_function (void*)
{
  try {
    do_some_work ();
  }
  catch (ThreadExitException ex) {
    /* Some function indicated that we should exit the thread.  */
    ex.DoThreadExit ();
  }
  return NULL;
}
```

4.4 Synchronization and Critical Sections

Programming with threads is very tricky because most threaded programs are concurrent programs. In particular, there's no way to know when the system will schedule one thread to run and when it will run another. One thread might run for a very long time, or the system might switch among threads very quickly. On a system with multiple processors, the system might even schedule multiple threads to run at literally the same time.

Debugging a threaded program is difficult because you cannot always easily reproduce the behavior that caused the problem. You might run the program once and have everything work fine; the next time you run it, it might crash. There's no way to make the system schedule the threads exactly the same way it did before.

The ultimate cause of most bugs involving threads is that the threads are accessing the same data. As mentioned previously, that's one of the powerful aspects of threads, but it can also be dangerous. If one thread is only partway through updating a data structure when another thread accesses the same data structure, chaos is likely to ensue. Often, buggy threaded programs contain a code that will work only if one thread gets scheduled more often—or sooner—than another thread. These bugs are called *race conditions*; the threads are racing one another to change the same data structure.

4.4.1 Race Conditions

Suppose that your program has a series of queued jobs that are processed by several concurrent threads. The queue of jobs is represented by a linked list of struct job objects.

After each thread finishes an operation, it checks the queue to see if an additional job is available. If job_queue is non-null, the thread removes the head of the linked list and sets job_queue to the next job on the list.

The thread function that processes jobs in the queue might look like Listing 4.10.

Listing 4.10   (*job-queue1.c*) **Thread Function to Process Jobs from the Queue**

```
#include <malloc.h>

struct job {
  /* Link field for linked list.  */
  struct job* next;

  /* Other fields describing work to be done... */
};

/* A linked list of pending jobs.  */
struct job* job_queue;

/* Process queued jobs until the queue is empty.  */

void* thread_function (void* arg)
{
  while (job_queue != NULL) {
    /* Get the next available job.  */
    struct job* next_job = job_queue;
    /* Remove this job from the list.  */
    job_queue = job_queue->next;
    /* Carry out the work.  */
    process_job (next_job);
    /* Clean up.  */
    free (next_job);
  }
  return NULL;
}
```

Now suppose that two threads happen to finish a job at about the same time, but only one job remains in the queue. The first thread checks whether job_queue is null; finding that it isn't, the thread enters the loop and stores the pointer to the job object in next_job. At this point, Linux happens to interrupt the first thread and schedules the second. The second thread also checks job_queue and finding it non-null, also assigns the same job pointer to next_job. By unfortunate coincidence, we now have two threads executing the same job.

To make matters worse, one thread will unlink the job object from the queue, leaving job_queue containing null. When the other thread evaluates job_queue->next, a segmentation fault will result.

This is an example of a race condition. Under "lucky" circumstances, this particular schedule of the two threads may never occur, and the race condition may never exhibit itself. Only under different circumstances, perhaps when running on a heavily loaded system (or on an important customer's new multiprocessor server!) may the bug exhibit itself.

To eliminate race conditions, you need a way to make operations *atomic*. An atomic operation is indivisible and uninterruptible; once the operation starts, it will not be paused or interrupted until it completes, and no other operation will take place meanwhile. In this particular example, you want to check job_queue; if it's not empty, remove the first job, all as a single atomic operation.

4.4.2 Mutexes

The solution to the job queue race condition problem is to let only one thread access the queue of jobs at a time. Once a thread starts looking at the queue, no other thread should be able to access it until the first thread has decided whether to process a job and, if so, has removed the job from the list.

Implementing this requires support from the operating system. GNU/Linux provides *mutexes*, short for *MUTual EXclusion locks*. A mutex is a special lock that only one thread may lock at a time. If a thread locks a mutex and then a second thread also tries to lock the same mutex, the second thread is *blocked*, or put on hold. Only when the first thread unlocks the mutex is the second thread *unblocked*—allowed to resume execution. GNU/Linux guarantees that race conditions do not occur among threads attempting to lock a mutex; only one thread will ever get the lock, and all other threads will be blocked.

Think of a mutex as the lock on a lavatory door. Whoever gets there first enters the lavatory and locks the door. If someone else attempts to enter the lavatory while it's occupied, that person will find the door locked and will be forced to wait outside until the occupant emerges.

To create a mutex, create a variable of type pthread_mutex_t and pass a pointer to it to pthread_mutex_init. The second argument to pthread_mutex_init is a pointer to a mutex attribute object, which specifies attributes of the mutex. As with `pthread_create`, if the attribute pointer is null, default attributes are assumed. The mutex variable should be initialized only once. This code fragment demonstrates the declaration and initialization of a mutex variable.

```
pthread_mutex_t mutex;
pthread_mutex_init (&mutex, NULL);
```

Another simpler way to create a mutex with default attributes is to initialize it with the special value `PTHREAD_MUTEX_INITIALIZER`. No additional call to `pthread_mutex_init` is necessary. This is particularly convenient for global variables (and, in C++, static data members). The previous code fragment could equivalently have been written like this:

```
pthread_mutex_t mutex = PTHREAD_MUTEX_INITIALIZER;
```

A thread may attempt to lock a mutex by calling `pthread_mutex_lock` on it. If the mutex was unlocked, it becomes locked and the function returns immediately. If the mutex was locked by another thread, `pthread_mutex_lock` blocks execution and returns only eventually when the mutex is unlocked by the other thread. More than one thread may be blocked on a locked mutex at one time. When the mutex is unlocked, only one of the blocked threads (chosen unpredictably) is unblocked and allowed to lock the mutex; the other threads stay blocked.

A call to `pthread_mutex_unlock` unlocks a mutex. This function should always be called from the same thread that locked the mutex.

Listing 4.11 shows another version of the job queue example. Now the queue is protected by a mutex. Before accessing the queue (either for read or write), each thread locks a mutex first. Only when the entire sequence of checking the queue and removing a job is complete is the mutex unlocked. This prevents the race condition previously described.

Listing 4.11   (*job-queue2.c*) **Job Queue Thread Function, Protected by a Mutex**

```
#include <malloc.h>
#include <pthread.h>

struct job {
  /* Link field for linked list.  */
  struct job* next;

  /* Other fields describing work to be done... */
};

/* A linked list of pending jobs.  */
struct job* job_queue;

/* A mutex protecting job_queue.  */
pthread_mutex_t job_queue_mutex = PTHREAD_MUTEX_INITIALIZER;
```

```
/* Process queued jobs until the queue is empty.  */

void* thread_function (void* arg)
{
  while (1) {
    struct job* next_job;

    /* Lock the mutex on the job queue.  */
    pthread_mutex_lock (&job_queue_mutex);
    /* Now it's safe to check if the queue is empty.  */
    if (job_queue == NULL)
      next_job = NULL;
    else {
      /* Get the next available job.  */
      next_job = job_queue;
      /* Remove this job from the list.  */
      job_queue = job_queue->next;
    }
    /* Unlock the mutex on the job queue because we're done with the
       queue for now.  */
    pthread_mutex_unlock (&job_queue_mutex);

    /* Was the queue empty?  If so, end the thread.  */
    if (next_job == NULL)
      break;

    /* Carry out the work.  */
    process_job (next_job);
    /* Clean up.  */
    free (next_job);
  }
  return NULL;
}
```

All accesses to `job_queue`, the shared data pointer, come between the call to `pthread_mutex_lock` and the call to `pthread_mutex_unlock`. A job object, stored in `next_job`, is accessed outside this region only after that object has been removed from the queue and is therefore inaccessible to other threads.

Note that if the queue is empty (that is, `job_queue` is null), we don't break out of the loop immediately because this would leave the mutex permanently locked and would prevent any other thread from accessing the job queue ever again. Instead, we remember this fact by setting `next_job` to null and breaking out only after unlocking the mutex.

Use of the mutex to lock `job_queue` is not automatic; it's up to you to add code to lock the mutex before accessing that variable and then to unlock it afterward. For example, a function to add a job to the job queue might look like this:

```
void enqueue_job (struct job* new_job)
{
  pthread_mutex_lock (&job_queue_mutex);
```

```
    new_job->next = job_queue;
    job_queue = new_job;
    pthread_mutex_unlock (&job_queue_mutex);
}
```

4.4.3   Mutex Deadlocks

Mutexes provide a mechanism for allowing one thread to block the execution of another. This opens up the possibility of a new class of bugs, called *deadlocks*. A deadlock occurs when one or more threads are stuck waiting for something that never will occur.

A simple type of deadlock may occur when the same thread attempts to lock a mutex twice in a row. The behavior in this case depends on what kind of mutex is being used. Three kinds of mutexes exist:

- Locking a *fast mutex* (the default kind) will cause a deadlock to occur. An attempt to lock the mutex blocks until the mutex is unlocked. But because the thread that locked the mutex is blocked on the same mutex, the lock cannot ever be released.

- Locking a *recursive mutex* does not cause a deadlock. A recursive mutex may safely be locked many times by the same thread. The mutex remembers how many times pthread_mutex_lock was called on it by the thread that holds the lock; that thread must make the same number of calls to pthread_mutex_unlock before the mutex is actually unlocked and another thread is allowed to lock it.

- GNU/Linux will detect and flag a double lock on an *error-checking mutex* that would otherwise cause a deadlock. The second consecutive call to pthread_mutex_lock returns the failure code EDEADLK.

By default, a GNU/Linux mutex is of the fast kind. To create a mutex of one of the other two kinds, first create a mutex attribute object by declaring a pthread_mutexattr_t variable and calling pthread_mutexattr_init on a pointer to it. Then set the mutex kind by calling pthread_mutexattr_setkind_np; the first argument is a pointer to the mutex attribute object, and the second is PTHREAD_MUTEX_RECURSIVE_NP for a recursive mutex, or PTHREAD_MUTEX_ERRORCHECK_NP for an error-checking mutex. Pass a pointer to this attribute object to pthread_mutex_init to create a mutex of this kind, and then destroy the attribute object with pthread_mutexattr_destroy.

This code sequence illustrates creation of an error-checking mutex, for instance:

```
pthread_mutexattr_t attr;
pthread_mutex_t mutex;

pthread_mutexattr_init (&attr);
pthread_mutexattr_setkind_np (&attr, PTHREAD_MUTEX_ERRORCHECK_NP);
pthread_mutex_init (&mutex, &attr);
pthread_mutexattr_destroy (&attr);
```

As suggested by the "np" suffix, the recursive and error-checking mutex kinds are specific to GNU/Linux and are not portable. Therefore, it is generally not advised to use them in programs. (Error-checking mutexes can be useful when debugging, though.)

4.4.4   Nonblocking Mutex Tests

Occasionally, it is useful to test whether a mutex is locked without actually blocking on it. For instance, a thread may need to lock a mutex but may have other work to do instead of blocking if the mutex is already locked. Because `pthread_mutex_lock` will not return until the mutex becomes unlocked, some other function is necessary.

GNU/Linux provides `pthread_mutex_trylock` for this purpose. If you call `pthread_mutex_trylock` on an unlocked mutex, you will lock the mutex as if you had called `pthread_mutex_lock`, and `pthread_mutex_trylock` will return zero. However, if the mutex is already locked by another thread, `pthread_mutex_trylock` will not block. Instead, it will return immediately with the error code `EBUSY`. The mutex lock held by the other thread is not affected. You may try again later to lock the mutex.

4.4.5   Semaphores for Threads

In the preceding example, in which several threads process jobs from a queue, the main thread function of the threads carries out the next job until no jobs are left and then exits the thread. This scheme works if all the jobs are queued in advance or if new jobs are queued at least as quickly as the threads process them. However, if the threads work too quickly, the queue of jobs will empty and the threads will exit. If new jobs are later enqueued, no threads may remain to process them. What we might like instead is a mechanism for blocking the threads when the queue empties until new jobs become available.

A *semaphore* provides a convenient method for doing this. A semaphore is a counter that can be used to synchronize multiple threads. As with a mutex, GNU/Linux guarantees that checking or modifying the value of a semaphore can be done safely, without creating a race condition.

Each semaphore has a counter value, which is a non-negative integer. A semaphore supports two basic operations:

- A *wait* operation decrements the value of the semaphore by 1. If the value is already zero, the operation blocks until the value of the semaphore becomes positive (due to the action of some other thread). When the semaphore's value becomes positive, it is decremented by 1 and the wait operation returns.

- A *post* operation increments the value of the semaphore by 1. If the semaphore was previously zero and other threads are blocked in a wait operation on that semaphore, one of those threads is unblocked and its wait operation completes (which brings the semaphore's value back to zero).

Note that GNU/Linux provides two slightly different semaphore implementations. The one we describe here is the POSIX standard semaphore implementation. Use these semaphores when communicating among threads The other implementation, used for communication among processes, is described in Section 5.2, "Process Semaphores." If you use semaphores, include `<semaphore.h>`.

A semaphore is represented by a `sem_t` variable. Before using it, you must initialize it using the `sem_init` function, passing a pointer to the `sem_t` variable. The second parameter should be zero,[2] and the third parameter is the semaphore's initial value. If you no longer need a semaphore, it's good to deallocate it with `sem_destroy`.

To wait on a semaphore, use `sem_wait`. To post to a semaphore, use `sem_post`. A nonblocking wait function, `sem_trywait`, is also provided. It's similar to `pthread_mutex_trylock`—if the wait would have blocked because the semaphore's value was zero, the function returns immediately, with error value `EAGAIN`, instead of blocking.

GNU/Linux also provides a function to retrieve the current value of a semaphore, `sem_getvalue`, which places the value in the `int` variable pointed to by its second argument. You should not use the semaphore value you get from this function to make a decision whether to post to or wait on the semaphore, though. To do this could lead to a race condition: Another thread could change the semaphore's value between the call to `sem_getvalue` and the call to another semaphore function. Use the atomic post and wait functions instead.

Returning to our job queue example, we can use a semaphore to count the number of jobs waiting in the queue. Listing 4.12 controls the queue with a semaphore. The function `enqueue_job` adds a new job to the queue.

Listing 4.12   (*job-queue3.c*) **Job Queue Controlled by a Semaphore**

```
#include <malloc.h>
#include <pthread.h>
#include <semaphore.h>

struct job {
  /* Link field for linked list.  */
  struct job* next;

  /* Other fields describing work to be done... */
};

/* A linked list of pending jobs.  */
struct job* job_queue;

/* A mutex protecting job_queue.  */
pthread_mutex_t job_queue_mutex = PTHREAD_MUTEX_INITIALIZER;
```

2. A nonzero value would indicate a semaphore that can be shared across processes, which is not supported by GNU/Linux for this type of semaphore.

```
/* A semaphore counting the number of jobs in the queue.  */
sem_t job_queue_count;

/* Perform one-time initialization of the job queue.  */

void initialize_job_queue ()
{
  /* The queue is initially empty.  */
  job_queue = NULL;
  /* Initialize the semaphore which counts jobs in the queue.  Its
     initial value should be zero.  */
  sem_init (&job_queue_count, 0, 0);
}

/* Process queued jobs until the queue is empty.  */

void* thread_function (void* arg)
{
  while (1) {
    struct job* next_job;

    /* Wait on the job queue semaphore.  If its value is positive,
       indicating that the queue is not empty, decrement the count by
       1.  If the queue is empty, block until a new job is enqueued.  */
    sem_wait (&job_queue_count);

    /* Lock the mutex on the job queue.  */
    pthread_mutex_lock (&job_queue_mutex);
    /* Because of the semaphore, we know the queue is not empty.  Get
       the next available job.  */
    next_job = job_queue;
    /* Remove this job from the list.  */
    job_queue = job_queue->next;
    /* Unlock the mutex on the job queue because we're done with the
       queue for now.  */
    pthread_mutex_unlock (&job_queue_mutex);

    /* Carry out the work.  */
    process_job (next_job);
    /* Clean up.  */
    free (next_job);
  }
  return NULL;
}

/* Add a new job to the front of the job queue.  */

void enqueue_job (/* Pass job-specific data here...  */)
{
  struct job* new_job;
```

continues

Listing 4.12   **Continued**

```
    /* Allocate a new job object.  */
    new_job = (struct job*) malloc (sizeof (struct job));
    /* Set the other fields of the job struct here...  */

    /* Lock the mutex on the job queue before accessing it.  */
    pthread_mutex_lock (&job_queue_mutex);
    /* Place the new job at the head of the queue.  */
    new_job->next = job_queue;
    job_queue = new_job;

    /* Post to the semaphore to indicate that another job is available.  If
       threads are blocked, waiting on the semaphore, one will become
       unblocked so it can process the job.  */
    sem_post (&job_queue_count);

    /* Unlock the job queue mutex.  */
    pthread_mutex_unlock (&job_queue_mutex);
}
```

Before taking a job from the front of the queue, each thread will first wait on the semaphore. If the semaphore's value is zero, indicating that the queue is empty, the thread will simply block until the semaphore's value becomes positive, indicating that a job has been added to the queue.

The enqueue_job function adds a job to the queue. Just like thread_function, it needs to lock the queue mutex before modifying the queue. After adding a job to the queue, it posts to the semaphore, indicating that a new job is available. In the version shown in Listing 4.12, the threads that process the jobs never exit; if no jobs are available for a while, all the threads simply block in sem_wait.

4.4.6   Condition Variables

We've shown how to use a mutex to protect a variable against simultaneous access by two threads and how to use semaphores to implement a shared counter. A *condition variable* is a third synchronization device that GNU/Linux provides; with it, you can implement more complex conditions under which threads execute.

Suppose that you write a thread function that executes a loop infinitely, performing some work on each iteration. The thread loop, however, needs to be controlled by a flag: The loop runs only when the flag is set; when the flag is not set, the loop pauses.

Listing 4.13 shows how you might implement this by spinning in a loop. During each iteration of the loop, the thread function checks that the flag is set. Because the flag is accessed by multiple threads, it is protected by a mutex. This implementation may be correct, but it is not efficient. The thread function will spend lots of CPU whenever the flag is not set, checking and rechecking the flag, each time locking and unlocking the mutex. What you really want is a way to put the thread to sleep when the flag is not set, until some circumstance changes that might cause the flag to become set.

Listing 4.13 *(spin-condvar.c)* **A Simple Condition Variable Implementation**

```
#include <pthread.h>

int thread_flag;
pthread_mutex_t thread_flag_mutex;

void initialize_flag ()
{
  pthread_mutex_init (&thread_flag_mutex, NULL);
  thread_flag = 0;
}

/* Calls do_work repeatedly while the thread flag is set; otherwise
   spins.  */

void* thread_function (void* thread_arg)
{
  while (1) {
    int flag_is_set;

    /* Protect the flag with a mutex lock.  */
    pthread_mutex_lock (&thread_flag_mutex);
    flag_is_set = thread_flag;
    pthread_mutex_unlock (&thread_flag_mutex);

    if (flag_is_set)
      do_work ();
    /* Else don't do anything.  Just loop again.  */
  }
  return NULL;
}

/* Sets the value of the thread flag to FLAG_VALUE.  */

void set_thread_flag (int flag_value)
{
  /* Protect the flag with a mutex lock.  */
  pthread_mutex_lock (&thread_flag_mutex);
  thread_flag = flag_value;
  pthread_mutex_unlock (&thread_flag_mutex);
}
```

A condition variable enables you to implement a condition under which a thread executes and, inversely, the condition under which the thread is blocked. As long as every thread that potentially changes the sense of the condition uses the condition variable properly, Linux guarantees that threads blocked on the condition will be unblocked when the condition changes.

As with a semaphore, a thread may *wait* on a condition variable. If thread A waits on a condition variable, it is blocked until some other thread, thread B, signals the same condition variable. Unlike a semaphore, a condition variable has no counter or memory; thread A must wait on the condition variable *before* thread B signals it. If thread B signals the condition variable before thread A waits on it, the signal is lost, and thread A blocks until some other thread signals the condition variable again.

This is how you would use a condition variable to make the previous sample more efficient:

- The loop in `thread_function` checks the flag. If the flag is not set, the thread waits on the condition variable.

- The `set_thread_flag` function signals the condition variable after changing the flag value. That way, if `thread_function` is blocked on the condition variable, it will be unblocked and will check the condition again.

There's one problem with this: There's a race condition between checking the flag value and signaling or waiting on the condition variable. Suppose that `thread_function` checked the flag and found that it was not set. At that moment, the Linux scheduler paused that thread and resumed the main one. By some coincidence, the main thread is in `set_thread_flag`. It sets the flag and then signals the condition variable. Because no thread is waiting on the condition variable at the time (remember that `thread_function` was paused before it could wait on the condition variable), the signal is lost. Now, when Linux reschedules the other thread, it starts waiting on the condition variable and may end up blocked forever.

To solve this problem, we need a way to lock the flag and the condition variable together with a single mutex. Fortunately, GNU/Linux provides exactly this mechanism. Each condition variable must be used in conjunction with a mutex, to prevent this sort of race condition. Using this scheme, the thread function follows these steps:

1. The loop in `thread_function` locks the mutex and reads the flag value.

2. If the flag is set, it unlocks the mutex and executes the work function.

3. If the flag is not set, it atomically unlocks the mutex and waits on the condition variable.

The critical feature here is in step 3, in which GNU/Linux allows you to unlock the mutex and wait on the condition variable atomically, without the possibility of another thread intervening. This eliminates the possibility that another thread may change the flag value and signal the condition variable in between `thread_function`'s test of the flag value and wait on the condition variable.

A condition variable is represented by an instance of `pthread_cond_t`. Remember that each condition variable should be accompanied by a mutex. These are the functions that manipulate condition variables:

- `pthread_cond_init` initializes a condition variable. The first argument is a pointer to a `pthread_cond_t` instance. The second argument, a pointer to a condition variable attribute object, is ignored under GNU/Linux.

  The mutex must be initialized separately, as described in Section 4.4.2, "Mutexes."

- `pthread_cond_signal` signals a condition variable. A single thread that is blocked on the condition variable will be unblocked. If no other thread is blocked on the condition variable, the signal is ignored. The argument is a pointer to the `pthread_cond_t` instance.

  A similar call, `pthread_cond_broadcast`, unblocks *all* threads that are blocked on the condition variable, instead of just one.

- `pthread_cond_wait` blocks the calling thread until the condition variable is signaled. The argument is a pointer to the `pthread_cond_t` instance. The second argument is a pointer to the `pthread_mutex_t` mutex instance.

  When `pthread_cond_wait` is called, the mutex must already be locked by the calling thread. That function atomically unlocks the mutex and blocks on the condition variable. When the condition variable is signaled and the calling thread unblocks, `pthread_cond_wait` automatically reacquires a lock on the mutex.

Whenever your program performs an action that may change the sense of the condition you're protecting with the condition variable, it should perform these steps. (In our example, the condition is the state of the thread flag, so these steps must be taken whenever the flag is changed.)

1. Lock the mutex accompanying the condition variable.
2. Take the action that may change the sense of the condition (in our example, set the flag).
3. Signal or broadcast the condition variable, depending on the desired behavior.
4. Unlock the mutex accompanying the condition variable.

Listing 4.14 shows the previous example again, now using a condition variable to protect the thread flag. Note that in `thread_function`, a lock on the mutex is held before checking the value of `thread_flag`. That lock is automatically released by `pthread_cond_wait` before blocking and is automatically reacquired afterward. Also note that `set_thread_flag` locks the mutex before setting the value of `thread_flag` and signaling the mutex.

Listing 4.14   *(condvar.c)* **Control a Thread Using a Condition Variable**

```
#include <pthread.h>

int thread_flag;
pthread_cond_t thread_flag_cv;
pthread_mutex_t thread_flag_mutex;

void initialize_flag ()
{
  /* Initialize the mutex and condition variable.  */
  pthread_mutex_init (&thread_flag_mutex, NULL);
  pthread_cond_init (&thread_flag_cv, NULL);
  /* Initialize the flag value.  */
  thread_flag = 0;
}

/* Calls do_work repeatedly while the thread flag is set; blocks if
   the flag is clear.  */

void* thread_function (void* thread_arg)
{
  /* Loop infinitely.  */
  while (1) {
    /* Lock the mutex before accessing the flag value.  */
    pthread_mutex_lock (&thread_flag_mutex);
    while (!thread_flag)
      /* The flag is clear.  Wait for a signal on the condition
         variable, indicating that the flag value has changed.  When the
         signal arrives and this thread unblocks, loop and check the
         flag again.  */
      pthread_cond_wait (&thread_flag_cv, &thread_flag_mutex);
    /* When we've gotten here, we know the flag must be set.  Unlock
       the mutex.  */
    pthread_mutex_unlock (&thread_flag_mutex);
    /* Do some work.  */
    do_work ();
  }
  return NULL;
}

/* Sets the value of the thread flag to FLAG_VALUE.  */

void set_thread_flag (int flag_value)
{
  /* Lock the mutex before accessing the flag value.  */
  pthread_mutex_lock (&thread_flag_mutex);
  /* Set the flag value, and then signal in case thread_function is
     blocked, waiting for the flag to become set.  However,
     thread_function can't actually check the flag until the mutex is
     unlocked.  */
```

```
    thread_flag = flag_value;
    pthread_cond_signal (&thread_flag_cv);
    /* Unlock the mutex.  */
    pthread_mutex_unlock (&thread_flag_mutex);
  }
```

The condition protected by a condition variable can be arbitrarily complex. However, before performing any operation that may change the sense of the condition, a mutex lock should be required, and the condition variable should be signaled afterward.

A condition variable may also be used without a condition, simply as a mechanism for blocking a thread until another thread "wakes it up." A semaphore may also be used for that purpose. The principal difference is that a semaphore "remembers" the wake-up call even if no thread was blocked on it at the time, while a condition variable discards the wake-up call unless some thread is actually blocked on it at the time. Also, a semaphore delivers only a single wake-up per post; with pthread_cond_broadcast, an arbitrary and unknown number of blocked threads may be awoken at the same time.

4.4.7 Deadlocks with Two or More Threads

Deadlocks can occur when two (or more) threads are each blocked, waiting for a condition to occur that only the other one can cause. For instance, if thread A is blocked on a condition variable waiting for thread B to signal it, and thread B is blocked on a condition variable waiting for thread A to signal it, a deadlock has occurred because neither thread will ever signal the other. You should take care to avoid the possibility of such situations because they are quite difficult to detect.

One common error that can cause a deadlock involves a problem in which more than one thread is trying to lock the same set of objects. For example, consider a program in which two different threads, running two different thread functions, need to lock the same two mutexes. Suppose that thread A locks mutex 1 and then mutex 2, and thread B happens to lock mutex 2 before mutex 1. In a sufficiently unfortunate scheduling scenario, Linux may schedule thread A long enough to lock mutex 1, and then schedule thread B, which promptly locks mutex 2. Now neither thread can progress because each is blocked on a mutex that the other thread holds locked.

This is an example of a more general deadlock problem, which can involve not only synchronization objects such as mutexes, but also other resources, such as locks on files or devices. The problem occurs when multiple threads try to lock the same set of resources in different orders. The solution is to make sure that all threads that lock more than one resource lock them in the same order.

4.5   GNU/Linux Thread Implementation

The implementation of POSIX threads on GNU/Linux differs from the thread implementation on many other UNIX-like systems in an important way: on GNU/Linux, threads are implemented as processes. Whenever you call pthread_create to create a new thread, Linux creates a new process that runs that thread. However, this process is not the same as a process you would create with fork; in particular, it shares the same address space and resources as the original process rather than receiving copies.

The program thread-pid shown in Listing 4.15 demonstrates this. The program creates a thread; both the original thread and the new one call the getpid function and print their respective process IDs and then spin infinitely.

Listing 4.15   (thread-pid) Print Process IDs for Threads

```
#include <pthread.h>
#include <stdio.h>
#include <unistd.h>

void* thread_function (void* arg)
{
  fprintf (stderr, "child thread pid is %d\n", (int) getpid ());
  /* Spin forever.  */
  while (1);
  return NULL;
}

int main ()
{
  pthread_t thread;
  fprintf (stderr, "main thread pid is %d\n", (int) getpid ());
  pthread_create (&thread, NULL, &thread_function, NULL);
  /* Spin forever.  */
  while (1);
  return 0;
}
```

Run the program in the background, and then invoke ps x to display your running processes. Don't forget to kill the thread-pid program afterward—it consumes lots of CPU doing nothing. Here's what the output might look like:

```
% cc thread-pid.c -o thread-pid -lpthread
% ./thread-pid &
[1] 14608
main thread pid is 14608
child thread pid is 14610
% ps x
  PID TTY       STAT   TIME COMMAND
14042 pts/9     S      0:00 bash
14608 pts/9     R      0:01 ./thread-pid
```

```
14609 pts/9    S     0:00 ./thread-pid
14610 pts/9    R     0:01 ./thread-pid
14611 pts/9    R     0:00 ps x
% kill 14608
[1]+  Terminated              ./thread-pid
```

Job Control Notification in the Shell

The lines starting with [1] are from the shell. When you run a program in the background, the shell assigns a job number to it—in this case, 1—and prints out the program's pid. If a background job terminates, the shell reports that fact the next time you invoke a command.

Notice that there are three processes running the thread-pid program. The first of these, with pid 14608, is the main thread in the program; the third, with pid 14610, is the thread we created to execute thread_function.

How about the second thread, with pid 14609? This is the "manager thread," which is part of the internal implementation of GNU/Linux threads. The manager thread is created the first time a program calls pthread_create to create a new thread.

4.5.1 Signal Handling

Suppose that a multithreaded program receives a signal. In which thread is the signal handler invoked? The behavior of the interaction between signals and threads varies from one UNIX-like system to another. In GNU/Linux, the behavior is dictated by the fact that threads are implemented as processes.

Because each thread is a separate process, and because a signal is delivered to a particular process, there is no ambiguity about which thread receives the signal. Typically, signals sent from outside the program are sent to the process corresponding to the main thread of the program. For instance, if a program forks and the child process execs a multithreaded program, the parent process will hold the process id of the main thread of the child process's program and will use that process id to send signals to its child. This is generally a good convention to follow yourself when sending signals to a multithreaded program.

Note that this aspect of GNU/Linux's implementation of pthreads is at variance with the POSIX thread standard. Do not rely on this behavior in programs that are meant to be portable.

Within a multithreaded program, it is possible for one thread to send a signal specifically to another thread. Use the pthread_kill function to do this. Its first parameter is a thread ID, and its second parameter is a signal number.

4.5.2 The *clone* System Call

Although GNU/Linux threads created in the same program are implemented as separate processes, they share their virtual memory space and other resources. A child process created with fork, however, gets copies of these items. How is the former type of process created?

The Linux `clone` system call is a generalized form of `fork` and `pthread_create` that allows the caller to specify which resources are shared between the calling process and the newly created process. Also, `clone` requires you to specify the memory region for the execution stack that the new process will use. Although we mention `clone` here to satisfy the reader's curiosity, that system call should not ordinarily be used in programs. Use `fork` to create new processes or `pthread_create` to create threads.

4.6   Processes Vs. Threads

For some programs that benefit from concurrency, the decision whether to use processes or threads can be difficult. Here are some guidelines to help you decide which concurrency model best suits your program:

- All threads in a program must run the same executable. A child process, on the other hand, may run a different executable by calling an `exec` function.

- An errant thread can harm other threads in the same process because threads share the same virtual memory space and other resources. For instance, a wild memory write through an uninitialized pointer in one thread can corrupt memory visible to another thread.

  An errant process, on the other hand, cannot do so because each process has a copy of the program's memory space.

- Copying memory for a new process adds an additional performance overhead relative to creating a new thread. However, the copy is performed only when the memory is changed, so the penalty is minimal if the child process only reads memory.

- Threads should be used for programs that need fine-grained parallelism. For example, if a problem can be broken into multiple, nearly identical tasks, threads may be a good choice. Processes should be used for programs that need coarser parallelism.

- Sharing data among threads is trivial because threads share the same memory. (However, great care must be taken to avoid race conditions, as described previously.) Sharing data among processes requires the use of IPC mechanisms, as described in Chapter 5. This can be more cumbersome but makes multiple processes less likely to suffer from concurrency bugs.

5

Interprocess Communication

Cʜᴀᴘᴛᴇʀ 3, "Pʀᴏᴄᴇꜱꜱᴇꜱ," ᴅɪꜱᴄᴜꜱꜱᴇᴅ ᴛʜᴇ ᴄʀᴇᴀᴛɪᴏɴ ᴏꜰ ᴘʀᴏᴄᴇꜱꜱᴇꜱ and showed how one process can obtain the exit status of a child process. That's the simplest form of communication between two processes, but it's by no means the most powerful. The mechanisms of Chapter 3 don't provide any way for the parent to communicate with the child except via command-line arguments and environment variables, nor any way for the child to communicate with the parent except via the child's exit status. None of these mechanisms provides any means for communicating with the child process while it is actually running, nor do these mechanisms allow communication with a process outside the parent-child relationship.

This chapter describes means for interprocess communication that circumvent these limitations. We will present various ways for communicating between parents and children, between "unrelated" processes, and even between processes on different machines.

Interprocess communication (IPC) is the transfer of data among processes. For example, a Web browser may request a Web page from a Web server, which then sends HTML data. This transfer of data usually uses sockets in a telephone-like connection. In another example, you may want to print the filenames in a directory using a command such as ls | lpr. The shell creates an ls process and a separate lpr process, connecting the two with a *pipe*, represented by the "|" symbol. A pipe permits one-way communication between two related processes. The ls process writes data into the pipe, and the lpr process reads data from the pipe.

In this chapter, we discuss five types of interprocess communication:

- Shared memory permits processes to communicate by simply reading and writing to a specified memory location.

- Mapped memory is similar to shared memory, except that it is associated with a file in the filesystem.

- Pipes permit sequential communication from one process to a related process.

- FIFOs are similar to pipes, except that unrelated processes can communicate because the pipe is given a name in the filesystem.

- Sockets support communication between unrelated processes even on different computers.

These types of IPC differ by the following criteria:

- Whether they restrict communication to related processes (processes with a common ancestor), to unrelated processes sharing the same filesystem, or to any computer connected to a network

- Whether a communicating process is limited to only write data or only read data

- The number of processes permitted to communicate

- Whether the communicating processes are synchronized by the IPC—for example, a reading process halts until data is available to read

In this chapter, we omit discussion of IPC permitting communication only a limited number of times, such as communicating via a child's exit value.

5.1 Shared Memory

One of the simplest interprocess communication methods is using shared memory. Shared memory allows two or more processes to access the same memory as if they all called malloc and were returned pointers to the same actual memory. When one process changes the memory, all the other processes see the modification.

5.1.1 Fast Local Communication

Shared memory is the fastest form of interprocess communication because all processes share the same piece of memory. Access to this shared memory is as fast as accessing a process's nonshared memory, and it does not require a system call or entry to the kernel. It also avoids copying data unnecessarily.

Because the kernel does not synchronize accesses to shared memory, you must provide your own synchronization. For example, a process should not read from the memory until after data is written there, and two processes must not write to the same memory location at the same time. A common strategy to avoid these race conditions is to use semaphores, which are discussed in the next section. Our illustrative programs, though, show just a single process accessing the memory, to focus on the shared memory mechanism and to avoid cluttering the sample code with synchronization logic.

5.1.2   The Memory Model

To use a shared memory segment, one process must allocate the segment. Then each process desiring to access the segment must attach the segment. After finishing its use of the segment, each process detaches the segment. At some point, one process must deallocate the segment.

Understanding the Linux memory model helps explain the allocation and attachment process. Under Linux, each process's virtual memory is split into pages. Each process maintains a mapping from its memory addresses to these virtual memory pages, which contain the actual data. Even though each process has its own addresses, multiple processes' mappings can point to the same page, permitting sharing of memory. Memory pages are discussed further in Section 8.8, "The `mlock` Family: Locking Physical Memory," of Chapter 8, "Linux System Calls."

Allocating a new shared memory segment causes virtual memory pages to be created. Because all processes desire to access the same shared segment, only one process should allocate a new shared segment. Allocating an existing segment does not create new pages, but it does return an identifier for the existing pages. To permit a process to use the shared memory segment, a process attaches it, which adds entries mapping from its virtual memory to the segment's shared pages. When finished with the segment, these mapping entries are removed. When no more processes want to access these shared memory segments, exactly one process must deallocate the virtual memory pages.

All shared memory segments are allocated as integral multiples of the system's *page size*, which is the number of bytes in a page of memory. On Linux systems, the page size is 4KB, but you should obtain this value by calling the `getpagesize` function.

5.1.3   Allocation

A process allocates a shared memory segment using `shmget` ("SHared Memory GET"). Its first parameter is an integer key that specifies which segment to create. Unrelated processes can access the same shared segment by specifying the same key value. Unfortunately, other processes may have also chosen the same fixed key, which could lead to conflict. Using the special constant `IPC_PRIVATE` as the key value guarantees that a brand new memory segment is created.

Its second parameter specifies the number of bytes in the segment. Because segments are allocated using pages, the number of actually allocated bytes is rounded up to an integral multiple of the page size.

The third parameter is the bitwise or of flag values that specify options to `shmget`. The flag values include these:

- `IPC_CREAT`—This flag indicates that a new segment should be created. This permits creating a new segment while specifying a key value.

- `IPC_EXCL`—This flag, which is always used with `IPC_CREAT`, causes `shmget` to fail if a segment key is specified that already exists. Therefore, it arranges for the calling process to have an "exclusive" segment. If this flag is not given and the key of an existing segment is used, `shmget` returns the existing segment instead of creating a new one.

- Mode flags—This value is made of 9 bits indicating permissions granted to owner, group, and world to control access to the segment. Execution bits are ignored. An easy way to specify permissions is to use the constants defined in `<sys/stat.h>` and documented in the section 2 `stat` man page.[1] For example, `S_IRUSR` and `S_IWUSR` specify read and write permissions for the owner of the shared memory segment, and `S_IROTH` and `S_IWOTH` specify read and write permissions for others.

For example, this invocation of `shmget` creates a new shared memory segment (or access to an existing one, if `shm_key` is already used) that's readable and writeable to the owner but not other users.

```
int segment_id = shmget (shm_key, getpagesize (),
                    IPC_CREAT | S_IRUSR |  S_IWUSER);
```

If the call succeeds, `shmget` returns a segment identifier. If the shared memory segment already exists, the access permissions are verified and a check is made to ensure that the segment is not marked for destruction.

5.1.4   Attachment and Detachment

To make the shared memory segment available, a process must use `shmat`, "SHared Memory ATtach." Pass it the shared memory segment identifier `SHMID` returned by `shmget`. The second argument is a pointer that specifies where in your process's address space you want to map the shared memory; if you specify NULL, Linux will choose an available address. The third argument is a flag, which can include the following:

- `SHM_RND` indicates that the address specified for the second parameter should be rounded down to a multiple of the page size. If you don't specify this flag, you must page-align the second argument to `shmat` yourself.

- `SHM_RDONLY` indicates that the segment will be only read, not written.

---

1. These permission bits are the same as those used for files. They are described in Section 10.3, "File System Permissions."

If the call succeeds, it returns the address of the attached shared segment. Children created by calls to fork inherit attached shared segments; they can detach the shared memory segments, if desired.

When you're finished with a shared memory segment, the segment should be detached using shmdt ("SHared Memory DeTach"). Pass it the address returned by shmat. If the segment has been deallocated and this was the last process using it, it is removed. Calls to exit and any of the exec family automatically detach segments.

5.1.5   Controlling and Deallocating Shared Memory

The shmctl ("SHared Memory ConTroL") call returns information about a shared memory segment and can modify it. The first parameter is a shared memory segment identifier.

To obtain information about a shared memory segment, pass IPC_STAT as the second argument and a pointer to a struct shmid_ds.

To remove a segment, pass IPC_RMID as the second argument, and pass NULL as the third argument. The segment is removed when the last process that has attached it finally detaches it.

Each shared memory segment should be explicitly deallocated using shmctl when you're finished with it, to avoid violating the systemwide limit on the total number of shared memory segments. Invoking exit and exec detaches memory segments but does not deallocate them.

See the shmctl man page for a description of other operations you can perform on shared memory segments.

5.1.6   An Example Program

The program in Listing 5.1 illustrates the use of shared memory.

Listing 5.1   *(shm.c)* **Exercise Shared Memory**

```
#include <stdio.h>
#include <sys/shm.h>
#include <sys/stat.h>

int main ()
{
  int segment_id;
  char* shared_memory;
  struct shmid_ds shmbuffer;
  int segment_size;
  const int shared_segment_size = 0x6400;

  /* Allocate a shared memory segment.  */
  segment_id = shmget (IPC_PRIVATE, shared_segment_size,
                       IPC_CREAT | IPC_EXCL | S_IRUSR | S_IWUSR);
```

continues

Listing 5.1 **Continued**

```
    /* Attach the shared memory segment.  */
    shared_memory = (char*) shmat (segment_id, 0, 0);
    printf ("shared memory attached at address %p\n", shared_memory);
    /* Determine the segment's size.  */
    shmctl (segment_id, IPC_STAT, &shmbuffer);
    segment_size = shmbuffer.shm_segsz;
    printf ("segment size: %d\n", segment_size);
    /* Write a string to the shared memory segment.  */
    sprintf (shared_memory, "Hello, world.");
    /* Detach the shared memory segment.  */
    shmdt (shared_memory);

    /* Reattach the shared memory segment, at a different address.  */
    shared_memory = (char*) shmat (segment_id, (void*) 0x5000000, 0);
    printf ("shared memory reattached at address %p\n", shared_memory);
    /* Print out the string from shared memory.  */
    printf ("%s\n", shared_memory);
    /* Detach the shared memory segment.  */
    shmdt (shared_memory);

    /* Deallocate the shared memory segment.  */
    shmctl (segment_id, IPC_RMID, 0);

    return 0;
}
```

5.1.7 Debugging

The ipcs command provides information on interprocess communication facilities, including shared segments. Use the -m flag to obtain information about shared memory. For example, this code illustrates that one shared memory segment, numbered 1627649, is in use:

```
% ipcs -m

------ Shared Memory Segments --------
key        shmid      owner   perms   bytes    nattch    status
0x00000000 1627649    user    640     25600    0
```

If this memory segment was erroneously left behind by a program, you can use the ipcrm command to remove it.

```
% ipcrm shm 1627649
```

5.1.8 Pros and Cons

Shared memory segments permit fast bidirectional communication among any number of processes. Each user can both read and write, but a program must establish and follow some protocol for preventing race conditions such as overwriting information before it is read. Unfortunately, Linux does not strictly guarantee exclusive access even if you create a new shared segment with `IPC_PRIVATE`.

Also, for multiple processes to use a shared segment, they must make arrangements to use the same key.

5.2 Processes Semaphores

As noted in the previous section, processes must coordinate access to shared memory. As we discussed in Section 4.4.5, "Semaphores for Threads," in Chapter 4, "Threads," semaphores are counters that permit synchronizing multiple threads. Linux provides a distinct alternate implementation of semaphores that can be used for synchronizing processes (called process semaphores or sometimes System V semaphores). Process semaphores are allocated, used, and deallocated like shared memory segments. Although a single semaphore is sufficient for almost all uses, process semaphores come in sets. Throughout this section, we present system calls for process semaphores, showing how to implement single binary semaphores using them.

5.2.1 Allocation and Deallocation

The calls `semget` and `semctl` allocate and deallocate semaphores, which is analogous to `shmget` and `shmctl` for shared memory. Invoke `semget` with a key specifying a semaphore set, the number of semaphores in the set, and permission flags as for `shmget`; the return value is a semaphore set identifier. You can obtain the identifier of an existing semaphore set by specifying the right key value; in this case, the number of semaphores can be zero.

Semaphores continue to exist even after all processes using them have terminated. The last process to use a semaphore set must explicitly remove it to ensure that the operating system does not run out of semaphores. To do so, invoke `semctl` with the semaphore identifier, the number of semaphores in the set, `IPC_RMID` as the third argument, and any `union semun` value as the fourth argument (which is ignored). The effective user ID of the calling process must match that of the semaphore's allocator (or the caller must be `root`). Unlike shared memory segments, removing a semaphore set causes Linux to deallocate immediately.

Listing 5.2 presents functions to allocate and deallocate a binary semaphore.

Listing 5.2 *(sem_all_deall.c)* **Allocating and Deallocating a Binary Semaphore**

```
#include <sys/ipc.h>
#include <sys/sem.h>
#include <sys/types.h>

/* We must define union semun ourselves.  */

union semun {
  int val;
  struct semid_ds *buf;
  unsigned short int *array;
  struct seminfo *__buf;
};

/* Obtain a binary semaphore's ID, allocating if necessary.  */

int binary_semaphore_allocation (key_t key, int sem_flags)
{
  return semget (key, 1, sem_flags);
}

/* Deallocate a binary semaphore.  All users must have finished their
   use.  Returns -1 on failure.  */

int binary_semaphore_deallocate (int semid)
{
  union semun ignored_argument;
  return semctl (semid, 1, IPC_RMID, ignored_argument);
}
```

5.2.2 Initializing Semaphores

Allocating and initializing semaphores are two separate operations. To initialize a semaphore, use semctl with zero as the second argument and SETALL as the third argument. For the fourth argument, you must create a union semun object and point its array field at an array of unsigned short values. Each value is used to initialize one semaphore in the set.

Listing 5.3 presents a function that initializes a binary semaphore.

Listing 5.3 *(sem_init.c)* **Initializing a Binary Semaphore**

```
#include <sys/types.h>
#include <sys/ipc.h>
#include <sys/sem.h>
```

```
/* We must define union semun ourselves.  */

union semun {
  int val;
  struct semid_ds *buf;
  unsigned short int *array;
  struct seminfo *__buf;
};

/* Initialize a binary semaphore with a value of 1.  */

int binary_semaphore_initialize (int semid)
{
  union semun argument;
  unsigned short values[1];
  values[0] = 1;
  argument.array = values;
  return semctl (semid, 0, SETALL, argument);
}
```

5.2.3 Wait and Post Operations

Each semaphore has a non-negative value and supports wait and post operations. The `semop` system call implements both operations. Its first parameter specifies a semaphore set identifier. Its second parameter is an array of `struct sembuf` elements, which specify the operations you want to perform. The third parameter is the length of this array.

The fields of `struct sembuf` are listed here:

- `sem_num` is the semaphore number in the semaphore set on which the operation is performed.

- `sem_op` is an integer that specifies the semaphore operation.

  If `sem_op` is a positive number, that number is added to the semaphore value immediately.

  If `sem_op` is a negative number, the absolute value of that number is subtracted from the semaphore value. If this would make the semaphore value negative, the call blocks until the semaphore value becomes as large as the absolute value of `sem_op` (because some other process increments it).

  If `sem_op` is zero, the operation blocks until the semaphore value becomes zero.

- `sem_flg` is a flag value. Specify `IPC_NOWAIT` to prevent the operation from blocking; if the operation would have blocked, the call to `semop` fails instead. If you specify `SEM_UNDO`, Linux automatically undoes the operation on the semaphore when the process exits.

Listing 5.4 illustrates wait and post operations for a binary semaphore.

Listing 5.4   (*sem_pv.c*) **Wait and Post Operations for a Binary Semaphore**

```
#include <sys/types.h>
#include <sys/ipc.h>
#include <sys/sem.h>

/* Wait on a binary semaphore.  Block until the semaphore value is positive, then
   decrement it by 1.  */

int binary_semaphore_wait (int semid)
{
  struct sembuf operations[1];
  /* Use the first (and only) semaphore.  */
  operations[0].sem_num = 0;
  /* Decrement by 1.  */
  operations[0].sem_op = -1;
  /* Permit undo'ing.  */
  operations[0].sem_flg = SEM_UNDO;

  return semop (semid, operations, 1);
}

/* Post to a binary semaphore: increment its value by 1.
   This returns immediately.  */

int binary_semaphore_post (int semid)
{
  struct sembuf operations[1];
  /* Use the first (and only) semaphore.  */
  operations[0].sem_num = 0;
  /* Increment by 1.  */
  operations[0].sem_op = 1;
  /* Permit undo'ing.  */
  operations[0].sem_flg = SEM_UNDO;

  return semop (semid, operations, 1);
}
```

Specifying the SEM_UNDO flag permits dealing with the problem of terminating a
process while it has resources allocated through a semaphore. When a process terminates, either voluntarily or involuntarily, the semaphore's values are automatically
adjusted to "undo" the process's effects on the semaphore. For example, if a process
that has decremented a semaphore is killed, the semaphore's value is incremented.

5.2.4 Debugging Semaphores

Use the command `ipcs -s` to display information about existing semaphore sets. Use the `ipcrm sem` command to remove a semaphore set from the command line. For example, to remove the semaphore set with identifier 5790517, use this line:

```
% ipcrm sem 5790517
```

5.3 Mapped Memory

Mapped memory permits different processes to communicate via a shared file. Although you can think of mapped memory as using a shared memory segment with a name, you should be aware that there are technical differences. Mapped memory can be used for interprocess communication or as an easy way to access the contents of a file.

Mapped memory forms an association between a file and a process's memory. Linux splits the file into page-sized chunks and then copies them into virtual memory pages so that they can be made available in a process's address space. Thus, the process can read the file's contents with ordinary memory access. It can also modify the file's contents by writing to memory. This permits fast access to files.

You can think of mapped memory as allocating a buffer to hold a file's entire contents, and then reading the file into the buffer and (if the buffer is modified) writing the buffer back out to the file afterward. Linux handles the file reading and writing operations for you.

There are uses for memory-mapped files other than interprocess communication. Some of these are discussed in Section 5.3.5, "Other Uses for `mmap`."

5.3.1 Mapping an Ordinary File

To map an ordinary file to a process's memory, use the `mmap` ("Memory MAPped," pronounced "em-map") call. The first argument is the address at which you would like Linux to map the file into your process's address space; the value NULL allows Linux to choose an available start address. The second argument is the length of the map in bytes. The third argument specifies the protection on the mapped address range. The protection consists of a bitwise "or" of `PROT_READ`, `PROT_WRITE`, and `PROT_EXEC`, corresponding to read, write, and execution permission, respectively. The fourth argument is a flag value that specifies additional options. The fifth argument is a file descriptor opened to the file to be mapped. The last argument is the offset from the beginning of the file from which to start the map. You can map all or part of the file into memory by choosing the starting offset and length appropriately.

The flag value is a bitwise "or" of these constraints:

- `MAP_FIXED`—If you specify this flag, Linux uses the address you request to map the file rather than treating it as a hint. This address must be page-aligned.
- `MAP_PRIVATE`—Writes to the memory range should not be written back to the attached file, but to a private copy of the file. No other process sees these writes. This mode may not be used with `MAP_SHARED`.

- `MAP_SHARED`—Writes are immediately reflected in the underlying file rather than
  buffering writes. Use this mode when using mapped memory for IPC. This
  mode may not be used with `MAP_PRIVATE`.

If the call succeeds, it returns a pointer to the beginning of the memory. On failure, it
returns `MAP_FAILED`.

When you're finished with a memory mapping, release it by using `munmap`. Pass it
the start address and length of the mapped memory region. Linux automatically
unmaps mapped regions when a process terminates.

5.3.2 Example Programs

Let's look at two programs to illustrate using memory-mapped regions to read and
write to files. The first program, Listing 5.5, generates a random number and writes it
to a memory-mapped file. The second program, Listing 5.6, reads the number, prints
it, and replaces it in the memory-mapped file with double the value. Both take a
command-line argument of the file to map.

Listing 5.5 (*mmap-write.c*) **Write a Random Number to a Memory-Mapped File**

```c
#include <stdlib.h>
#include <stdio.h>
#include <fcntl.h>
#include <sys/mman.h>
#include <sys/stat.h>
#include <time.h>
#include <unistd.h>
#define FILE_LENGTH 0x100

/* Return a uniformly random number in the range [low,high].  */

int random_range (unsigned const low, unsigned const high)
{
  unsigned const range = high - low + 1;
  return low + (int) (((double) range) * rand () / (RAND_MAX + 1.0));
}

int main (int argc, char* const argv[])
{
  int fd;
  void* file_memory;

  /* Seed the random number generator.  */
  srand (time (NULL));

  /* Prepare a file large enough to hold an unsigned integer.  */
  fd = open (argv[1], O_RDWR | O_CREAT, S_IRUSR | S_IWUSR);
  lseek (fd, FILE_LENGTH+1, SEEK_SET);
```

```
write (fd, "", 1);
lseek (fd, 0, SEEK_SET);

/* Create the memory mapping.  */
file_memory = mmap (0, FILE_LENGTH, PROT_WRITE, MAP_SHARED, fd, 0);
close (fd);
/* Write a random integer to memory-mapped area.  */
sprintf((char*) file_memory, "%d\n", random_range (-100, 100));
/* Release the memory (unnecessary because the program exits).  */
munmap (file_memory, FILE_LENGTH);

return 0;
}
```

The mmap-write program opens the file, creating it if it did not previously exist. The
third argument to open specifies that the file is opened for reading and writing.
Because we do not know the file's length, we use lseek to ensure that the file is large
enough to store an integer and then move back the file position to its beginning.

The program maps the file and then closes the file descriptor because it's no longer
needed. The program then writes a random integer to the mapped memory, and thus
the file, and unmaps the memory. The munmap call is unnecessary because Linux would
automatically unmap the file when the program terminates.

Listing 5.6 *(mmap-read.c)* **Read an Integer from a Memory-Mapped File, and**
Double It

```
#include <stdlib.h>
#include <stdio.h>
#include <fcntl.h>
#include <sys/mman.h>
#include <sys/stat.h>
#include <unistd.h>
#define FILE_LENGTH 0x100

int main (int argc, char* const argv[])
{
  int fd;
  void* file_memory;
  int integer;

  /* Open the file.  */
  fd = open (argv[1], O_RDWR, S_IRUSR | S_IWUSR);
  /* Create the memory mapping.  */
  file_memory = mmap (0, FILE_LENGTH, PROT_READ | PROT_WRITE,
                      MAP_SHARED, fd, 0);
  close (fd);
```

continues

Listing 5.6 **Continued**

```
    /* Read the integer, print it out, and double it.  */
    scanf (file_memory, "%d", &integer);
    printf ("value: %d\n", integer);
    sprintf ((char*) file_memory, "%d\n", 2 * integer);
    /* Release the memory (unnecessary because the program exits).  */
    munmap (file_memory, FILE_LENGTH);

    return 0;
}
```

The `mmap-read` program reads the number out of the file and then writes the doubled value to the file. First, it opens the file and maps it for reading and writing. Because we can assume that the file is large enough to store an unsigned integer, we need not use `lseek`, as in the previous program. The program reads and parses the value out of memory using `sscanf` and then formats and writes the double value using `sprintf`.

Here's an example of running these example programs. It maps the file `/tmp/integer-file`.

```
% ./mmap-write /tmp/integer-file
% cat /tmp/integer-file
42
% ./mmap-read /tmp/integer-file
value: 42
% cat /tmp/integer-file
84
```

Observe that the text `42` was written to the disk file without ever calling `write`, and was read back in again without calling `read`. Note that these sample programs write and read the integer as a string (using `sprintf` and `sscanf`) for demonstration purposes only—there's no need for the contents of a memory-mapped file to be text. You can store and retrieve arbitrary binary in a memory-mapped file.

5.3.3 Shared Access to a File

Different processes can communicate using memory-mapped regions associated with the same file. Specify the `MAP_SHARED` flag so that any writes to these regions are immediately transferred to the underlying file and made visible to other processes. If you don't specify this flag, Linux may buffer writes before transferring them to the file.

Alternatively, you can force Linux to incorporate buffered writes into the disk file by calling `msync`. Its first two parameters specify a memory-mapped region, as for `munmap`. The third parameter can take these flag values:

- `MS_ASYNC`—The update is scheduled but not necessarily run before the call returns.
- `MS_SYNC`—The update is immediate; the call to `msync` blocks until it's done. `MS_SYNC` and `MS_ASYNC` may not both be used.

- MS_INVALIDATE—All other file mappings are invalidated so that they can see the updated values.

For example, to flush a shared file mapped at address mem_addr of length mem_length bytes, call this:

```
msync (mem_addr, mem_length, MS_SYNC | MS_INVALIDATE);
```

As with shared memory segments, users of memory-mapped regions must establish and follow a protocol to avoid race conditions. For example, a semaphore can be used to prevent more than one process from accessing the mapped memory at one time. Alternatively, you can use fcntl to place a read or write lock on the file, as described in Section 8.3, "fcntl: Locks and Other File Operations," in Chapter 8.

5.3.4 Private Mappings

Specifying MAP_PRIVATE to mmap creates a copy-on-write region. Any write to the region is reflected only in this process's memory; other processes that map the same file won't see the changes. Instead of writing directly to a page shared by all processes, the process writes to a private copy of this page. All subsequent reading and writing by the process use this page.

5.3.5 Other Uses for *mmap*

The mmap call can be used for purposes other than interprocess communications. One common use is as a replacement for read and write. For example, rather than explicitly reading a file's contents into memory, a program might map the file into memory and scan it using memory reads. For some programs, this is more convenient and may also run faster than explicit file I/O operations.

One advanced and powerful technique used by some programs is to build data structures (ordinary struct instances, for example) in a memory-mapped file. On a subsequent invocation, the program maps that file back into memory, and the data structures are restored to their previous state. Note, though, that pointers in these data structures will be invalid unless they all point within the same mapped region of memory and unless care is taken to map the file back into the same address region that it occupied originally.

Another handy technique is to map the special /dev/zero file into memory. That file, which is described in Section 6.5.2, "/dev/zero," of Chapter 6, "Devices," behaves as if it were an infinitely long file filled with 0 bytes. A program that needs a source of 0 bytes can mmap the file /dev/zero. Writes to /dev/zero are discarded, so the mapped memory may be used for any purpose. Custom memory allocators often map /dev/zero to obtain chunks of preinitialized memory.

5.4 Pipes

A *pipe* is a communication device that permits unidirectional communication. Data written to the "write end" of the pipe is read back from the "read end." Pipes are serial devices; the data is always read from the pipe in the same order it was written. Typically, a pipe is used to communicate between two threads in a single process or between parent and child processes.

In a shell, the symbol | creates a pipe. For example, this shell command causes the shell to produce two child processes, one for ls and one for less:

```
% ls | less
```

The shell also creates a pipe connecting the standard output of the ls subprocess with the standard input of the less process. The filenames listed by ls are sent to less in exactly the same order as if they were sent directly to the terminal.

A pipe's data capacity is limited. If the writer process writes faster than the reader process consumes the data, and if the pipe cannot store more data, the writer process blocks until more capacity becomes available. If the reader tries to read but no data is available, it blocks until data becomes available. Thus, the pipe automatically synchronizes the two processes.

5.4.1 Creating Pipes

To create a pipe, invoke the pipe command. Supply an integer array of size 2. The call to pipe stores the reading file descriptor in array position 0 and the writing file descriptor in position 1. For example, consider this code:

```
int pipe_fds[2];
int read_fd;
int write_fd;

pipe (pipe_fds);
read_fd = pipe_fds[0];
write_fd = pipe_fds[1];
```

Data written to the file descriptor read_fd can be read back from write_fd.

5.4.2 Communication Between Parent and Child Processes

A call to pipe creates file descriptors, which are valid only within that process and its children. A process's file descriptors cannot be passed to unrelated processes; however, when the process calls fork, file descriptors are copied to the new child process. Thus, pipes can connect only related processes.

In the program in Listing 5.7, a fork spawns a child process. The child inherits the pipe file descriptors. The parent writes a string to the pipe, and the child reads it out. The sample program converts these file descriptors into FILE* streams using fdopen. Because we use streams rather than file descriptors, we can use the higher-level standard C library I/O functions such as printf and fgets.

Listing 5.7 (*pipe.c*) **Using a Pipe to Communicate with a Child Process**

```c
#include <stdlib.h>
#include <stdio.h>
#include <unistd.h>

/* Write COUNT copies of MESSAGE to STREAM, pausing for a second
   between each.  */

void writer (const char* message, int count, FILE* stream)
{
  for (; count > 0; --count) {
    /* Write the message to the stream, and send it off immediately.  */
    fprintf (stream, "%s\n", message);
    fflush (stream);
    /* Snooze a while.  */
    sleep (1);
  }
}

/* Read random strings from the stream as long as possible.  */

void reader (FILE* stream)
{
  char buffer[1024];
  /* Read until we hit the end of the stream.  fgets reads until
     either a newline or the end-of-file.  */
  while (!feof (stream)
         && !ferror (stream)
         && fgets (buffer, sizeof (buffer), stream) != NULL)
    fputs (buffer, stdout);
}

int main ()
{
  int fds[2];
  pid_t pid;

  /* Create a pipe.  File descriptors for the two ends of the pipe are
     placed in fds.  */
  pipe (fds);
  /* Fork a child process.  */
  pid = fork ();
  if (pid == (pid_t) 0) {
    FILE* stream;
    /* This is the child process.  Close our copy of the write end of
       the file descriptor.  */
    close (fds[1]);
    /* Convert the read file descriptor to a FILE object, and read
       from it.  */
    stream = fdopen (fds[0], "r");
    reader (stream);
```

continues

Listing 5.7   **Continued**

```
    close (fds[0]);
  }
  else {
    /* This is the parent process.  */
    FILE* stream;
    /* Close our copy of the read end of the file descriptor.  */
    close (fds[0]);
    /* Convert the write file descriptor to a FILE object, and write
       to it.  */
    stream = fdopen (fds[1], "w");
    writer ("Hello, world.", 5, stream);
    close (fds[1]);
  }

  return 0;
}
```

At the beginning of main, fds is declared to be an integer array with size 2. The pipe
call creates a pipe and places the read and write file descriptors in that array. The program then forks a child process. After closing the read end of the pipe, the parent
process starts writing strings to the pipe. After closing the write end of the pipe, the
child reads strings from the pipe.

Note that after writing in the writer function, the parent flushes the pipe by
calling fflush. Otherwise, the string may not be sent through the pipe immediately.

When you invoke the command ls | less, two forks occur: one for the ls child
process and one for the less child process. Both of these processes inherit the pipe file
descriptors so they can communicate using a pipe. To have unrelated processes communicate, use a FIFO instead, as discussed in Section 5.4.5, "FIFOs."

5.4.3   Redirecting the Standard Input, Output, and Error Streams

Frequently, you'll want to create a child process and set up one end of a pipe as its
standard input or standard output. Using the dup2 call, you can equate one file
descriptor with another. For example, to redirect a process's standard input to a file
descriptor fd, use this line:

```
dup2 (fd, STDIN_FILENO);
```

The symbolic constant STDIN_FILENO represents the file descriptor for the standard
input, which has the value 0. The call closes standard input and then reopens it as a
duplicate of fd so that the two may be used interchangeably. Equated file descriptors
share the same file position and the same set of file status flags. Thus, characters read
from fd are not reread from standard input.

The program in Listing 5.8 uses dup2 to send the output from a pipe to the sort command.[2] After creating a pipe, the program forks. The parent process prints some strings to the pipe. The child process attaches the read file descriptor of the pipe to its standard input using dup2. It then executes the sort program.

Listing 5.8   (*dup2.c*) **Redirect Output from a Pipe with** *dup2*

```
#include <stdio.h>
#include <sys/types.h>
#include <sys/wait.h>
#include <unistd.h>

int main ()
{
  int fds[2];
  pid_t pid;

  /* Create a pipe.  File descriptors for the two ends of the pipe are
     placed in fds.  */
  pipe (fds);
  /* Fork a child process.  */
  pid = fork ();
  if (pid == (pid_t) 0) {
    /* This is the child process.  Close our copy of the write end of
       the file descriptor.  */
    close (fds[1]);
    /* Connect the read end of the pipe to standard input.  */
    dup2 (fds[0], STDIN_FILENO);
    /* Replace the child process with the "sort" program.  */
    execlp ("sort", "sort", 0);
  }
  else {
    /* This is the parent process.  */
    FILE* stream;
    /* Close our copy of the read end of the file descriptor.  */
    close (fds[0]);
    /* Convert the write file descriptor to a FILE object, and write
       to it.  */
    stream = fdopen (fds[1], "w");
    fprintf (stream, "This is a test.\n");
    fprintf (stream, "Hello, world.\n");
    fprintf (stream, "My dog has fleas.\n");
    fprintf (stream, "This program is great.\n");
    fprintf (stream, "One fish, two fish.\n");
    fflush (stream);
    close (fds[1]);
    /* Wait for the child process to finish.  */
    waitpid (pid, NULL, 0);
  }

  return 0;
}
```

2. sort reads lines of text from standard input, sorts them into alphabetical order, and prints them to standard output.

5.4.4 *popen* and *pclose*

A common use of pipes is to send data to or receive data from a program being run in a subprocess. The popen and pclose functions ease this paradigm by eliminating the need to invoke pipe, fork, dup2, exec, and fdopen.

Compare Listing 5.9, which uses popen and pclose, to the previous example (Listing 5.8).

Listing 5.9   *(popen.c)* **Example Using** *popen*

```
#include <stdio.h>
#include <unistd.h>

int main ()
{
  FILE* stream = popen ("sort", "w");
  fprintf (stream, "This is a test.\n");
  fprintf (stream, "Hello, world.\n");
  fprintf (stream, "My dog has fleas.\n");
  fprintf (stream, "This program is great.\n");
  fprintf (stream, "One fish, two fish.\n");
  return pclose (stream);
}
```

The call to popen creates a child process executing the sort command, replacing calls to pipe, fork, dup2, and execlp. The second argument, "w", indicates that this process wants to write to the child process. The return value from popen is one end of a pipe; the other end is connected to the child process's standard input. After the writing finishes, pclose closes the child process's stream, waits for the process to terminate, and returns its status value.

The first argument to popen is executed as a shell command in a subprocess running /bin/sh. The shell searches the PATH environment variable in the usual way to find programs to execute. If the second argument is "r", the function returns the child process's standard output stream so that the parent can read the output. If the second argument is "w", the function returns the child process's standard input stream so that the parent can send data. If an error occurs, popen returns a null pointer.

Call pclose to close a stream returned by popen. After closing the specified stream, pclose waits for the child process to terminate.

5.4.5 FIFOs

A *first-in, first-out (FIFO)* file is a pipe that has a name in the filesystem. Any process can open or close the FIFO; the processes on either end of the pipe need not be related to each other. FIFOs are also called *named pipes*.

You can make a FIFO using the `mkfifo` command. Specify the path to the FIFO on the command line. For example, create a FIFO in `/tmp/fifo` by invoking this:

```
% mkfifo /tmp/fifo
% ls -l /tmp/fifo
prw-rw-rw-   1 samuel   users          0 Jan 16 14:04 /tmp/fifo
```

The first character of the output from `ls` is `p`, indicating that this file is actually a FIFO (named pipe). In one window, read from the FIFO by invoking the following:

```
% cat < /tmp/fifo
```

In a second window, write to the FIFO by invoking this:

```
% cat > /tmp/fifo
```

Then type in some lines of text. Each time you press Enter, the line of text is sent through the FIFO and appears in the first window. Close the FIFO by pressing Ctrl+D in the second window. Remove the FIFO with this line:

```
% rm /tmp/fifo
```

Creating a FIFO

Create a FIFO programmatically using the `mkfifo` function. The first argument is the path at which to create the FIFO; the second parameter specifies the pipe's owner, group, and world permissions, as discussed in Chapter 10, "Security," Section 10.3, "File System Permissions." Because a pipe must have a reader and a writer, the permissions must include both read and write permissions. If the pipe cannot be created (for instance, if a file with that name already exists), `mkfifo` returns −1. Include `<sys/types.h>` and `<sys/stat.h>` if you call `mkfifo`.

Accessing a FIFO

Access a FIFO just like an ordinary file. To communicate through a FIFO, one program must open it for writing, and another program must open it for reading. Either low-level I/O functions (`open`, `write`, `read`, `close`, and so on, as listed in Appendix B, "Low-Level I/O") or C library I/O functions (`fopen`, `fprintf`, `fscanf`, `fclose`, and so on) may be used.

For example, to write a buffer of data to a FIFO using low-level I/O routines, you could use this code:

```
int fd = open (fifo_path, O_WRONLY);
write (fd, data, data_length);
close (fd);
```

To read a string from the FIFO using C library I/O functions, you could use this code:

```
FILE* fifo = fopen (fifo_path, "r");
fscanf (fifo, "%s", buffer);
fclose (fifo);
```

A FIFO can have multiple readers or multiple writers. Bytes from each writer are written atomically up to a maximum size of `PIPE_BUF` (4KB on Linux). Chunks from simultaneous writers can be interleaved. Similar rules apply to simultaneous reads.

Differences from Windows Named Pipes

Pipes in the Win32 operating systems are very similar to Linux pipes. (Refer to the Win32 library documentation for technical details about these.) The main differences concern named pipes, which, for Win32, function more like sockets. Win32 named pipes can connect processes on separate computers connected via a network. On Linux, sockets are used for this purpose. Also, Win32 allows multiple reader-writer connections on a named pipe without interleaving data, and pipes can be used for two-way communication.[3]

5.5 Sockets

A *socket* is a bidirectional communication device that can be used to communicate with another process on the same machine or with a process running on other machines. Sockets are the only interprocess communication we'll discuss in this chapter that permit communication between processes on different computers. Internet programs such as Telnet, rlogin, FTP, talk, and the World Wide Web use sockets.

For example, you can obtain the WWW page from a Web server using the Telnet program because they both use sockets for network communications.[4] To open a connection to a WWW server at www.codesourcery.com, use `telnet www.codesourcery.com 80`. The magic constant 80 specifies a connection to the Web server programming running www.codesourcery.com instead of some other process. Try typing `GET /` after the connection is established. This sends a message through the socket to the Web server, which replies by sending the home page's HTML source and then closing the connection—for example:

```
% telnet www.codesourcery.com 80
Trying 206.168.99.1...
Connected to merlin.codesourcery.com (206.168.99.1).
Escape character is '^]'.
GET /
<html>
<head>
  <meta http-equiv="Content-Type" content="text/html; charset=iso-8859-1">
...
```

---

3. Note that only Windows NT can create a named pipe; Windows 9*x* programs can form only client connections.

4. Usually, you'd use `telnet` to connect a Telnet server for remote logins. But you can also use `telnet` to connect to a server of a different kind and then type comments directly at it.

5.5.1 Socket Concepts

When you create a socket, you must specify three parameters: communication style, namespace, and protocol.

A communication style controls how the socket treats transmitted data and specifies the number of communication partners. When data is sent through a socket, it is packaged into chunks called *packets*. The communication style determines how these packets are handled and how they are addressed from the sender to the receiver.

- *Connection* styles guarantee delivery of all packets in the order they were sent. If packets are lost or reordered by problems in the network, the receiver automatically requests their retransmission from the sender.

  A connection-style socket is like a telephone call: The addresses of the sender and receiver are fixed at the beginning of the communication when the connection is established.

- *Datagram* styles do not guarantee delivery or arrival order. Packets may be lost or reordered in transit due to network errors or other conditions. Each packet must be labeled with its destination and is not guaranteed to be delivered. The system guarantees only "best effort," so packets may disappear or arrive in a different order than shipping.

  A datagram-style socket behaves more like postal mail. The sender specifies the receiver's address for each individual message.

A socket namespace specifies how *socket addresses* are written. A socket address identifies one end of a socket connection. For example, socket addresses in the "local namespace" are ordinary filenames. In "Internet namespace," a socket address is composed of the Internet address (also known as an *Internet Protocol address* or *IP address*) of a host attached to the network and a port number. The port number distinguishes among multiple sockets on the same host.

A protocol specifies how data is transmitted. Some protocols are TCP/IP, the primary networking protocols used by the Internet; the AppleTalk network protocol; and the UNIX local communication protocol. Not all combinations of styles, namespaces, and protocols are supported.

5.5.2 System Calls

Sockets are more flexible than previously discussed communication techniques. These are the system calls involving sockets:

`socket`—Creates a socket

`closes`—Destroys a socket

`connect`—Creates a connection between two sockets

`bind`—Labels a server socket with an address

`listen`—Configures a socket to accept conditions

`accept`—Accepts a connection and creates a new socket for the connection

Sockets are represented by file descriptors.

Creating and Destroying Sockets

The socket and close functions create and destroy sockets, respectively. When you create a socket, specify the three socket choices: namespace, communication style, and protocol. For the namespace parameter, use constants beginning with PF_ (abbreviating "protocol families"). For example, PF_LOCAL or PF_UNIX specifies the local namespace, and PF_INET specifies Internet namespaces. For the communication style parameter, use constants beginning with SOCK_. Use SOCK_STREAM for a connection-style socket, or use SOCK_DGRAM for a datagram-style socket.

The third parameter, the protocol, specifies the low-level mechanism to transmit and receive data. Each protocol is valid for a particular namespace-style combination. Because there is usually one best protocol for each such pair, specifying 0 is usually the correct protocol. If socket succeeds, it returns a file descriptor for the socket. You can read from or write to the socket using read, write, and so on, as with other file descriptors. When you are finished with a socket, call close to remove it.

Calling *connect*

To create a connection between two sockets, the client calls connect, specifying the address of a server socket to connect to. A *client* is the process initiating the connection, and a *server* is the process waiting to accept connections. The client calls connect to initiate a connection from a local socket to the server socket specified by the second argument. The third argument is the length, in bytes, of the address structure pointed to by the second argument. Socket address formats differ according to the socket namespace.

Sending Information

Any technique to write to a file descriptor can be used to write to a socket. See Appendix B for a discussion of Linux's low-level I/O functions and some of the issues surrounding their use. The send function, which is specific to the socket file descriptors, provides an alternative to write with a few additional choices; see the man page for information.

5.5.3   Servers

A server's life cycle consists of the creation of a connection-style socket, binding an address to its socket, placing a call to listen that enables connections to the socket, placing calls to accept incoming connections, and then closing the socket. Data isn't read and written directly via the server socket; instead, each time a program accepts a new connection, Linux creates a separate socket to use in transferring data over that connection. In this section, we introduce bind, listen, and accept.

An address must be bound to the server's socket using `bind` if a client is to find it. Its first argument is the socket file descriptor. The second argument is a pointer to a socket address structure; the format of this depends on the socket's address family. The third argument is the length of the address structure, in bytes. When an address is bound to a connection-style socket, it must invoke `listen` to indicate that it is a server. Its first argument is the socket file descriptor. The second argument specifies how many pending connections are queued. If the queue is full, additional connections will be rejected. This does not limit the total number of connections that a server can handle; it limits just the number of clients attempting to connect that have not yet been accepted.

A server accepts a connection request from a client by invoking `accept`. The first argument is the socket file descriptor. The second argument points to a socket address structure, which is filled with the client socket's address. The third argument is the length, in bytes, of the socket address structure. The server can use the client address to determine whether it really wants to communicate with the client. The call to accept creates a new socket for communicating with the client and returns the corresponding file descriptor. The original server socket continues to accept new client connections. To read data from a socket without removing it from the input queue, use `recv`. It takes the same arguments as `read`, plus an additional `FLAGS` argument. A flag of `MSG_PEEK` causes data to be read but not removed from the input queue.

5.5.4 Local Sockets

Sockets connecting processes on the same computer can use the local namespace represented by the synonyms `PF_LOCAL` and `PF_UNIX`. These are called *local sockets* or *UNIX-domain sockets*. Their socket addresses, specified by filenames, are used only when creating connections.

The socket's name is specified in `struct sockaddr_un`. You must set the `sun_family` field to `AF_LOCAL`, indicating that this is a local namespace. The `sun_path` field specifies the filename to use and may be, at most, 108 bytes long. The actual length of `struct sockaddr_un` should be computed using the `SUN_LEN` macro. Any filename can be used, but the process must have directory write permissions, which permit adding files to the directory. To connect to a socket, a process must have read permission for the file. Even though different computers may share the same filesystem, only processes running on the same computer can communicate with local namespace sockets.

The only permissible protocol for the local namespace is 0.

Because it resides in a file system, a local socket is listed as a file. For example, notice the initial `s`:

```
% ls -l /tmp/socket
srwxrwx--x  1 user    group     0 Nov 13 19:18 /tmp/socket
```

Call `unlink` to remove a local socket when you're done with it.

5.5.5 An Example Using Local Namespace Sockets

We illustrate sockets with two programs. The server program, in Listing 5.10, creates a
local namespace socket and listens for connections on it. When it receives a connection, it reads text messages from the connection and prints them until the connection
closes. If one of these messages is "quit," the server program removes the socket and
ends. The socket-server program takes the path to the socket as its command-line
argument.

Listing 5.10   (*socket-server.c*) **Local Namespace Socket Server**

```c
#include <stdio.h>
#include <stdlib.h>
#include <string.h>
#include <sys/socket.h>
#include <sys/un.h>
#include <unistd.h>

/* Read text from the socket and print it out.  Continue until the
   socket closes.  Return nonzero if the client sent a "quit"
   message, zero otherwise.  */

int server (int client_socket)
{
  while (1) {
    int length;
    char* text;

    /* First, read the length of the text message from the socket.  If
       read returns zero, the client closed the connection.  */
    if (read (client_socket, &length, sizeof (length)) == 0)
      return 0;
    /* Allocate a buffer to hold the text.  */
    text = (char*) malloc (length);
    /* Read the text itself, and print it.  */

    read (client_socket, text, length);
    printf ("%s\n", text);
    /* Free the buffer.  */
    free (text);
    /* If the client sent the message "quit," we're all done.  */
    if (!strcmp (text, "quit"))
      return 1;
  }
}

int main (int argc, char* const argv[])
{
const char* const socket_name = argv[1];
```

```
  int socket_fd;
  struct sockaddr_un name;
  int client_sent_quit_message;

  /* Create the socket.  */
  socket_fd = socket (PF_LOCAL, SOCK_STREAM, 0);
  /* Indicate that this is a server.  */
  name.sun_family = AF_LOCAL;
  strcpy (name.sun_path, socket_name);
  bind (socket_fd, &name, SUN_LEN (&name));
  /* Listen for connections.  */
  listen (socket_fd, 5);

  /* Repeatedly accept connections, spinning off one server() to deal
     with each client.  Continue until a client sends a "quit" message.  */
  do {
    struct sockaddr_un client_name;
    socklen_t client_name_len;
    int client_socket_fd;

    /* Accept a connection.  */
    client_socket_fd = accept (socket_fd, &client_name, &client_name_len);
    /* Handle the connection.  */
    client_sent_quit_message = server (client_socket_fd);
    /* Close our end of the connection.  */
    close (client_socket_fd);
  }
  while (!client_sent_quit_message);

  /* Remove the socket file.  */
  close (socket_fd);
  unlink (socket_name);

  return 0;
}
```

The client program, in Listing 5.11, connects to a local namespace socket and sends a message. The name path to the socket and the message are specified on the command line.

Listing 5.11   *(socket-client.c)* **Local Namespace Socket Client**

```
#include <stdio.h>
#include <string.h>
#include <sys/socket.h>
#include <sys/un.h>
#include <unistd.h>
```

continues

Listing 5.11 **Continued**

```c
/* Write TEXT to the socket given by file descriptor SOCKET_FD.  */

void write_text (int socket_fd, const char* text)
{
  /* Write the number of bytes in the string, including
     NUL-termination.  */
  int length = strlen (text) + 1;
  write (socket_fd, &length, sizeof (length));
  /* Write the string.  */
  write (socket_fd, text, length);
}

int main (int argc, char* const argv[])
{
  const char* const socket_name = argv[1];
  const char* const message = argv[2];
  int socket_fd;
  struct sockaddr_un name;

  /* Create the socket.  */
  socket_fd = socket (PF_LOCAL, SOCK_STREAM, 0);
  /* Store the server's name in the socket address.  */
  name.sun_family = AF_LOCAL;
  strcpy (name.sun_path, socket_name);
  /* Connect the socket.  */
  connect (socket_fd, &name, SUN_LEN (&name));
  /* Write the text on the command line to the socket.  */
  write_text (socket_fd, message);
  close (socket_fd);
  return 0;
}
```

Before the client sends the message text, it sends the length of that text by sending the bytes of the integer variable length. Likewise, the server reads the length of the text by reading from the socket into an integer variable. This allows the server to allocate an appropriately sized buffer to hold the message text before reading it from the socket.

To try this example, start the server program in one window. Specify a path to a socket—for example, /tmp/socket.

```
% ./socket-server /tmp/socket
```

In another window, run the client a few times, specifying the same socket path plus messages to send to the client:

```
% ./socket-client /tmp/socket "Hello, world."
% ./socket-client /tmp/socket "This is a test."
```

The server program receives and prints these messages. To close the server, send the message "quit" from a client:

```
% ./socket-client /tmp/socket "quit"
```

The server program terminates.

5.5.6 Internet-Domain Sockets

UNIX-domain sockets can be used only for communication between two processes on the same computer. *Internet-domain sockets*, on the other hand, may be used to connect processes on different machines connected by a network.

Sockets connecting processes through the Internet use the Internet namespace represented by `PF_INET`. The most common protocols are TCP/IP. The *Internet Protocol (IP)*, a low-level protocol, moves packets through the Internet, splitting and rejoining the packets, if necessary. It guarantees only "best-effort" delivery, so packets may vanish or be reordered during transport. Every participating computer is specified using a unique IP number. The *Transmission Control Protocol (TCP)*, layered on top of IP, provides reliable connection-ordered transport. It permits telephone-like connections to be established between computers and ensures that data is delivered reliably and in order.

> **DNS Names**
>
> Because it is easier to remember names than numbers, the *Domain Name Service (DNS)* associates names such as www.codesourcery.com with computers' unique IP numbers. DNS is implemented by a world-wide hierarchy of name servers, but you don't need to understand DNS protocols to use Internet host names in your programs.

Internet socket addresses contain two parts: a machine and a port number. This information is stored in a `struct sockaddr_in` variable. Set the `sin_family` field to `AF_INET` to indicate that this is an Internet namespace address. The `sin_addr` field stores the Internet address of the desired machine as a 32-bit integer IP number. A *port number* distinguishes a given machine's different sockets. Because different machines store multibyte values in different byte orders, use `htons` to convert the port number to *network byte order*. See the man page for `ip` for more information.

To convert human-readable hostnames, either numbers in standard dot notation (such as 10.0.0.1) or DNS names (such as www.codesourcery.com) into 32-bit IP numbers, you can use `gethostbyname`. This returns a pointer to the `struct hostent` structure; the `h_addr` field contains the host's IP number. See the sample program in Listing 5.12.

Listing 5.12 illustrates the use of Internet-domain sockets. The program obtains the home page from the Web server whose hostname is specified on the command line.

Listing 5.12   (*socket-inet.c*) **Read from a WWW Server**

```c
#include <stdlib.h>
#include <stdio.h>
#include <netinet/in.h>
#include <netdb.h>
#include <sys/socket.h>
#include <unistd.h>
#include <string.h>

/* Print the contents of the home page for the server's socket.
   Return an indication of success.  */

void get_home_page (int socket_fd)
{
  char buffer[10000];
  ssize_t number_characters_read;

  /* Send the HTTP GET command for the home page.  */
  sprintf (buffer, "GET /\n");
  write (socket_fd, buffer, strlen (buffer));
  /* Read from the socket.  The call to read may not
  return all the data at one time, so keep
  trying until we run out.  */
  while (1) {
    number_characters_read = read (socket_fd, buffer, 10000);
    if (number_characters_read == 0)
      return;
    /* Write the data to standard output.  */
    fwrite (buffer, sizeof (char), number_characters_read, stdout);
  }
}

int main (int argc, char* const argv[])
{
  int socket_fd;
  struct sockaddr_in name;
  struct hostent* hostinfo;

  /* Create the socket.  */
  socket_fd = socket (PF_INET, SOCK_STREAM, 0);
  /* Store the server's name in the socket address.  */
  name.sin_family = AF_INET;
  /* Convert from strings to numbers.  */
  hostinfo = gethostbyname (argv[1]);
  if (hostinfo == NULL)
    return 1;
  else
    name.sin_addr = *((struct in_addr *) hostinfo->h_addr);
  /* Web servers use port 80.  */
  name.sin_port = htons (80);
```

```
  /* Connect to the Web server  */
  if (connect (socket_fd, &name, sizeof (struct sockaddr_in)) == -1) {
    perror ("connect");
    return 1;
  }
  /* Retrieve the server's home page.  */
  get_home_page (socket_fd);

  return 0;
}
```

This program takes the hostname of the Web server on the command line (not a URL—that is, without the "http://"). It calls `gethostbyname` to translate the hostname into a numerical IP address and then connects a stream (TCP) socket to port 80 on that host. Web servers speak the *Hypertext Transport Protocol (HTTP)*, so the program issues the HTTP `GET` command and the server responds by sending the text of the home page.

Standard Port Numbers

By convention, Web servers listen for connections on port 80. Most Internet network services are associated with a standard port number. For example, secure Web servers that use SSL listen for connections on port 443, and mail servers (which speak SMTP) use port 25.

On GNU/Linux systems, the associations between protocol/service names and standard port numbers are listed in the file `/etc/services`. The first column is the protocol or service name. The second column lists the port number and the connection type: `tcp` for connection-oriented, or `udp` for datagram.

If you implement custom network services using Internet-domain sockets, use port numbers greater than 1024.

For example, to retrieve the home page from the Web site `www.codesourcery.com`, invoke this:

```
% ./socket-inet www.codesourcery.com
<html>
  <meta http-equiv="Content-Type" content="text/html; charset=iso-8859-1">

  ...
```

5.5.7 Socket Pairs

As we saw previously, the `pipe` function creates two file descriptors for the beginning and end of a pipe. Pipes are limited because the file descriptors must be used by related processes and because communication is unidirectional. The `socketpair` function creates two file descriptors for two connected sockets on the same computer. These file descriptors permit two-way communication between related processes.

Its first three parameters are the same as those of the socket call: They specify the domain, connection style, and protocol. The last parameter is a two-integer array, which is filled with the file descriptions of the two sockets, similar to pipe. When you call socketpair, you must specify PF_LOCAL as the domain.

II

Mastering Linux

6

Devices

LINUX, LIKE MOST OPERATING SYSTEMS, INTERACTS WITH HARDWARE devices via modularized software components called *device drivers*. A device driver hides the peculiarities of a hardware device's communication protocols from the operating system and allows the system to interact with the device through a standardized interface.

Under Linux, device drivers are part of the kernel and may be either linked statically into the kernel or loaded on demand as kernel modules. Device drivers run as part of the kernel and aren't directly accessible to user processes. However, Linux provides a mechanism by which processes can communicate with a device driver—and through it with a hardware device—via file-like objects. These objects appear in the file system, and programs can open them, read from them, and write to them practically as if they were normal files. Using either Linux's low-level I/O operations (see Appendix B, "Low-Level I/O") or the standard C library's I/O operations, your programs can communicate with hardware devices through these file-like objects.

Linux also provides several file-like objects that communicate directly with the kernel rather than with device drivers. These aren't linked to hardware devices; instead, they provide various kinds of specialized behavior that can be of use to application and system programs.

Exercise Caution When Accessing Devices!

The techniques in this chapter provide direct access to device drivers running in the Linux kernel, and through them to hardware devices connected to the system. Use these techniques with care because misuse can cause impair or damage the GNU/Linux system.

See especially the sidebar "Dangers of Block Devices."

6.1   Device Types

Device files aren't ordinary files—they do not represent regions of data on a disk-based file system. Instead, data read from or written to a device file is communicated to the corresponding device driver, and from there to the underlying device. Device files come in two flavors:

- A *character device* represents a hardware device that reads or writes a serial stream of data bytes. Serial and parallel ports, tape drives, terminal devices, and sound cards are examples of character devices.

- A *block device* represents a hardware device that reads or writes data in fixed-size blocks. Unlike a character device, a block device provides random access to data stored on the device. A disk drive is an example of a block device.

Typical application programs will never use block devices. While a disk drive is represented as block devices, the contents of each disk partition typically contain a file system, and that file system is mounted into GNU/Linux's root file system tree. Only the kernel code that implements the file system needs to access the block device directly; application programs access the disk's contents through normal files and directories.

Dangers of Block Devices

Block devices provide direct access to disk drive data. Although most GNU/Linux systems are configured to prevent nonroot processes from accessing these devices directly, a root process can inflict severe damage by changing the contents of the disk. By writing to a disk block device, a program can modify or destroy file system control information and even a disk's partition table and master boot record, thus rendering a drive or even the entire system unusable. Always access these devices with great care.

Applications sometimes make use of character devices, though. We'll discuss several of them in the following sections.

6.2   Device Numbers

Linux identifies devices using two numbers: the *major device number* and the *minor device number*. The major device number specifies which driver the device corresponds to. The correspondence from major device numbers to drivers is fixed and part of the Linux kernel sources. Note that the same major device number may correspond to two different drivers, one a character device and one a block device. Minor device numbers distinguish individual devices or components controlled by a single driver. The meaning of a minor device number depends on the device driver.

For example, major device no. 3 corresponds to the primary IDE controller on the system. An IDE controller can have two devices (disk, tape, or CD-ROM drives) attached to it; the "master" device has minor device no. 0, and the "slave" device has minor device no. 64. Individual partitions on the master device (if the device supports partitions) are represented by minor device numbers 1, 2, 3, and so on. Individual partitions on the slave device are represented by minor device numbers 65, 66, 67, and so on.

Major device numbers are listed in the Linux kernel sources documentation. On many GNU/Linux distributions, this documentation can be found in `/usr/src/linux/Documentation/devices.txt`. The special entry `/proc/devices` lists major device numbers corresponding to active device drivers currently loaded into the kernel. (See Chapter 7, "The `/proc` File System," for more information about `/proc` file system entries.)

6.3 Device Entries

A device entry is in many ways the same as a regular file. You can move it using the `mv` command and delete it using the `rm` command. If you try to copy a device entry using `cp`, though, you'll read bytes from the device (if the device supports reading) and write them to the destination file. If you try to overwrite a device entry, you'll write bytes to the corresponding device instead.

You can create a device entry in the file system using the `mknod` command (invoke `man 1 mknod` for the man page) or the `mknod` system call (invoke `man 2 mknod` for the man page). Creating a device entry in the file system doesn't automatically imply that the corresponding device driver or hardware device is present or available; the device entry is merely a portal for communicating with the driver, if it's there. Only superuser processes can create block and character devices using the `mknod` command or the `mknod` system call.

To create a device using the `mknod` command, specify as the first argument the path at which the entry will appear in the file system. For the second argument, specify `b` for a block device or `c` for a character device. Provide the major and minor device numbers as the third and fourth arguments, respectively. For example, this command makes a character device entry named `lp0` in the current directory. The device has major device no. 6 and minor device no. 0. These numbers correspond to the first parallel port on the Linux system.

```
% mknod ./lp0 c 6 0
```

Remember that only superuser processes can create block and character devices, so you must be logged in as root to invoke this command successfully.

The ls command displays device entries specially. If you invoke ls with the -l or -o options, the first character on each line of output specifies the type of the entry. Recall that - (a hyphen) designates a normal file, while d designates a directory. Similarly, b designates a block device, and c designates a character device. For the latter two, ls prints the major and minor device numbers where it would the size of an ordinary file. For example, we can display the block device that we just created:

```
% ls -l lp0
crw-r-----   1 root     root       6,   0 Mar  7 17:03 lp0
```

In a program, you can determine whether a file system entry is a block or character device and then retrieve its device numbers using stat. See Section B.2, "stat," in Appendix B, for instructions.

To remove the entry, use rm. This doesn't remove the device or device driver; it simply removes the device entry from the file system.

```
% rm ./lp0
```

6.3.1   The /dev Directory

By convention, a GNU/Linux system includes a directory /dev containing the full complement of character and block device entries for devices that Linux knows about. Entries in /dev have standardized names corresponding to major and minor device numbers.

For example, the master device attached to the primary IDE controller, which has major and minor device numbers 3 and 0, has the standard name /dev/hda. If this device supports partitions, the first partition on it, which has minor device no. 1, has the standard name /dev/hda1. You can check that this is true on your system:

```
% ls -l /dev/hda /dev/hda1
brw-rw----   1 root     disk       3,   0 May  5 1998 /dev/hda
brw-rw----   1 root     disk       3,   1 May  5 1998 /dev/hda1
```

Similarly, /dev has an entry for the parallel port character device that we used previously:

```
% ls -l /dev/lp0
crw-rw----   1 root     daemon     6,   0 May  5 1998 /dev/lp0
```

In most cases, you should not use mknod to create your own device entries. Use the entries in /dev instead. Non-superuser programs have no choice but to use preexisting device entries because they cannot create their own. Typically, only system administrators and developers working with specialized hardware devices will need to create device entries. Most GNU/Linux distributions include facilities to help system administrators create standard device entries with the correct names.

6.3.2 Accessing Devices by Opening Files

How do you use these devices? In the case of character devices, it can be quite simple:
Open the device as if it were a normal file, and read from or write to it. You can even
use normal file commands such as `cat`, or your shell's redirection syntax, to send data
to or from the device.

For example, if you have a printer connected to your computer's first parallel port,
you can print files by sending them directly to `/dev/lp0`.[1] To print the contents of
`document.txt`, invoke the following:

```
% cat document.txt > /dev/lp0
```

You must have permission to write to the device entry for this to succeed; on many
GNU/Linux systems, the permissions are set so that only `root` and the system's printer
daemon (`lpd`) can write to the file. Also, what comes out of your printer depends on
how your printer interprets the contents of the data you send it. Some printers will
print plain text files that are sent to them,[2] while others will not. PostScript printers
will render and print PostScript files that you send to them.

In a program, sending data to a device is just as simple. For example, this code fragment uses low-level I/O functions to send the contents of a buffer to `/dev/lp0`.

```
int fd = open ("/dev/lp0", O_WRONLY);
write (fd, buffer, buffer_length);
close (fd);
```

6.4 Hardware Devices

Some common block devices are listed in Table 6.1. Device numbers for similar
devices follow the obvious pattern (for instance, the second partition on the first SCSI
drive is `/dev/sda2`). It's occasionally useful to know which devices these device names
correspond to when examining mounted file systems in `/proc/mounts` (see Section
7.5, "Drives, Mounts, and File Systems," in Chapter 7, for more about this).

Table 6.1 **Partial Listing of Common Block Devices**

Device	Name	Major	Minor
First floppy drive	/dev/fd0	2	0
Second floppy drive	/dev/fd1	2	1
Primary IDE controller, master device	/dev/hda	3	0
Primary IDE controller, master device, first partition	/dev/hda1	3	1

continues

1. Windows users will recognize that this device is similar to the magic Windows file `LPR1`.
2. Your printer may require explicit carriage return characters, ASCII code 14, at the end of
   each line, and may require a form feed character, ASCII code 12, at the end of each page.

Table 6.1 **Continued**

Device	Name	Major	Minor
Primary IDE controller, secondary device	/dev/hdb	3	64
Primary IDE controller, secondary device, first partition	/dev/hdb1	3	65
Secondary IDE controller, master device	/dev/hdc	22	0
Secondary IDE controller, secondary device	/dev/hdd	22	64
First SCSI drive	/dev/sda	8	0
First SCSI drive, first partition	/dev/sda1	8	1
Second SCSI disk	/dev/sdb	8	16
Second SCSI disk, first partition	/dev/sdb1	8	17
First SCSI CD-ROM drive	/dev/scd0	11	0
Second SCSI CD-ROM drive	/dev/scd1	11	1

Table 6.2 lists some common character devices.

Table 6.2 **Some Common Character Devices**

Device	Name	Major	Minor
Parallel port 0	/dev/lp0 or /dev/par0	6	0
Parallel port 1	/dev/lp1 or /dev/par1	6	1
First serial port	/dev/ttyS0	4	64
Second serial port	/dev/ttyS1	4	65
IDE tape drive	/dev/ht0	37	0
First SCSI tape drive	/dev/st0	9	0
Second SCSI tape drive	/dev/st1	9	1
System console	/dev/console	5	1
First virtual terminal	/dev/tty1	4	1
Second virtual terminal	/dev/tty2	4	2
Process's current terminal device	/dev/tty	5	0
Sound card	/dev/audio	14	4

You can access certain hardware components through more than one character device; often, the different character devices provide different semantics. For example, when you use the IDE tape device /dev/ht0, Linux automatically rewinds the tape in the drive when you close the file descriptor. You can use the device /dev/nht0 to access the same tape drive, except that Linux will not automatically rewind the tape when you close the file descriptor. You sometimes might see programs using /dev/cua0 and similar devices; these are older interfaces to serial ports such as /dev/ttyS0.

Occasionally, you'll want to write data directly to character devices—for example:

- A terminal program might access a modem directly through a serial port device. Data written to or read from the devices is transmitted via the modem to a remote computer.

- A tape backup program might write data directly to a tape device. The backup program could implement its own compression and error-checking format.

- A program can write directly to the first virtual terminal[3] writing data to /dev/tty1.

  Terminal windows running in a graphical environment, or remote login terminal sessions, are not associated with virtual terminals; instead, they're associated with pseudo-terminals. See Section 6.6, "PTYs," for information about these.

- Sometimes a program needs to access the terminal device with which it is associated.

  For example, your program may need to prompt the user for a password. For security reasons, you might want to ignore redirection of standard input and output and always read the password from the terminal, no matter how the user invokes the command. One way to do this is to open /dev/tty, which always corresponds to the terminal device associated with the process that opens it. Write the prompt message to that device, and read the password from it. By ignoring standard input and output, this prevents the user from feeding your program a password from a file using shell syntax such as this:

  ```
  % secure_program < my-password.txt
  ```

  If you need to authenticate users in your program, you should learn about GNU/Linux's PAM facility. See Section 10.5, "Authenticating Users," in Chapter 10, "Security," for more information.

- A program can play sounds through the system's sound card by sending audio data to /dev/audio. Note that the audio data must be in Sun audio format (usually associated with the .au extension).

  For example, many GNU/Linux distributions come with the classic sound file /usr/share/sndconfig/sample.au. If your system includes this file, try playing it by invoking the following:

  ```
  % cat /usr/share/sndconfig/sample.au > /dev/audio
  ```

  If you're planning on using sound in your program, though, you should investigate the various sound libraries and services available for GNU/Linux. The Gnome windowing environment uses the Enlightenment Sound Daemon (EsounD), at http://www.tux.org/~ricdude/EsounD.html. KDE uses aRts, at http://space.twc.de/~stefan/kde/arts-mcop-doc/. If you use one of these sound systems instead of writing directly to /dev/audio, your program will cooperate better with other programs that use the computer's sound card.

3. On most GNU/Linux systems, you can switch to the first virtual terminal by pressing Ctrl+Alt+F1. Use Ctrl+Alt+F2 for the second virtual terminal, and so on.

6.5   Special Devices

Linux also provides several character devices that don't correspond to hardware devices. These entries all use the major device no. 1, which is associated with the Linux kernel's memory device instead of a device driver.

6.5.1   */dev/null*

The entry /dev/null, the *null device*, is very handy. It serves two purposes; you are probably familiar at least with the first one:

- Linux discards any data written to /dev/null. A common trick is to specify /dev/null as an output file in some context where the output is unwanted.

  For example, to run a command and discard its standard output (without printing it or writing it to a file), redirect standard output to /dev/null:

  ```
  % verbose_command > /dev/null
  ```

- Reading from /dev/null always results in an end-of-file. For instance, if you open a file descriptor to /dev/null using open and then attempt to read from the file descriptor, read will read no bytes and will return 0. If you copy from /dev/null to another file, the destination will be a zero-length file:

  ```
  % cp /dev/null empty-file
  % ls -l empty-file
  -rw-rw----   1 samuel    samuel          0 Mar  8 00:27 empty-file
  ```

6.5.2   */dev/zero*

The device entry /dev/zero behaves as if it were an infinitely long file filled with 0 bytes. As much data as you'd try to read from /dev/zero, Linux "generates" enough 0 bytes.

To illustrate this, let's run the hex dump program presented in Listing B.4 in Section B.1.4, "Reading Data," of Appendix B. This program prints the contents of a file in hexadecimal form.

```
% ./hexdump /dev/zero
0x000000 : 00 00 00 00 00 00 00 00 00 00 00 00 00 00 00 00
0x000010 : 00 00 00 00 00 00 00 00 00 00 00 00 00 00 00 00
0x000020 : 00 00 00 00 00 00 00 00 00 00 00 00 00 00 00 00
0x000030 : 00 00 00 00 00 00 00 00 00 00 00 00 00 00 00 00
...
```

Hit Ctrl+C when you're convinced that it will go on indefinitely.

Memory mapping /dev/zero is an advanced technique for allocating memory. See Section 5.3.5, "Other Uses for mmap," in Chapter 5, "Interprocess Communication," for more information, and see the sidebar "Obtaining Page-Aligned Memory" in Section 8.9, "mprotect: Setting Memory Permissions," in Chapter 8, "Linux System Calls," for an example.

6.5.3 */dev/full*

The entry /dev/full behaves as if it were a file on a file system that has no more room. A write to /dev/full fails and sets errno to ENOSPC, which ordinarily indicates that the written-to device is full.

For example, you can try to write to /dev/full using the cp command:

```
% cp /etc/fstab /dev/full
cp: /dev/full: No space left on device
```

The /dev/full entry is primarily useful to test how your program behaves if it runs out of disk space while writing to a file.

6.5.4 Random Number Devices

The special devices /dev/random and /dev/urandom provide access to the Linux kernel's built-in random number–generation facility.

Most software functions for generating random numbers, such as the rand function in the standard C library, actually generate *pseudorandom* numbers. Although these numbers satisfy some properties of random numbers, they are reproducible: If you start with the same seed value, you'll obtain the same sequence of pseudorandom numbers every time. This behavior is inevitable because computers are intrinsically deterministic and predictable. For certain applications, though, this behavior is undesirable; for instance, it is sometimes possible to break a cryptographic algorithm if you can obtain the sequence of random numbers that it employs.

To obtain better random numbers in computer programs requires an external source of randomness. The Linux kernel harnesses a particularly good source of randomness: *you!* By measuring the time delay between your input actions, such as keystrokes and mouse movements, Linux is capable of generating an unpredictable stream of high-quality random numbers. You can access this stream by reading from /dev/random and /dev/urandom. The data that you read is a stream of randomly generated bytes.

The difference between the two devices exhibits itself when Linux exhausts its store of randomness. If you try to read a large number of bytes from /dev/random but don't generate any input actions (you don't type, move the mouse, or perform a similar action), Linux blocks the read operation. Only when you provide some randomness does Linux generate some more random bytes and return them to your program.

For example, try displaying the contents of /dev/random using the od command.[4] Each row of output shows 16 random bytes.

---

4. We use od here instead of the hexdump program presented in Listing B.4, even though they do pretty much the same thing, because hexdump terminates when it runs out of data, while od waits for more data to become available. The -t x1 option tells od to print file contents in hexadecimal.

```
% od -t x1 /dev/random
0000000 2c 9c 7a db 2e 79 3d 65 36 c2 e3 1b 52 75 1e 1a
0000020 d3 6d 1e a7 91 05 2d 4d c3 a6 de 54 29 f4 46 04
0000040 b3 b0 8d 94 21 57 f3 90 61 dd 26 ac 94 c3 b9 3a
0000060 05 a3 02 cb 22 0a bc c9 45 dd a6 59 40 22 53 d4
```

The number of lines of output that you see will vary—there may be quite a few—but the output will eventually pause when Linux exhausts its store of randomness. Now try moving your mouse or typing on the keyboard, and watch additional random numbers appear. For even better randomness, let your cat walk on the keyboard.

A read from /dev/urandom, in contrast, will never block. If Linux runs out of randomness, it uses a cryptographic algorithm to generate pseudorandom bytes from the past sequence of random bytes. Although these bytes are random enough for many purposes, they don't pass as many tests of randomness as those obtained from /dev/random.

For instance, if you invoke the following, the random bytes will fly by forever, until you kill the program with Ctrl+C:

```
% od -t x1 /dev/urandom
0000000 62 71 d6 3e af dd de 62 c0 42 78 bd 29 9c 69 49
0000020 26 3b 95 bc b9 6c 15 16 38 fd 7e 34 f0 ba ce c3
0000040 95 31 e5 2c 8d 8a dd f4 c4 3b 9b 44 2f 20 d1 54
...
```

Using random numbers from /dev/random in a program is easy, too. Listing 6.1 presents a function that generates a random number using bytes read from in /dev/random. Remember that /dev/random blocks a read until there is enough randomness available to satisfy it; you can use /dev/urandom instead if fast execution is more important and you can live with the potential lower quality of random numbers.

Listing 6.1   (*random_number.c*) **Function to Generate a Random Number Using** */dev/random*

```
#include <assert.h>
#include <sys/stat.h>
#include <sys/types.h>
#include <fcntl.h>
#include <unistd.h>

/* Return a random integer between MIN and MAX, inclusive.  Obtain
   randomness from /dev/random.  */

int random_number (int min, int max)
{
  /* Store a file descriptor opened to /dev/random in a static
     variable.  That way, we don't need to open the file every time
     this function is called.  */
  static int dev_random_fd = -1;
```

```
  char* next_random_byte;
  int bytes_to_read;
  unsigned random_value;

  /* Make sure MAX is greater than MIN.  */
  assert (max > min);

  /* If this is the first time this function is called, open a file
     descriptor to /dev/random.  */
  if (dev_random_fd == -1) {
    dev_random_fd = open ("/dev/random", O_RDONLY);
    assert (dev_random_fd != -1);
  }

  /* Read enough random bytes to fill an integer variable.  */
  next_random_byte = (char*) &random_value;
  bytes_to_read = sizeof (random_value);
  /* Loop until we've read enough bytes.  Because /dev/random is filled
     from user-generated actions, the read may block and may only
     return a single random byte at a time.  */
  do {
    int bytes_read;
    bytes_read = read (dev_random_fd, next_random_byte, bytes_to_read);
    bytes_to_read -= bytes_read;
    next_random_byte += bytes_read;
  } while (bytes_to_read > 0);

  /* Compute a random number in the correct range.  */
  return min + (random_value % (max - min + 1));
}
```

6.5.5 Loopback Devices

A *loopback device* enables you to simulate a block device using an ordinary disk file. Imagine a disk drive device for which data is written to and read from a file named disk-image rather than to and from the tracks and sectors of an actual physical disk drive or disk partition. (Of course, the file disk-image must reside on an actual disk, which must be larger than the simulated disk.) A loopback device enables you to use a file in this manner.

Loopback devices are named /dev/loop0, /dev/loop1, and so on. Each can be used to simulate a single block device at one time. Note that only the superuser can set up a loopback device.

A loopback device can be used in the same way as any other block device. In particular, you can construct a file system on the device and then mount that file system as you would mount the file system on an ordinary disk or partition. Such a file system, which resides in its entirety within an ordinary disk file, is called a *virtual file system*.

To construct a virtual file system and mount it with a loopback device, follow these steps:

1. Create an empty file to hold the virtual file system. The size of the file will be the apparent size of the loopback device after it is mounted.

    One convenient way to construct a file of a fixed size is with the dd command. This command copies blocks (by default, 512 bytes each) from one file to another. The /dev/zero file is a convenient source of bytes to copy from.

    To construct a 10MB file named disk-image, invoke the following:

    ```
    % dd if=/dev/zero of=/tmp/disk-image count=20480
    20480+0 records in
    20480+0 records out
    % ls -l /tmp/disk-image
    -rw-rw----   1 root      root      10485760 Mar  8 01:56 /tmp/disk-image
    ```

2. The file that you've just created is filled with 0 bytes. Before you mount it, you must construct a file system. This sets up the various control structures needed to organize and store files, and builds the root directory.

    You can build any type of file system you like in your disk image. To construct an ext2 file system (the type most commonly used for Linux disks), use the mke2fs command. Because it's usually run on a block device, not an ordinary file, it asks for confirmation:

    ```
    % mke2fs -q /tmp/disk-image
    mke2fs 1.18, 11-Nov-1999 for EXT2 FS 0.5b, 95/08/09
    disk-image is not a block special device.
    Proceed anyway? (y,n) y
    ```

    The -q option suppresses summary information about the newly created file system. Leave this option out if you're curious about it.

    Now disk-image contains a brand-new file system, as if it were a freshly initialized 10MB disk drive.

3. Mount the file system using a loopback device. To do this, use the `mount` command, specifying the disk image file as the mount device. Also specify `loop=loopback-device` as a mount option, using the `-o` option to `mount` to tell `mount` which loopback device to use.

   For example, to mount our `disk-image` file system, invoke these commands. Remember, only the superuser may use a loopback device. The first command creates a directory, `/tmp/virtual-fs`, to use as the mount point for the virtual file system.

   ```
   % mkdir /tmp/virtual-fs
   % mount -o loop=/dev/loop0 /tmp/disk-image /tmp/virtual-fs
   ```

   Now your disk image is mounted as if it were an ordinary 10MB disk drive.

   ```
   % df -h /tmp/virtual-fs
   Filesystem          Size  Used Avail Use% Mounted on
   /tmp/disk-image     9.7M   13k  9.2M   0% /tmp/virtual-fs
   ```

   You can use it like any other disk:

   ```
   % cd /tmp/virtual-fs
   % echo 'Hello, world!' > test.txt
   % ls -l
   total 13
   drwxr-xr-x   2 root     root        12288 Mar  8 02:00 lost+found
   -rw-rw----   1 root     root           14 Mar  8 02:12 test.txt
   % cat test.txt
   Hello, world!
   ```

   Note that `lost+found` is a directory that was automatically added by `mke2fs`.[5]

---

5. If the file system is ever damaged, and some data is recovered but not associated with a file, it is placed in `lost+found`.

When you're done, unmount the virtual file system.

```
% cd /tmp
% umount /tmp/virtual-fs
```

You can delete disk-image if you like, or you can mount it later to access the files on the virtual file system. You can also copy it to another computer and mount it there—the whole file system that you created on it will be intact.

Instead of creating a file system from scratch, you can copy one directly from a device. For instance, you can create an image of the contents of a CD-ROM simply by copying it from the CD-ROM device.

If you have an IDE CD-ROM drive, use the corresponding device name, such as /dev/hda, described previously. If you have a SCSI CD-ROM drive, the device name will be /dev/scd0 or similar. Your system may also have a symbolic link /dev/cdrom that points to the appropriate device. Consult your /etc/fstab file to determine what device corresponds to your computer's CD-ROM drive.

Simply copy that device to a file. The resulting file will be a complete disk image of the file system on the CD-ROM in the drive—for example:

```
% cp /dev/cdrom /tmp/cdrom-image
```

This may take several minutes, depending on the CD-ROM you're copying and the speed of your drive. The resulting image file will be quite large—as large as the contents of the CD-ROM.

Now you can mount this CD-ROM image without having the original CD-ROM in the drive. For example, to mount it on /mnt/cdrom, use this line:

```
% mount -o loop=/dev/loop0 /tmp/cdrom-image /mnt/cdrom
```

Because the image is on a hard disk drive, it'll perform much faster than the actual CD-ROM disk. Note that most CD-ROMs use the file system type iso9660.

6.6   PTYs

If you run the mount command with no command-line arguments, which displays the file systems mounted on your system, you'll notice a line that looks something like this:

```
none on /dev/pts type devpts (rw,gid=5,mode=620)
```

This indicates that a special type of file system, devpts, is mounted at /dev/pts. This file system, which isn't associated with any hardware device, is a "magic" file system that is created by the Linux kernel. It's similar to the /proc file system; see Chapter 7 for more information about how this works.

Like the /dev directory, /dev/pts contains entries corresponding to devices. But unlike /dev, which is an ordinary directory, /dev/pts is a special directory that is created dynamically by the Linux kernel. The contents of the directory vary with time and reflect the state of the running system.

The entries in /dev/pts correspond to *pseudo-terminals* (or *pseudo-TTYs*, or *PTYs*). Linux creates a PTY for every new terminal window you open and displays a corresponding entry in /dev/pts. The PTY device acts like a terminal device—it accepts input from the keyboard and displays text output from the programs that run in it. PTYs are numbered, and the PTY number is the name of the corresponding entry in /dev/pts.

You can display the terminal device associated with a process using the ps command. Specify tty as one of the fields of a custom format with the -o option. To display the process ID, TTY, and command line of each process sharing the same terminal, invoke ps -o pid,tty,cmd.

6.6.1 A PTY Demonstration

For example, you can determine the PTY associated with a given terminal window by invoking in the window this command:

```
% ps -o pid,tty,cmd
  PID TT     CMD
28832 pts/4    bash
29287 pts/4    ps -o pid,tty,cmd
```

This particular terminal window is running in PTY 4.

The PTY has a corresponding entry in /dev/pts:

```
% ls -l /dev/pts/4
crw--w---- 1 samuel   tty      136,   4 Mar  8 02:56 /dev/pts/4
```

Note that it is a character device, and its owner is the owner of the process for which it was created.

You can read from or write to the PTY device. If you read from it, you'll hijack keyboard input that would otherwise be sent to the program running in the PTY. If you write to it, the data will appear in that window.

Try opening a new terminal window, and determine its PTY number by invoking ps -o pid,tty,cmd. From another window, write some text to the PTY device. For example, if the new terminal window's PTY number is 7, invoke this command from another window:

```
% echo 'Hello, other window!' > /dev/pts/7
```

The output appears in the new terminal window. If you close the new terminal window, the entry 7 in /dev/pts disappears.

If you invoke `ps` to determine the TTY from a text-mode virtual terminal (press Ctrl+Alt+F1 to switch to the first virtual terminal, for instance), you'll see that it's running in an ordinary terminal device instead of a PTY:

```
% ps -o pid,tty,cmd
  PID TT      CMD
29325 tty1    -bash
29353 tty1    ps -o pid,tty,cmd
```

6.7   *ioctl*

The `ioctl` system call is an all-purpose interface for controlling hardware devices. The first argument to `ioctl` is a file descriptor, which should be opened to the device that you want to control. The second argument is a request code that indicates the operation that you want to perform. Various request codes are available for different devices. Depending on the request code, there may be additional arguments supplying data to `ioctl`.

Many of the available requests codes for various devices are listed in the `ioctl_list` man page. Using `ioctl` generally requires a detailed understanding of the device driver corresponding to the hardware device that you want to control. Most of these are quite specialized and are beyond the scope of this book. However, we'll present one example to give you a taste of how `ioctl` is used.

Listing 6.2   *(cdrom-eject.c)* **Eject a CD-ROM**

```c
#include <fcntl.h>
#include <linux/cdrom.h>
#include <sys/ioctl.h>
#include <sys/stat.h>
#include <sys/types.h>
#include <unistd.h>

int main (int argc, char* argv[])
{
  /* Open a file descriptor to the device specified on the command line.  */
  int fd = open (argv[1], O_RDONLY);
  /* Eject the CD-ROM.  */
  ioctl (fd, CDROMEJECT);
  /* Close the file descriptor.  */
  close (fd);

  return 0;
}
```

Listing 6.2 presents a short program that ejects the disk in a CD-ROM drive (if the drive supports this). It takes a single command-line argument, the CD-ROM drive device. It opens a file descriptor to the device and invokes `ioctl` with the request code `CDROMEJECT`. This request, defined in the header `<linux/cdrom.h>`, instructs the device to eject the disk.

For example, if your system has an IDE CD-ROM drive connected as the master device on the secondary IDE controller, the corresponding device is `/dev/hdc`. To eject the disk from the drive, invoke this line:

```
% ./cdrom-eject /dev/hdc
```

7

The /proc File System

T RY INVOKING THE mount COMMAND WITHOUT ARGUMENTS—this displays the file systems currently mounted on your GNU/Linux computer. You'll see one line that looks like this:

```
none on /proc type proc (rw)
```

This is the special /proc *file system*. Notice that the first field, none, indicates that this file system isn't associated with a hardware device such as a disk drive. Instead, /proc is a window into the running Linux kernel. Files in the /proc file system don't correspond to actual files on a physical device. Instead, they are magic objects that behave like files but provide access to parameters, data structures, and statistics in the kernel. The "contents" of these files are not always fixed blocks of data, as ordinary file contents are. Instead, they are generated on the fly by the Linux kernel when you read from the file. You can also change the configuration of the running kernel by writing to certain files in the /proc file system.

Let's look at an example:

```
% ls -l /proc/version
-r--r--r--   1 root     root            0 Jan 17 18:09 /proc/version
```

Note that the file size is zero; because the file's contents are generated by the kernel, the concept of file size is not applicable. Also, if you try this command yourself, you'll notice that the modification time on the file is the current time.

What's in this file? The contents of /proc/version consist of a string describing the Linux kernel version number. It contains the version information that would be obtained by the uname system call, described in Chapter 8, "Linux System Calls," in Section 8.15, "uname," plus additional information such as the version of the compiler that was used to compile the kernel. You can read from /proc/version like you would any other file. For instance, an easy way to display its contents is with the cat command.

```
% cat /proc/version
Linux version 2.2.14-5.0 (root@porky.devel.redhat.com) (gcc version egcs-2.91.
66 19990314/Linux (egcs-1.1.2 release)) #1 Tue Mar 7 21:07:39 EST 2000
```

The various entries in the /proc file system are described extensively in the proc man page (Section 5). To view it, invoke this command:

```
% man 5 proc
```

In this chapter, we'll describe some of the features of the /proc file system that are most likely to be useful to application programmers, and we'll give examples of using them. Some of the features of /proc are handy for debugging, too.

If you're interested in exactly how /proc works, take a look at the source code in the Linux kernel sources, under /usr/src/linux/fs/proc/.

7.1   Extracting Information from /proc

Most of the entries in /proc provide information formatted to be readable by humans, but the formats are simple enough to be easily parsed. For example, /proc/cpuinfo contains information about the system CPU (or CPUs, for a multiprocessor machine). The output is a table of values, one per line, with a description of the value and a colon preceding each value.

For example, the output might look like this:

```
% cat /proc/cpuinfo
processor       : 0
vendor_id       : GenuineIntel
cpu family      : 6
model           : 5
model name      : Pentium II (Deschutes)
stepping        : 2
cpu MHz         : 400.913520
cache size      : 512 KB
fdiv_bug        : no
hlt_bug         : no
sep_bug         : no
f00f_bug        : no
coma_bug        : no
fpu             : yes
fpu_exception   : yes
cpuid level     : 2
wp              : yes
flags           : fpu vme de pse tsc msr pae mce cx8 apic sep
mtrr pge mca cmov pat pse36 mmx fxsr
bogomips        : 399.77
```

We'll describe the interpretation of some of these fields in Section 7.3.1, "CPU Information."

A simple way to extract a value from this output is to read the file into a buffer and parse it in memory using sscanf. Listing 7.1 shows an example of this. The program includes the function get_cpu_clock_speed that reads from /proc/cpuinfo into memory and extracts the first CPU's clock speed.

Listing 7.1   **(*clock-speed.c*) Extract CPU Clock Speed from** */proc/cpuinfo*

```c
#include <stdio.h>
#include <string.h>

/* Returns the clock speed of the system's CPU in MHz, as reported by
   /proc/cpuinfo.  On a multiprocessor machine, returns the speed of
   the first CPU.  On error returns zero.  */

float get_cpu_clock_speed ()
{
  FILE* fp;
  char buffer[1024];
  size_t bytes_read;
  char* match;
  float clock_speed;

  /* Read the entire contents of /proc/cpuinfo into the buffer.  */
  fp = fopen ("/proc/cpuinfo", "r");
  bytes_read = fread (buffer, 1, sizeof (buffer), fp);
  fclose (fp);
  /* Bail if read failed or if buffer isn't big enough.  */
  if (bytes_read == 0 || bytes_read == sizeof (buffer))
    return 0;
  /* NUL-terminate the text.  */
  buffer[bytes_read] = '\0';
  /* Locate the line that starts with "cpu MHz".  */
  match = strstr (buffer, "cpu MHz");
  if (match == NULL)
    return 0;
  /* Parse the line to extract the clock speed.  */
  sscanf (match, "cpu MHz : %f", &clock_speed);
  return clock_speed;
}


int main ()
{
  printf ("CPU clock speed: %4.0f MHz\n", get_cpu_clock_speed ());
  return 0;
}
```

Be aware, however, that the names, semantics, and output formats of entries in the /proc file system might change in new Linux kernel revisions. If you use them in a program, you should make sure that the program's behavior degrades gracefully if the /proc entry is missing or is formatted unexpectedly.

7.2 Process Entries

The /proc file system contains a directory entry for each process running on the GNU/Linux system. The name of each directory is the process ID of the corresponding process.[1] These directories appear and disappear dynamically as processes start and terminate on the system. Each directory contains several entries providing access to information about the running process. From these process directories the /proc file system gets its name.

Each process directory contains these entries:

- cmdline contains the argument list for the process. The cmdline entry is described in Section 7.2.2, "Process Argument List."

- cwd is a symbolic link that points to the current working directory of the process (as set, for instance, with the chdir call).

- environ contains the process's environment. The environ entry is described in Section 7.2.3, "Process Environment."

- exe is a symbolic link that points to the executable image running in the process. The exe entry is described in Section 7.2.4, "Process Executable."

- fd is a subdirectory that contains entries for the file descriptors opened by the process. These are described in Section 7.2.5, "Process File Descriptors."

- maps displays information about files mapped into the process's address. See Chapter 5, "Interprocess Communication," Section 5.3, "Mapped Memory," for details of how memory-mapped files work. For each mapped file, maps displays the range of addresses in the process's address space into which the file is mapped, the permissions on these addresses, the name of the file, and other information.

  The maps table for each process displays the executable running in the process, any loaded shared libraries, and other files that the process has mapped in.

- root is a symbolic link to the root directory for this process. Usually, this is a symbolic link to /, the system root directory. The root directory for a process can be changed using the chroot call or the chroot command.[2]

---

1. On some UNIX systems, the process IDs are padded with zeros. On GNU/Linux, they are not.

2. The chroot call and command are outside the scope of this book. See the chroot man page in Section 1 for information about the command (invoke man 1 chroot), or the chroot man page in Section 2 (invoke man 2 chroot) for information about the call.

- `stat` contains lots of status and statistical information about the process. These are the same data as presented in the `status` entry, but in raw numerical format, all on a single line. The format is difficult to read but might be more suitable for parsing by programs.

  If you want to use the `stat` entry in your programs, see the `proc` man page, which describes its contents, by invoking `man 5 proc`.

- `statm` contains information about the memory used by the process. The `statm` entry is described in Section 7.2.6, "Process Memory Statistics."

- `status` contains lots of status and statistical information about the process, formatted to be comprehensible by humans. Section 7.2.7, "Process Statistics," contains a description of the `status` entry.

- The `cpu` entry appears only on SMP Linux kernels. It contains a breakdown of process time (user and system) by CPU.

Note that for security reasons, the permissions of some entries are set so that only the user who owns the process (or the superuser) can access them.

7.2.1 /proc/self

One additional entry in the /proc file system makes it easy for a program to use /proc to find information about its own process. The entry /proc/self is a symbolic link to the /proc directory corresponding to the current process. The destination of the /proc/self link depends on which process looks at it: Each process sees its own process directory as the target of the link.

For example, the program in Listing 7.2 reads the target of the /proc/self link to determine its process ID. (We're doing it this way for illustrative purposes only; calling the `getpid` function, described in Chapter 3, "Processes," in Section 3.1.1, "Process IDs," is a much easier way to do the same thing.) This program uses the `readlink` system call, described in Section 8.11, "`readlink`: Reading Symbolic Links," to extract the target of the symbolic link.

Listing 7.2   (*get-pid.c*) **Obtain the Process ID from** */proc/self*

```
#include <stdio.h>
#include <sys/types.h>
#include <unistd.h>

/* Returns the process ID of the calling processes, as determined from
   the /proc/self symlink.  */

pid_t get_pid_from_proc_self ()
{
  char target[32];
  int pid;
  /* Read the target of the symbolic link.  */
  readlink ("/proc/self", target, sizeof (target));
```

continues

Listing 7.2 **Continued**

```
  /* The target is a directory named for the process ID.  */
  sscanf (target, "%d", &pid);
  return (pid_t) pid;
}

int main ()
{
  printf ("/proc/self reports process id %d\n",
          (int) get_pid_from_proc_self ());
  printf ("getpid() reports process id %d\n", (int) getpid ());
  return 0;
}
```

7.2.2 Process Argument List

The cmdline entry contains the process argument list (see Chapter 2, "Writing Good GNU/Linux Software," Section 2.1.1, "The Argument List"). The arguments are presented as a single character string, with arguments separated by NULs. Most string functions expect that the entire character string is terminated with a single NUL and will not handle NULs embedded within strings, so you'll have to handle the contents specially.

> **NUL vs. NULL**
>
> NUL is the character with integer value 0. It's different from NULL, which is a pointer with value 0.
>
> In C, a character string is usually terminated with a NUL character. For instance, the character string "Hello, world!" occupies 14 bytes because there is an implicit NUL after the exclamation point indicating the end of the string.
>
> NULL, on the other hand, is a pointer value that you can be sure will never correspond to a real memory address in your program.
>
> In C and C++, NUL is expressed as the character constant '\0', or (char) 0. The definition of NULL differs among operating systems; on Linux, it is defined as ((void*)0) in C and simply 0 in C++.

In Section 2.1.1, we presented a program in Listing 2.1 that printed out its own argument list. Using the cmdline entries in the /proc file system, we can implement a program that prints the argument of another process. Listing 7.3 is such a program; it prints the argument list of the process with the specified process ID. Because there may be several NULs in the contents of cmdline rather than a single one at the end, we can't determine the length of the string with strlen (which simply counts the number of characters until it encounters a NUL). Instead, we determine the length of cmdline from read, which returns the number of bytes that were read.

Listing 7.3 (*print-arg-list.c*) **Print the Argument List of a Running Process**

```c
#include <fcntl.h>
#include <stdio.h>
#include <stdlib.h>
#include <sys/stat.h>
#include <sys/types.h>
#include <unistd.h>

/* Prints the argument list, one argument to a line, of the process
   given by PID.  */

void print_process_arg_list (pid_t pid)
{
  int fd;
  char filename[24];
  char arg_list[1024];
  size_t length;
  char* next_arg;

  /* Generate the name of the cmdline file for the process. */
  snprintf (filename, sizeof (filename), "/proc/%d/cmdline", (int) pid);
  /* Read the contents of the file. */
  fd = open (filename, O_RDONLY);
  length = read (fd, arg_list, sizeof (arg_list));
  close (fd);
  /* read does not NUL-terminate the buffer, so do it here. */
  arg_list[length] = '\0';

  /* Loop over arguments.  Arguments are separated by NULs. */
  next_arg = arg_list;
  while (next_arg < arg_list + length) {
    /* Print the argument.  Each is NUL-terminated, so just treat it
       like an ordinary string.  */
    printf ("%s\n", next_arg);
    /* Advance to the next argument.  Since each argument is
       NUL-terminated, strlen counts the length of the next argument,
       not the entire argument list.  */
    next_arg += strlen (next_arg) + 1;
  }
}

int main (int argc, char* argv[])
{
  pid_t pid = (pid_t) atoi (argv[1]);
  print_process_arg_list (pid);
  return 0;
}
```

For example, suppose that process 372 is the system logger daemon, `syslogd`.

```
% ps 372
  PID TTY        STAT   TIME COMMAND
  372 ?          S      0:00 syslogd -m 0
% ./print-arg-list 372
syslogd
-m
0
```

In this case, `syslogd` was invoked with the arguments `-m 0`.

7.2.3 Process Environment

The `environ` entry contains a process's environment (see Section 2.1.6, "The
Environment"). As with `cmdline`, the individual environment variables are separated by
NULs. The format of each element is the same as that used in the `environ` variable,
namely *VARIABLE=value*.

Listing 7.4 presents a generalization of the program in Listing 2.3 in Section 2.1.6.
This version takes a process ID number on its command line and prints the environment for that process by reading it from `/proc`.

Listing 7.4 (*print-environment.c*) **Display the Environment of a Process**

```
#include <fcntl.h>
#include <stdio.h>
#include <stdlib.h>
#include <sys/stat.h>
#include <sys/types.h>
#include <unistd.h>

/* Prints the environment, one environment variable to a line, of the
   process given by PID.  */

void print_process_environment (pid_t pid)
{
  int fd;
  char filename[24];
  char environment[8192];
  size_t length;
  char* next_var;

  /* Generate the name of the environ file for the process. */
  snprintf (filename, sizeof (filename), "/proc/%d/environ", (int) pid);
  /* Read the contents of the file. */
  fd = open (filename, O_RDONLY);
  length = read (fd, environment, sizeof (environment));
  close (fd);
  /* read does not NUL-terminate the buffer, so do it here. */
  environment[length] = '\0';
```

7.2 Process Entries 155

```
  /* Loop over variables.  Variables are separated by NULs. */
  next_var = environment;
  while (next_var < environment + length) {
    /* Print the variable.  Each is NUL-terminated, so just treat it
       like an ordinary string.  */
    printf ("%s\n", next_var);
    /* Advance to the next variable.  Since each variable is
       NUL-terminated, strlen counts the length of the next variable,
       not the entire variable list.  */
    next_var += strlen (next_var) + 1;
  }
}

int main (int argc, char* argv[])
{
  pid_t pid = (pid_t) atoi (argv[1]);
  print_process_environment (pid);
  return 0;
}
```

7.2.4 Process Executable

The exe entry points to the executable file being run in a process. In Section 2.1.1, we explained that typically the program executable name is passed as the first element of the argument list. Note, though, that this is purely conventional; a program may be invoked with any argument list. Using the exe entry in the /proc file system is a more reliable way to determine which executable is running.

One useful technique is to extract the path containing the executable from the /proc file system. For many programs, auxiliary files are installed in directories with known paths relative to the main program executable, so it's necessary to determine where that executable actually is. The function get_executable_path in Listing 7.5 determines the path of the executable running in the calling process by examining the symbolic link /proc/self/exe.

Listing 7.5 (*get-exe-path.c*) **Get the Path of the Currently Running Program Executable**

```
#include <limits.h>
#include <stdio.h>
#include <string.h>
#include <unistd.h>

/* Finds the path containing the currently running program executable.
   The path is placed into BUFFER, which is of length LEN.  Returns
   the number of characters in the path, or -1 on error.  */
```

continues

Listing 7.5   **Continued**

```
size_t get_executable_path (char* buffer, size_t len)
{
  char* path_end;
  /* Read the target of /proc/self/exe.  */
  if (readlink ("/proc/self/exe", buffer, len) <= 0)
    return -1;
  /* Find the last occurrence of a forward slash, the path separator.  */
  path_end = strrchr (buffer, '/');
  if (path_end == NULL)
    return -1;
  /* Advance to the character past the last slash.  */
  ++path_end;
  /* Obtain the directory containing the program by truncating the
     path after the last slash.  */
  *path_end = '\0';
  /* The length of the path is the number of characters up through the
     last slash.  */
  return (size_t) (path_end - buffer);
}

int main ()
{
  char path[PATH_MAX];
  get_executable_path (path, sizeof (path));
  printf ("this program is in the directory %s\n", path);
  return 0;
}
```

7.2.5   Process File Descriptors

The fd entry is a subdirectory that contains entries for the file descriptors opened by a process. Each entry is a symbolic link to the file or device opened on that file descriptor. You can write to or read from these symbolic links; this writes to or reads from the corresponding file or device opened in the target process. The entries in the fd subdirectory are named by the file descriptor numbers.

Here's a neat trick you can try with fd entries in /proc. Open a new window, and find the process ID of the shell process by running ps.

```
% ps
  PID TTY          TIME CMD
 1261 pts/4    00:00:00 bash
 2455 pts/4    00:00:00 ps
```

In this case, the shell (bash) is running in process 1261. Now open a second window, and look at the contents of the fd subdirectory for that process.

```
% ls -l /proc/1261/fd
total 0
lrwx------   1 samuel    samuel           64 Jan 30 01:02 0 -> /dev/pts/4
lrwx------   1 samuel    samuel           64 Jan 30 01:02 1 -> /dev/pts/4
lrwx------   1 samuel    samuel           64 Jan 30 01:02 2 -> /dev/pts/4
```

(There may be other lines of output corresponding to other open file descriptors as well.) Recall that we mentioned in Section 2.1.4, "Standard I/O," that file descriptors 0, 1, and 2 are initialized to standard input, output, and error, respectively. Thus, by writing to /proc/1261/fd/1, you can write to the device attached to stdout for the shell process—in this case, the pseudo TTY in the first window. In the second window, try writing a message to that file:

```
% echo "Hello, world." >> /proc/1261/fd/1
```

The text appears in the first window.

File descriptors besides standard input, output, and error appear in the fd subdirectory, too. Listing 7.6 presents a program that simply opens a file descriptor to a file specified on the command line and then loops forever.

Listing 7.6   (*open-and-spin.c*) **Open a File for Reading**

```c
#include <fcntl.h>
#include <stdio.h>
#include <sys/stat.h>
#include <sys/types.h>
#include <unistd.h>

int main (int argc, char* argv[])
{
  const char* const filename = argv[1];
  int fd = open (filename, O_RDONLY);
  printf ("in process %d, file descriptor %d is open to %s\n",
          (int) getpid (), (int) fd, filename);
  while (1);
  return 0;
}
```

Try running it in one window:

```
%  ./open-and-spin /etc/fstab
in process 2570, file descriptor 3 is open to /etc/fstab
```

In another window, take a look at the fd subdirectory corresponding to this process in /proc.

```
% ls -l /proc/2570/fd
total 0
lrwx------   1 samuel    samuel           64 Jan 30 01:30 0 -> /dev/pts/2
```

```
lrwx------    1 samuel    samuel       64 Jan 30 01:30 1 -> /dev/pts/2
lrwx------    1 samuel    samuel       64 Jan 30 01:30 2 -> /dev/pts/2
lr-x------    1 samuel    samuel       64 Jan 30 01:30 3 -> /etc/fstab
```

Notice the entry for file descriptor 3, linked to the file /etc/fstab opened on this descriptor.

File descriptors can be opened on sockets or pipes, too (see Chapter 5 for more information about these). In such a case, the target of the symbolic link corresponding to the file descriptor will state "socket" or "pipe" instead of pointing to an ordinary file or device.

7.2.6   Process Memory Statistics

The statm entry contains a list of seven numbers, separated by spaces. Each number is a count of the number of pages of memory used by the process in a particular category. The categories, in the order the numbers appear, are listed here:

- The total process size
- The size of the process resident in physical memory
- The memory shared with other processes—that is, memory mapped both by this process and at least one other (such as shared libraries or untouched copy-on-write pages)
- The text size of the process—that is, the size of loaded executable code
- The size of shared libraries mapped into this process
- The memory used by this process for its stack
- The number of dirty pages—that is, pages of memory that have been modified by the program

7.2.7   Process Statistics

The status entry contains a variety of information about the process, formatted for comprehension by humans. Among this information is the process ID and parent process ID, the real and effective user and group IDs, memory usage, and bit masks specifying which signals are caught, ignored, and blocked.

7.3   Hardware Information

Several of the other entries in the /proc file system provide access to information about the system hardware. Although these are typically of interest to system configurators and administrators, the information may occasionally be of use to application programmers as well. We'll present some of the more useful entries here.

7.3.1 CPU Information

As shown previously, `/proc/cpuinfo` contains information about the CPU or CPUs running the GNU/Linux system. The Processor field lists the processor number; this is 0 for single-processor systems. The Vendor, CPU Family, Model, and Stepping fields enable you to determine the exact model and revision of the CPU. More useful, the Flags field shows which CPU flags are set, which indicates the features available in this CPU. For example, "mmx" indicates the availability of the extended MMX instructions.[3]

Most of the information returned from `/proc/cpuinfo` is derived from the `cpuid` x86 assembly instruction. This instruction is the low-level mechanism by which a program obtains information about the CPU. For a greater understanding of the output of `/proc/cpuinfo`, see the documentation of the `cpuid` instruction in Intel's *IA-32 Intel Architecture Software Developer's Manual, Volume 2: Instruction Set Reference.* This manual is available from `http://developer.intel.com/design`.

The last element, `bogomips`, is a Linux-specific value. It is a measurement of the processor's speed spinning in a tight loop and is therefore a rather poor indicator of overall processor speed.

7.3.2 Device Information

The `/proc/devices` file lists major device numbers for character and block devices available to the system. See Chapter 6, "Devices," for information about types of devices and device numbers.

7.3.3 PCI Bus Information

The `/proc/pci` file lists a summary of devices attached to the PCI bus or buses. These are actual PCI expansion cards and may also include devices built into the system's motherboard, plus AGP graphics cards. The listing includes the device type; the device and vendor ID; a device name, if available; information about the features offered by the device; and information about the PCI resources used by the device.

7.3.4 Serial Port Information

The `/proc/tty/driver/serial` file lists configuration information and statistics about serial ports. Serial ports are numbered from 0.[4] Configuration information about serial ports can also be obtained, as well as modified, using the `setserial` command. However, `/proc/tty/driver/serial` displays additional statistics about each serial port's interrupt counts.

---

3. See the *IA-32 Intel Architecture Software Developer's Manual* for documentation about MMX instructions, and see Chapter 9, "Inline Assembly Code," in this book for information on how to use these and other special assembly instructions in GNU/Linux programs.

4. Note that under DOS and Windows, serial ports are numbered from 1, so `COM1` corresponds to serial port number 0 under Linux.

For example, this line from /proc/tty/driver/serial might describe serial port 1 (which would be COM2 under Windows):

```
1: uart:16550A port:2F8 irq:3 baud:9600 tx:11 rx:0
```

This indicates that the serial port is run by a 16550A-type UART, uses I/O port 0x2f8 and IRQ 3 for communication, and runs at 9,600 baud. The serial port has seen 11 transmit interrupts and 0 receive interrupts.

See Section 6.4, "Hardware Devices," for information about serial devices.

7.4 Kernel Information

Many of the entries in /proc provide access to information about the running kernel's configuration and state. Some of these entries are at the top level of /proc; others are under /proc/sys/kernel.

7.4.1 Version Information

The file /proc/version contains a long string describing the kernel's release number and build version. It also includes information about how the kernel was built: the user who compiled it, the machine on which it was compiled, the date it was compiled, and the compiler release that was used—for example:

```
% cat /proc/version
Linux version 2.2.14-5.0 (root@porky.devel.redhat.com) (gcc version
egcs-2.91.66 19990314/Linux (egcs-1.1.2 release)) #1 Tue Mar 7
21:07:39 EST 2000
```

This indicates that the system is running a 2.2.14 release of the Linux kernel, which was compiled with EGCS release 1.1.2. (EGCS, the *Experimental GNU Compiler System*, was a precursor to the current GCC project.)

The most important items in this output, the OS name and kernel version and revision, are available in separate /proc entries as well. These are /proc/sys/kernel/ostype, /proc/sys/kernel/osrelease, and /proc/sys/kernel/version, respectively.

```
% cat /proc/sys/kernel/ostype
Linux
% cat /proc/sys/kernel/osrelease
2.2.14-5.0
% cat /proc/sys/kernel/version
#1 Tue Mar 7 21:07:39 EST 2000
```

7.4.2 Hostname and Domain Name

The /proc/sys/kernel/hostname and /proc/sys/kernel/domainname entries contain the computer's hostname and domain name, respectively. This information is the same as that returned by the uname system call, described in Section 8.15.

7.4.3 Memory Usage

The /proc/meminfo entry contains information about the system's memory usage. Information is presented both for physical memory and for swap space. The first three lines present memory totals, in bytes; subsequent lines summarize this information in kilobytes—for example:

```
% cat /proc/meminfo
        total:    used:     free: shared: buffers: cached:
Mem: 529694720 519610368 10084352 82612224 10977280 82108416
Swap: 271392768 44003328 227389440
MemTotal:    517280 kB
MemFree:       9848 kB
MemShared:    80676 kB
Buffers:      10720 kB
Cached:       80184 kB
BigTotal:         0 kB
BigFree:          0 kB
SwapTotal:   265032 kB
SwapFree:    222060 kB
```

This shows 512MB physical memory, of which about 9MB is free, and 258MB of swap space, of which 216MB is free. In the row corresponding to physical memory, three other values are presented:

- The Shared column displays total shared memory currently allocated on the system (see Section 5.1, "Shared Memory").

- The Buffers column displays the memory allocated by Linux for block device buffers. These buffers are used by device drivers to hold blocks of data being read from and written to disk.

- The Cached column displays the memory allocated by Linux to the page cache. This memory is used to cache accesses to mapped files.

You can use the free command to display the same memory information.

7.5 Drives, Mounts, and File Systems

The /proc file system also contains information about the disk drives present in the system and the file systems mounted from them.

7.5.1 File Systems

The /proc/filesystems entry displays the file system types known to the kernel. Note that this list isn't very useful because it is not complete: File systems can be loaded and unloaded dynamically as kernel modules. The contents of /proc/filesystems list only file system types that either are statically linked into the kernel or are currently loaded. Other file system types may be available on the system as modules but might not be loaded yet.

7.5.2 Drives and Partitions

The /proc file system includes information about devices connected to both IDE controllers and SCSI controllers (if the system includes them).

On typical systems, the /proc/ide subdirectory may contain either or both of two subdirectories, ide0 and ide1, corresponding to the primary and secondary IDE controllers on the system.[5] These contain further subdirectories corresponding to physical devices attached to the controllers. The controller or device directories may be absent if Linux has not recognized any connected devices. The full paths corresponding to the four possible IDE devices are listed in Table 7.1.

Table 7.1 **Full Paths Corresponding to the Four Possible IDE Devices**

Controller	Device	Subdirectory
Primary	Master	/proc/ide/ide0/hda/
Primary	Slave	/proc/ide/ide0/hdb/
Secondary	Master	/proc/ide/ide1/hdc/
Secondary	Slave	/proc/ide/ide1/hdd/

See Section 6.4, "Hardware Devices," for more information about IDE device names.

Each IDE device directory contains several entries providing access to identification and configuration information for the device. A few of the most useful are listed here:

- model contains the device's model identification string.
- media contains the device's media type. Possible values are disk, cdrom, tape, floppy, and UNKNOWN.
- capacity contains the device's capacity, in 512-byte blocks. Note that for CD-ROM devices, the value will be $2^{31} - 1$, not the capacity of the disk in the drive. Note that the value in capacity represents the capacity of the entire physical disk; the capacity of file systems contained in partitions of the disk will be smaller.

For example, these commands show how to determine the media type and device identification for the master device on the secondary IDE controller. In this case, it turns out to be a Toshiba CD-ROM drive.

```
% cat /proc/ide/ide1/hdc/media
cdrom
% cat /proc/ide/ide1/hdc/model
TOSHIBA CD-ROM XM-6702B
```

---

5. If properly configured, the Linux kernel can support additional IDE controllers. These are numbered sequentially from ide2.

If SCSI devices are present in the system, /proc/scsi/scsi contains a summary of their identification values. For example, the contents might look like this:

```
% cat /proc/scsi/scsi
Attached devices:
Host: scsi0 Channel: 00 Id: 00 Lun: 00
   Vendor: QUANTUM  Model: ATLAS_V__9_WLS   Rev: 0230
   Type:   Direct-Access                    ANSI SCSI revision: 03
Host: scsi0 Channel: 00 Id: 04 Lun: 00
   Vendor: QUANTUM  Model: QM39100TD-SW     Rev: N491
   Type:   Direct-Access                    ANSI SCSI revision: 02
```

This computer contains one single-channel SCSI controller (designated "scsi0"), to which two Quantum disk drives are connected, with SCSI device IDs 0 and 4.

The /proc/partitions entry displays the partitions of recognized disk devices. For each partition, the output includes the major and minor device number, the number of 1024-byte blocks, and the device name corresponding to that partition.

The /proc/sys/dev/cdrom/info entry displays miscellaneous information about the capabilities of CD-ROM drives. The fields are self-explanatory:

```
% cat /proc/sys/dev/cdrom/info
CD-ROM information, Id: cdrom.c 2.56 1999/09/09

drive name:   hdc
drive speed:  48
drive # of slots:  0
Can close tray:  1
Can open tray:  1
Can lock tray:  1
Can change speed:  1
Can select disk:  0
Can read multisession:  1
Can read MCN:  1
Reports media changed:  1
Can play audio:  1
```

7.5.3 Mounts

The /proc/mounts file provides a summary of mounted file systems. Each line corresponds to a single *mount descriptor* and lists the mounted device, the mount point, and other information. Note that /proc/mounts contains the same information as the ordinary file /etc/mtab, which is automatically updated by the mount command.

These are the elements of a mount descriptor:

- The first element on the line is the mounted device (see Chapter 6). For special file systems such as the /proc file system, this is none.

- The second element is the *mount point*, the place in the root file system at which the file system contents appear. For the root file system itself, the mount point is listed as /. For swap drives, the mount point is listed as swap.

- The third element is the file system type. Currently, most GNU/Linux systems use the ext2 file system for disk drives, but DOS or Windows drives may be mounted with other file system types, such as fat or vfat. Most CD-ROMs contain an iso9660 file system. See the man page for the mount command for a list of file system types.
- The fourth element lists mount flags. These are options that were specified when the mount was added. See the man page for the mount command for an explanation of flags for the various file system types.

In /proc/mounts, the last two elements are always 0 and have no meaning.

See the man page for fstab for details about the format of mount descriptors.[6] GNU/Linux includes functions to help you parse mount descriptors; see the man page for the getmntent function for information on using these.

7.5.4   Locks

Section 8.3, "fcntl: Locks and Other File Operations," describes how to use the fcntl system call to manipulate read and write locks on files. The /proc/locks entry describes all the file locks currently outstanding in the system. Each row in the output corresponds to one lock.

For locks created with fcntl, the first two entries on the line are POSIX ADVISORY. The third is WRITE or READ, depending on the lock type. The next number is the process ID of the process holding the lock. The following three numbers, separated by colons, are the major and minor device numbers of the device on which the file resides and the *inode* number, which locates the file in the file system. The remainder of the line lists values internal to the kernel that are not of general utility.

Turning the contents of /proc/locks into useful information takes some detective work. You can watch /proc/locks in action, for instance, by running the program in Listing 8.2 to create a write lock on the file /tmp/test-file.

```
% touch /tmp/test-file
% ./lock-file /tmp/test-file
file /tmp/test-file
opening /tmp/test-file
locking
locked; hit enter to unlock...
```

In another window, look at the contents of /proc/locks.

```
% cat /proc/locks
1: POSIX  ADVISORY  WRITE 5467 08:05:181288 0 2147483647 d1b5f740 00000000
dfea7d40 00000000 00000000
```

6. The /etc/fstab file lists the static mount configuration of the GNU/Linux system.

There may be other lines of output, too, corresponding to locks held by other programs. In this case, 5467 is the process ID of the `lock-file` program. Use `ps` to figure out what this process is running.

```
% ps 5467
  PID TTY      STAT   TIME COMMAND
 5467 pts/28   S      0:00 ./lock-file /tmp/test-file
```

The locked file, `/tmp/test-file`, resides on the device that has major and minor device numbers 8 and 5, respectively. These numbers happen to correspond to `/dev/sda5`.

```
% df /tmp
Filesystem          1k-blocks      Used Available Use% Mounted on
/dev/sda5            8459764    5094292   2935736  63% /
% ls -l /dev/sda5
brw-rw----   1 root     disk       8,   5 May  5  1998 /dev/sda5
```

The file `/tmp/test-file` itself is at inode 181,288 on that device.

```
% ls --inode /tmp/test-file
 181288 /tmp/test-file
```

See Section 6.2, "Device Numbers," for more information about device numbers.

7.6   System Statistics

Two entries in `/proc` contain useful system statistics. The `/proc/loadavg` file contains information about the system load. The first three numbers represent the number of *active tasks* on the system—processes that are actually running—averaged over the last 1, 5, and 15 minutes. The next entry shows the instantaneous current number of *runnable tasks*—processes that are currently scheduled to run rather than being blocked in a system call—and the total number of processes on the system. The final entry is the process ID of the process that most recently ran.

The `/proc/uptime` file contains the length of time since the system was booted, as well as the amount of time since then that the system has been idle. Both are given as floating-point values, in seconds.

```
% cat /proc/uptime
3248936.18 3072330.49
```

The program in Listing 7.7 extracts the uptime and idle time from the system and displays them in friendly units.

Listing 7.7   (*print-uptime.c*) **Print the System Uptime and Idle Time**

```
#include <stdio.h>

/* Summarize a duration of time to standard output.  TIME is the
   amount of time, in seconds, and LABEL is a short descriptive label.  */

void print_time (char* label, long time)
{
```

continues

Listing 7.7 **Continued**

```
  /* Conversion constants.  */
  const long minute = 60;
  const long hour = minute * 60;
  const long day = hour * 24;
  /* Produce output.  */
  printf ("%s: %ld days, %ld:%02ld:%02ld\n", label, time / day,
          (time % day) / hour, (time % hour) / minute, time % minute);
}

int main ()
{
  FILE* fp;
  double uptime, idle_time;
  /* Read the system uptime and accumulated idle time from /proc/uptime.  */
  fp = fopen ("/proc/uptime", "r");
  fscanf (fp, "%lf %lf\n", &uptime, &idle_time);
  fclose (fp);
  /* Summarize it.  */
  print_time ("uptime   ", (long) uptime);
  print_time ("idle time", (long) idle_time);
  return 0;
}
```

The uptime command and the sysinfo system call (see Section 8.14, "sysinfo: Obtaining System Statistics") also can obtain the system's uptime. The uptime command also displays the load averages found in /proc/loadavg.

8

Linux System Calls

So FAR, WE'VE PRESENTED A VARIETY OF FUNCTIONS that your program can invoke
to perform system-related functions, such as parsing command-line options, manipulating processes, and mapping memory. If you look under the hood, you'll find that
these functions fall into two categories, based on how they are implemented.

- A *library function* is an ordinary function that resides in a library external to your
  program. Most of the library functions we've presented so far are in the standard
  C library, libc. For example, getopt_long and mkstemp are functions provided in
  the C library.

  A call to a library function is just like any other function call. The arguments are
  placed in processor registers or onto the stack, and execution is transferred to
  the start of the function's code, which typically resides in a loaded shared library.

- A *system call* is implemented in the Linux kernel. When a program makes a
  system call, the arguments are packaged up and handed to the kernel, which
  takes over execution of the program until the call completes. A system call isn't
  an ordinary function call, and a special procedure is required to transfer control
  to the kernel. However, the GNU C library (the implementation of the standard
  C library provided with GNU/Linux systems) wraps Linux system calls with
  functions so that you can call them easily. Low-level I/O functions such as open
  and read are examples of system calls on Linux.

The set of Linux system calls forms the most basic interface between programs and the Linux kernel. Each call presents a basic operation or capability.

Some system calls are very powerful and can exert great influence on the system. For instance, some system calls enable you to shut down the Linux system or to allocate system resources and prevent other users from accessing them. These calls have the restriction that only processes running with superuser privilege (programs run by the root account) can invoke them. These calls fail if invoked by a nonsuperuser process.

Note that a library function may invoke one or more other library functions or system calls as part of its implementation.

Linux currently provides about 200 different system calls. A listing of system calls for your version of the Linux kernel is in `/usr/include/asm/unistd.h`. Some of these are for internal use by the system, and others are used only in implementing specialized library functions. In this chapter, we'll present a selection of system calls that are likely to be the most useful to application and system programmers.

Most of these system calls are declared in `<unistd.h>`.

8.1 Using *strace*

Before we start discussing system calls, it will be useful to present a command with which you can learn about and debug system calls. The `strace` command traces the execution of another program, listing any system calls the program makes and any signals it receives.

To watch the system calls and signals in a program, simply invoke `strace`, followed by the program and its command-line arguments. For example, to watch the system calls that are invoked by the `hostname`[1] command, use this command:

```
% strace hostname
```

This produces a couple screens of output. Each line corresponds to a single system call. For each call, the system call's name is listed, followed by its arguments (or abbreviated arguments, if they are very long) and its return value. Where possible, `strace` conveniently displays symbolic names instead of numerical values for arguments and return values, and it displays the fields of structures passed by a pointer into the system call. Note that `strace` does *not* show ordinary function calls.

In the output from `strace hostname`, the first line shows the `execve` system call that invokes the `hostname` program:[2]

```
execve("/bin/hostname", ["hostname"], [/* 49 vars */]) = 0
```

1. `hostname` invoked without any flags simply prints out the computer's hostname to standard output.
2. In Linux, the `exec` family of functions is implemented via the `execve` system call.

The first argument is the name of the program to run; the second is its argument list, consisting of only a single element; and the third is its environment list, which strace omits for brevity. The next 30 or so lines are part of the mechanism that loads the standard C library from a shared library file.

Toward the end are system calls that actually help do the program's work. The uname system call is used to obtain the system's hostname from the kernel,

```
uname({sys="Linux", node="myhostname", ...}) = 0
```

Observe that strace helpfully labels the fields (sys and node) of the structure argument. This structure is filled in by the system call—Linux sets the sys field to the operating system name and the node field to the system's hostname. The uname call is discussed further in Section 8.15, "uname."

Finally, the write system call produces output. Recall that file descriptor 1 corresponds to standard output. The third argument is the number of characters to write, and the return value is the number of characters that were actually written.

```
write(1, "myhostname\n", 11)           = 11
```

This may appear garbled when you run strace because the output from the hostname program itself is mixed in with the output from strace.

If the program you're tracing produces lots of output, it is sometimes more convenient to redirect the output from strace into a file. Use the option -o *filename* to do this.

Understanding all the output from strace requires detailed familiarity with the design of the Linux kernel and execution environment. Much of this is of limited interest to application programmers. However, some understanding is useful for debugging tricky problems or understanding how other programs work.

8.2 *access*: Testing File Permissions

The access system call determines whether the calling process has access permission to a file. It can check any combination of read, write, and execute permission, and it can also check for a file's existence.

The access call takes two arguments. The first is the path to the file to check. The second is a bitwise or of R_OK, W_OK, and X_OK, corresponding to read, write, and execute permission. The return value is 0 if the process has all the specified permissions. If the file exists but the calling process does not have the specified permissions, access returns −1 and sets errno to EACCES (or EROFS, if write permission was requested for a file on a read-only file system).

If the second argument is F_OK, access simply checks for the file's existence. If the file exists, the return value is 0; if not, the return value is −1 and errno is set to ENOENT. Note that errno may instead be set to EACCES if a directory in the file path is inaccessible.

The program shown in Listing 8.1 uses `access` to check for a file's existence and to determine read and write permissions. Specify the name of the file to check on the command line.

Listing 8.1   *(check-access.c)* **Check File Access Permissions**

```
#include <errno.h>
#include <stdio.h>
#include <unistd.h>

int main (int argc, char* argv[])
{
  char* path = argv[1];
  int rval;

  /* Check file existence.  */
  rval = access (path, F_OK);
  if (rval == 0)
    printf ("%s exists\n", path);
  else {
    if (errno == ENOENT)
      printf ("%s does not exist\n", path);
    else if (errno == EACCES)
      printf ("%s is not accessible\n", path);
    return 0;
  }

  /* Check read access.  */
  rval = access (path, R_OK);
  if (rval == 0)
    printf ("%s is readable\n", path);
  else
    printf ("%s is not readable (access denied)\n", path);

  /* Check write access.  */
  rval = access (path, W_OK);
  if (rval == 0)
    printf ("%s is writable\n", path);
  else if (errno == EACCES)
    printf ("%s is not writable (access denied)\n", path);
  else if (errno == EROFS)
    printf ("%s is not writable (read-only filesystem)\n", path);
  return 0;
}
```

For example, to check access permissions for a file named README on a CD-ROM, invoke it like this:

```
% ./check-access /mnt/cdrom/README
/mnt/cdrom/README exists
/mnt/cdrom/README is readable
/mnt/cdrom/README is not writable (read-only filesystem)
```

8.3 *fcntl*: Locks and Other File Operations

The fcntl system call is the access point for several advanced operations on file descriptors. The first argument to fcntl is an open file descriptor, and the second is a value that indicates which operation is to be performed. For some operations, fcntl takes an additional argument. We'll describe here one of the most useful fcntl operations, file locking. See the fcntl man page for information about the others.

The fcntl system call allows a program to place a read lock or a write lock on a file, somewhat analogous to the mutex locks discussed in Chapter 5, "Interprocess Communication." A read lock is placed on a readable file descriptor, and a write lock is placed on a writable file descriptor. More than one process may hold a read lock on the same file at the same time, but only one process may hold a write lock, and the same file may not be both locked for read and locked for write. Note that placing a lock does not actually prevent other processes from opening the file, reading from it, or writing to it, unless they acquire locks with fcntl as well.

To place a lock on a file, first create and zero out a struct flock variable. Set the l_type field of the structure to F_RDLCK for a read lock or F_WRLCK for a write lock. Then call fcntl, passing a file descriptor to the file, the F_SETLCKW operation code, and a pointer to the struct flock variable. If another process holds a lock that prevents a new lock from being acquired, fcntl blocks until that lock is released.

The program in Listing 8.2 opens a file for writing whose name is provided on the command line, and then places a write lock on it. The program waits for the user to hit Enter and then unlocks and closes the file.

Listing 8.2 *(lock-file.c)* **Create a Write Lock with** *fcntl*

```
#include <fcntl.h>
#include <stdio.h>
#include <string.h>
#include <unistd.h>

int main (int argc, char* argv[])
{
  char* file = argv[1];
  int fd;
  struct flock lock;

  printf ("opening %s\n", file);
  /* Open a file descriptor to the file.  */
  fd = open (file, O_WRONLY);
  printf ("locking\n");
  /* Initialize the flock structure.  */
  memset (&lock, 0, sizeof(lock));
  lock.l_type = F_WRLCK;
  /* Place a write lock on the file.  */
  fcntl (fd, F_SETLKW, &lock);
```

continues

Listing 8.2   **Continued**

```
printf ("locked; hit Enter to unlock... ");
/* Wait for the user to hit Enter.  */
getchar ();

printf ("unlocking\n");
/* Release the lock.  */
lock.l_type = F_UNLCK;
fcntl (fd, F_SETLKW, &lock);

close (fd);
return 0;
}
```

Compile and run the program on a test file—say, /tmp/test-file—like this:

```
% cc -o lock-file lock-file.c
% touch /tmp/test-file
% ./lock-file /tmp/test-file
opening /tmp/test-file
locking
locked; hit Enter to unlock...
```

Now, in another window, try running it again on the same file.

```
% ./lock-file /tmp/test-file
opening /tmp/test-file
locking
```

Note that the second instance is blocked while attempting to lock the file. Go back to the first window and press Enter:

```
unlocking
```

The program running in the second window immediately acquires the lock.

If you prefer fcntl not to block if the call cannot get the lock you requested, use F_SETLK instead of F_SETLKW. If the lock cannot be acquired, fcntl returns −1 immediately.

Linux provides another implementation of file locking with the flock call. The fcntl version has a major advantage: It works with files on NFS[3] file systems (as long as the NFS server is reasonably recent and correctly configured). So, if you have access to two machines that both mount the same file system via NFS, you can repeat the previous example using two different machines. Run lock-file on one machine, specifying a file on an NFS file system, and then run it again on another machine, specifying the same file. NFS wakes up the second program when the lock is released by the first program.

3. *Network File System* (NFS) is a common network file sharing technology, comparable to Windows' shares and network drives.

8.4 *fsync* and *fdatasync*: Flushing Disk Buffers

On most operating systems, when you write to a file, the data is not immediately written to disk. Instead, the operating system caches the written data in a memory buffer, to reduce the number of required disk writes and improve program responsiveness. When the buffer fills or some other condition occurs (for instance, enough time elapses), the system writes the cached data to disk all at one time.

Linux provides caching of this type as well. Normally, this is a great boon to performance. However, this behavior can make programs that depend on the integrity of disk-based records unreliable. If the system goes down suddenly—for instance, due to a kernel crash or power outage—any data written by a program that is in the memory cache but has not yet been written to disk is lost.

For example, suppose that you are writing a transaction-processing program that keeps a journal file. The journal file contains records of all transactions that have been processed so that if a system failure occurs, the state of the transaction data can be reconstructed. It is obviously important to preserve the integrity of the journal file— whenever a transaction is processed, its journal entry should be sent to the disk drive immediately.

To help you implement this, Linux provides the `fsync` system call. It takes one argument, a writable file descriptor, and flushes to disk any data written to this file. The `fsync` call doesn't return until the data has physically been written.

The function in Listing 8.3 illustrates the use of `fsync`. It writes a single-line entry to a journal file.

Listing 8.3   (*write_journal_entry.c*) **Write and Sync a Journal Entry**

```
#include <fcntl.h>
#include <string.h>
#include <sys/stat.h>
#include <sys/types.h>
#include <unistd.h>

const char* journal_filename = "journal.log";

void write_journal_entry (char* entry)
{
  int fd = open (journal_filename, O_WRONLY | O_CREAT | O_APPEND, 0660);
  write (fd, entry, strlen (entry));
  write (fd, "\n", 1);
  fsync (fd);
  close (fd);
}
```

Another system call, `fdatasync` does the same thing. However, although `fsync` guarantees that the file's modification time will be updated, `fdatasync` does not; it guarantees only that the file's data will be written. This means that in principal, `fdatasync` can execute faster than `fsync` because it needs to force only one disk write instead of two.

However, in current versions of Linux, these two system calls actually do the same thing, both updating the file's modification time.

The fsync system call enables you to force a buffer write explicitly. You can also open a file for *synchronous I/O*, which causes all writes to be committed to disk immediately. To do this, specify the O_SYNC flag when opening the file with the open call.

8.5 *getrlimit* and *setrlimit*: Resource Limits

The getrlimit and setrlimit system calls allow a process to read and set limits on the system resources that it can consume. You may be familiar with the ulimit shell command, which enables you to restrict the resource usage of programs you run;[4] these system calls allow a program to do this programmatically.

For each resource there are two limits, the *hard limit* and the *soft limit*. The soft limit may never exceed the hard limit, and only processes with superuser privilege may change the hard limit. Typically, an application program will reduce the soft limit to place a throttle on the resources it uses.

Both getrlimit and setrlimit take as arguments a code specifying the resource limit type and a pointer to a structrlimit variable. The getrlimit call fills the fields of this structure, while the setrlimit call changes the limit based on its contents. The rlimit structure has two fields: rlim_cur is the soft limit, and rlim_max is the hard limit.

Some of the most useful resource limits that may be changed are listed here, with their codes:

- RLIMIT_CPU—The maximum CPU time, in seconds, used by a program. This is the amount of time that the program is actually executing on the CPU, which is not necessarily the same as wall-clock time. If the program exceeds this time limit, it is terminated with a SIGXCPU signal.

- RLIMIT_DATA—The maximum amount of memory that a program can allocate for its data. Additional allocation beyond this limit will fail.

- RLIMIT_NPROC—The maximum number of child processes that can be running for this user. If the process calls fork and too many processes belonging to this user are running on the system, fork fails.

- RLIMIT_NOFILE—The maximum number of file descriptors that the process may have open at one time.

See the setrlimit man page for a full list of system resources.

The program in Listing 8.4 illustrates setting the limit on CPU time consumed by a program. It sets a 1-second CPU time limit and then spins in an infinite loop. Linux kills the process soon afterward, when it exceeds 1 second of CPU time.

---

4. See the man page for your shell for more information about ulimit.

Listing 8.4   *(limit-cpu.c)* **CPU Time Limit Demonstration**

```
#include <sys/resource.h>
#include <sys/time.h>
#include <unistd.h>

int main ()
{
  struct rlimit rl;

  /* Obtain the current limits.  */
  getrlimit (RLIMIT_CPU, &rl);
  /* Set a CPU limit of 1 second.  */
  rl.rlim_cur = 1;
  setrlimit (RLIMIT_CPU, &rl);
  /* Do busy work.  */
  while (1);

  return 0;
}
```

When the program is terminated by SIGXCPU, the shell helpfully prints out a message interpreting the signal:

```
% ./limit_cpu
CPU time limit exceeded
```

8.6   *getrusage*: **Process Statistics**

The getrusage system call retrieves process statistics from the kernel. It can be used to obtain statistics either for the current process by passing RUSAGE_SELF as the first argument, or for all terminated child processes that were forked by this process and its children by passing RUSAGE_CHILDREN. The second argument to rusage is a pointer to a struct rusage variable, which is filled with the statistics.

A few of the more interesting fields in struct rusage are listed here:

- ru_utime—A struct timeval field containing the amount of *user time*, in seconds, that the process has used. User time is CPU time spent executing the user program, rather than in kernel system calls.

- ru_stime—A struct timeval field containing the amount of *system time*, in seconds, that the process has used. System time is the CPU time spent executing system calls on behalf of the process.

- ru_maxrss—The largest amount of physical memory occupied by the process's data at one time over the course of its execution.

The getrusage man page lists all the available fields. See Section 8.7, "gettimeofday: Wall-Clock Time," for information about struct timeval.

The function in Listing 8.5 prints out the current process's user and system time.

Listing 8.5   (*print-cpu-times.c*) **Display Process User and System Times**

```
#include <stdio.h>
#include <sys/resource.h>
#include <sys/time.h>
#include <unistd.h>

void print_cpu_time()
{
  struct rusage usage;
  getrusage (RUSAGE_SELF, &usage);
  printf ("CPU time: %ld.%06ld sec user, %ld.%06ld sec system\n",
          usage.ru_utime.tv_sec, usage.ru_utime.tv_usec,
          usage.ru_stime.tv_sec, usage.ru_stime.tv_usec);
}
```

8.7   *gettimeofday*: Wall-Clock Time

The `gettimeofday` system call gets the system's wall-clock time. It takes a pointer to a `struct timeval` variable. This structure represents a time, in seconds, split into two fields. The `tv_sec` field contains the integral number of seconds, and the `tv_usec` field contains an additional number of microseconds. This `struct timeval` value represents the number of seconds elapsed since the start of the *UNIX epoch*, on midnight UTC on January 1, 1970. The `gettimeofday` call also takes a second argument, which should be `NULL`. Include `<sys/time.h>` if you use this system call.

The number of seconds in the UNIX epoch isn't usually a very handy way of representing dates. The `localtime` and `strftime` library functions help manipulate the return value of `gettimeofday`. The `localtime` function takes a pointer to the number of seconds (the `tv_sec` field of `struct timeval`) and returns a pointer to a `struct tm` object. This structure contains more useful fields, which are filled according to the local time zone:

- `tm_hour`, `tm_min`, `tm_sec`—The time of day, in hours, minutes, and seconds.
- `tm_year`, `tm_mon`, `tm_day`—The year, month, and date.
- `tm_wday`—The day of the week. Zero represents Sunday.
- `tm_yday`—The day of the year.
- `tm_isdst`—A flag indicating whether daylight savings time is in effect.

The `strftime` function additionally can produce from the `struct tm` pointer a customized, formatted string displaying the date and time. The format is specified in a manner similar to `printf`, as a string with embedded codes indicating which time fields to include. For example, this format string

```
"%Y-%m-%d %H:%M:%S"
```

specifies the date and time in this form:

```
2001-01-14 13:09:42
```

Pass `strftime` a character buffer to receive the string, the length of that buffer, the format string, and a pointer to a `struct tm` variable. See the `strftime` man page for a complete list of codes that can be used in the format string. Notice that neither `localtime` nor `strftime` handles the fractional part of the current time more precise than 1 second (the `tv_usec` field of `struct timeval`). If you want this in your formatted time strings, you'll have to include it yourself.

Include `<time.h>` if you call `localtime` or `strftime`.

The function in Listing 8.6 prints the current date and time of day, down to the millisecond.

Listing 8.6   (*print-time.c*) **Print Date and Time**

```c
#include <stdio.h>
#include <sys/time.h>
#include <time.h>
#include <unistd.h>

void print_time ()
{
  struct timeval tv;
  struct tm* ptm;
  char time_string[40];
  long milliseconds;

  /* Obtain the time of day, and convert it to a tm struct.  */
  gettimeofday (&tv, NULL);
  ptm = localtime (&tv.tv_sec);
  /* Format the date and time, down to a single second.  */
  strftime (time_string, sizeof (time_string), "%Y-%m-%d %H:%M:%S", ptm);
  /* Compute milliseconds from microseconds.  */
  milliseconds = tv.tv_usec / 1000;
  /* Print the formatted time, in seconds, followed by a decimal point
     and the milliseconds.  */
  printf ("%s.%03ld\n", time_string, milliseconds);
}
```

8.8   The *mlock* Family: Locking Physical Memory

The `mlock` family of system calls allows a program to lock some or all of its address space into physical memory. This prevents Linux from paging this memory to swap space, even if the program hasn't accessed it for a while.

A time-critical program might lock physical memory because the time delay of paging memory out and back may be too long or too unpredictable. High-security applications may also want to prevent sensitive data from being written out to a swap file, where they might be recovered by an intruder after the program terminates.

Locking a region of memory is as simple as calling `mlock` with a pointer to the start of the region and the region's length. Linux divides memory into *pages* and can lock only entire pages at a time; each page that contains part of the memory region specified to `mlock` is locked. The `getpagesize` function returns the system's page size, which is 4KB on x86 Linux.

For example, to allocate 32MB of address space and lock it into RAM, you would use this code:

```
const int alloc_size = 32 * 1024 * 1024;
char* memory = malloc (alloc_size);
mlock (memory, alloc_size);
```

Note that simply allocating a page of memory and locking it with `mlock` doesn't reserve physical memory for the calling process because the pages may be copy-on-write.[5] Therefore, you should write a dummy value to each page as well:

```
size_t i;
size_t page_size = getpagesize ();
for (i = 0; i < alloc_size; i += page_size)
  memory[i] = 0;
```

The write to each page forces Linux to assign a unique, unshared memory page to the process for that page.

To unlock a region, call `munlock`, which takes the same arguments as `mlock`.

If you want your program's entire address space locked into physical memory, call `mlockall`. This system call takes a single flag argument: `MCL_CURRENT` locks all currently allocated memory, but future allocations are not locked; `MCL_FUTURE` locks all pages that are allocated after the call. Use `MCL_CURRENT|MCL_FUTURE` to lock into memory both current and subsequent allocations.

Locking large amounts of memory, especially using `mlockall`, can be dangerous to the entire Linux system. Indiscriminate memory locking is a good method of bringing your system to a grinding halt because other running processes are forced to compete for smaller physical memory resources and swap rapidly into and back out of memory (this is known as *thrashing*). If you lock too much memory, the system will run out of memory entirely and Linux will start killing off processes.

For this reason, only processes with superuser privilege may lock memory with `mlock` or `mlockall`. If a nonsuperuser process calls one of these functions, it will fail, return −1, and set `errno` to `EPERM`.

The `munlockall` call unlocks all memory locked by the current process, including memory locked with `mlock` and `mlockall`.

5. *Copy-on-write* means that Linux makes a private copy of a page of memory for a process only when that process writes a value somewhere into it.

A convenient way to monitor the memory usage of your program is to use the `top` command. In the output from `top`, the SIZE column displays the virtual address space size of each program (the total size of your program's code, data, and stack, some of which may be paged out to swap space). The RSS column (for *resident set size*) shows the size of physical memory that each program currently resides in. The sum of all the RSS values for all running programs cannot exceed your computer's physical memory size, and the sum of all address space sizes is limited to 2GB (for 32-bit versions of Linux).

Include `<sys/mman.h>` if you use any of the `mlock` system calls.

8.9   *mprotect*: Setting Memory Permissions

In Section 5.3, "Mapped Memory," we showed how to use the `mmap` system call to map a file into memory. Recall that the third argument to `mmap` is a bitwise or of memory protection flags `PROT_READ`, `PROT_WRITE`, and `PROT_EXEC` for read, write, and execute permission, respectively, or `PROT_NONE` for no memory access. If a program attempts to perform an operation on a memory location that is not allowed by these permissions, it is terminated with a `SIGSEGV` (segmentation violation) signal.

After memory has been mapped, these permissions can be modified with the `mprotect` system call. The arguments to `mprotect` are an address of a memory region, the size of the region, and a set of protection flags. The memory region must consist of entire pages: The address of the region must be aligned to the system's page size, and the length of the region must be a page size multiple. The protection flags for these pages are replaced with the specified value.

Obtaining Page-Aligned Memory

Note that memory regions returned by `malloc` are typically not page-aligned, even if the size of the memory is a multiple of the page size. If you want to protect memory obtained from `malloc`, you will have to allocate a larger memory region and find a page-aligned region within it.

Alternately, you can use the `mmap` system call to bypass `malloc` and allocate page-aligned memory directly from the Linux kernel. See Section 5.3, "Mapped Memory," for details.

For example, suppose that your program allocates a page of memory by mapping `/dev/zero`, as described in Section 5.3.5, "Other Uses for `mmap`." The memory is initially both readable and writable.

```
int fd = open ("/dev/zero", O_RDONLY);
char* memory = mmap (NULL, page_size, PROT_READ | PROT_WRITE,
                     MAP_PRIVATE, fd, 0);
close (fd);
```

Later, your program could make the memory read-only by calling `mprotect`:

```
mprotect (memory, page_size, PROT_READ);
```

An advanced technique to monitor memory access is to protect the region of memory using mmap or mprotect and then handle the SIGSEGV signal that Linux sends to the program when it tries to access that memory. The example in Listing 8.7 illustrates this technique.

Listing 8.7 *(mprotect.c)* **Detect Memory Access Using** *mprotect*

```c
#include <fcntl.h>
#include <signal.h>
#include <stdio.h>
#include <string.h>
#include <sys/mman.h>
#include <sys/stat.h>
#include <sys/types.h>
#include <unistd.h>

static int alloc_size;
static char* memory;

void segv_handler (int signal_number)
{
  printf ("memory accessed!\n");
  mprotect (memory, alloc_size, PROT_READ | PROT_WRITE);
}

int main ()
{
  int fd;
  struct sigaction sa;

  /* Install segv_handler as the handler for SIGSEGV.  */
  memset (&sa, 0, sizeof (sa));
  sa.sa_handler = &segv_handler;
  sigaction (SIGSEGV, &sa, NULL);

  /* Allocate one page of memory by mapping /dev/zero.  Map the memory
     as write-only, initially.  */
  alloc_size = getpagesize ();
  fd = open ("/dev/zero", O_RDONLY);
  memory = mmap (NULL, alloc_size, PROT_WRITE, MAP_PRIVATE, fd, 0);
  close (fd);
  /* Write to the page to obtain a private copy.  */
  memory[0] = 0;
  /* Make the memory unwritable.  */
  mprotect (memory, alloc_size, PROT_NONE);

  /* Write to the allocated memory region.  */
  memory[0] = 1;
```

```
    /* All done; unmap the memory.  */
    printf ("all done\n");
    munmap (memory, alloc_size);
    return 0;
  }
```

The program follows these steps:

1. The program installs a signal handler for `SIGSEGV`.

2. The program allocates a page of memory by mapping `/dev/zero` and writing a value to the allocated page to obtain a private copy.

3. The program protects the memory by calling `mprotect` with the `PROT_NONE` permission.

4. When the program subsequently writes to memory, Linux sends it `SIGSEGV`, which is handled by `segv_handler`. The signal handler unprotects the memory, which allows the memory access to proceed.

5. When the signal handler completes, control returns to `main`, where the program deallocates the memory using `munmap`.

8.10   *nanosleep*: **High-Precision Sleeping**

The `nanosleep` system call is a high-precision version of the standard UNIX `sleep` call. Instead of sleeping an integral number of seconds, `nanosleep` takes as its argument a pointer to a `struct timespec` object, which can express time to nanosecond precision. However, because of the details of how the Linux kernel works, the actual precision provided by `nanosleep` is 10 milliseconds—still better than that afforded by `sleep`. This additional precision can be useful, for instance, to schedule frequent operations with short time intervals between them.

The `struct timespec` structure has two fields: `tv_sec`, the integral number of seconds, and `tv_nsec`, an additional number of milliseconds. The value of `tv_nsec` must be less than 10^9.

The `nanosleep` call provides another advantage over `sleep`. As with `sleep`, the delivery of a signal interrupts the execution of `nanosleep`, which sets `errno` to `EINTR` and returns −1. However, `nanosleep` takes a second argument, another pointer to a `struct timespec` object, which, if not null, is filled with the amount of time remaining (that is, the difference between the requested sleep time and the actual sleep time). This makes it easy to resume the sleep operation.

The function in Listing 8.8 provides an alternate implementation of `sleep`. Unlike the ordinary system call, this function takes a floating-point value for the number of seconds to sleep and restarts the sleep operation if it's interrupted by a signal.

Listing 8.8   (*better_sleep.c*) **High-Precision Sleep Function**

```
#include <errno.h>
#include <time.h>

int better_sleep (double sleep_time)
{
  struct timespec tv;
  /* Construct the timespec from the number of whole seconds... */
  tv.tv_sec = (time_t) sleep_time;
  /* ... and the remainder in nanoseconds. */
  tv.tv_nsec = (long) ((sleep_time - tv.tv_sec) * 1e+9);

  while (1)
  {
    /* Sleep for the time specified in tv.  If interrupted by a
       signal, place the remaining time left to sleep back into tv. */
    int rval = nanosleep (&tv, &tv);
    if (rval == 0)
      /* Completed the entire sleep time; all done. */
      return 0;
    else if (errno == EINTR)
      /* Interrupted by a signal.  Try again. */
      continue;
    else
      /* Some other error; bail out. */
      return rval;
  }
  return 0;
}
```

8.11   *readlink*: **Reading Symbolic Links**

The readlink system call retrieves the target of a symbolic link. It takes three arguments: the path to the symbolic link, a buffer to receive the target of the link, and the
length of that buffer. Unusually, readlink does not NUL-terminate the target path
that it fills into the buffer. It does, however, return the number of characters in the
target path, so NUL-terminating the string is simple.

If the first argument to readlink points to a file that isn't a symbolic link, readlink
sets errno to EINVAL and returns −1.

The small program in Listing 8.9 prints the target of the symbolic link specified on
its command line.

Listing 8.9   (*print–symlink.c*) **Print the Target of a Symbolic Link**

```c
#include <errno.h>
#include <stdio.h>
#include <unistd.h>

int main (int argc, char* argv[])
{
  char target_path[256];
  char* link_path = argv[1];

  /* Attempt to read the target of the symbolic link.  */
  int len = readlink (link_path, target_path, sizeof (target_path));

  if (len == -1) {
    /* The call failed.  */
    if (errno == EINVAL)
      /* It's not a symbolic link; report that.  */
      fprintf (stderr, "%s is not a symbolic link\n", link_path);
    else
      /* Some other problem occurred; print the generic message.  */
      perror ("readlink");
    return 1;
  }
  else {
    /* NUL-terminate the target path.  */
    target_path[len] = '\0';
    /* Print it.  */
    printf ("%s\n", target_path);
    return 0;
  }
}
```

For example, here's how you could make a symbolic link and use print-symlink to read it back:

```
% ln -s /usr/bin/wc my_link
% ./print-symlink my_link
/usr/bin/wc
```

8.12   *sendfile*: Fast Data Transfers

The sendfile system call provides an efficient mechanism for copying data from one file descriptor to another. The file descriptors may be open to disk files, sockets, or other devices.

Typically, to copy from one file descriptor to another, a program allocates a fixed-size buffer, copies some data from one descriptor into the buffer, writes the buffer out to the other descriptor, and repeats until all the data has been copied. This is inefficient in both time and space because it requires additional memory for the buffer and performs an extra copy of the data into that buffer.

Using `sendfile`, the intermediate buffer can be eliminated. Call `sendfile`, passing the file descriptor to write to; the descriptor to read from; a pointer to an offset variable; and the number of bytes to transfer. The offset variable contains the offset in the input file from which the read should start (0 indicates the beginning of the file) and is updated to the position in the file after the transfer. The return value is the number of bytes transferred. Include `<sys/sendfile.h>` in your program if it uses `sendfile`.

The program in Listing 8.10 is a simple but extremely efficient implementation of a file copy. When invoked with two filenames on the command line, it copies the contents of the first file into a file named by the second. It uses `fstat` to determine the size, in bytes, of the source file.

Listing 8.10   *(copy.c)* **File Copy Using** *sendfile*

```c
#include <fcntl.h>
#include <stdlib.h>
#include <stdio.h>
#include <sys/sendfile.h>
#include <sys/stat.h>
#include <sys/types.h>
#include <unistd.h>

int main (int argc, char* argv[])
{
  int read_fd;
  int write_fd;
  struct stat stat_buf;
  off_t offset = 0;

  /* Open the input file.  */
  read_fd = open (argv[1], O_RDONLY);
  /* Stat the input file to obtain its size.  */
  fstat (read_fd, &stat_buf);
  /* Open the output file for writing, with the same permissions as the
     source file.  */
  write_fd = open (argv[2], O_WRONLY | O_CREAT, stat_buf.st_mode);
  /* Blast the bytes from one file to the other.  */
  sendfile (write_fd, read_fd, &offset, stat_buf.st_size);
  /* Close up.  */
  close (read_fd);
  close (write_fd);

  return 0;
}
```

The `sendfile` call can be used in many places to make copies more efficient. One good example is in a Web server or other network daemon, that serves the contents of a file over the network to a client program. Typically, a request is received from a socket connected to the client computer. The server program opens a local disk file to retrieve the data to serve and writes the file's contents to the network socket. Using `sendfile` can speed up this operation considerably. Other steps need to be taken to make the network transfer as efficient as possible, such as setting the socket parameters correctly. However, these are outside the scope of this book.

8.13   *setitimer*: Setting Interval Timers

The `setitimer` system call is a generalization of the `alarm` call. It schedules the delivery of a signal at some point in the future after a fixed amount of time has elapsed.

A program can set three different types of timers with `setitimer`:

- If the timer code is `ITIMER_REAL`, the process is sent a `SIGALRM` signal after the specified wall-clock time has elapsed.

- If the timer code is `ITIMER_VIRTUAL`, the process is sent a `SIGVTALRM` signal after the process has executed for the specified time. Time in which the process is not executing (that is, when the kernel or another process is running) is not counted.

- If the timer code is `ITIMER_PROF`, the process is sent a `SIGPROF` signal when the specified time has elapsed either during the process's own execution or the execution of a system call on behalf of the process.

The first argument to `setitimer` is the timer code, specifying which timer to set. The second argument is a pointer to a `struct itimerval` object specifying the new settings for that timer. The third argument, if not null, is a pointer to another `struct itimerval` object that receives the old timer settings.

A `struct itimerval` variable has two fields:

- `it_value` is a `struct timeval` field that contains the time until the timer next expires and a signal is sent. If this is 0, the timer is disabled.

- `it_interval` is another `struct timeval` field containing the value to which the timer will be reset after it expires. If this is 0, the timer will be disabled after it expires. If this is nonzero, the timer is set to expire repeatedly after this interval.

The `struct timeval` type is described in Section 8.7, "gettimeofday: Wall-Clock Time."

The program in Listing 8.11 illustrates the use of `setitimer` to track the execution time of a program. A timer is configured to expire every 250 milliseconds and send a `SIGVTALRM` signal.

Listing 8.11   (*itemer.c*) **Timer Example**

```
#include <signal.h>
#include <stdio.h>
#include <string.h>
#include <sys/time.h>
```

continues

Listing 8.11 **Continued**

```
void timer_handler (int signum)
{
  static int count = 0;
  printf ("timer expired %d times\n", ++count);
}

int main ()
{
  struct sigaction sa;
  struct itimerval timer;

  /* Install timer_handler as the signal handler for SIGVTALRM.  */
  memset (&sa, 0, sizeof (sa));
  sa.sa_handler = &timer_handler;
  sigaction (SIGVTALRM, &sa, NULL);

  /* Configure the timer to expire after 250 msec...  */
  timer.it_value.tv_sec = 0;
  timer.it_value.tv_usec = 250000;
  /* ... and every 250 msec after that.  */
  timer.it_interval.tv_sec = 0;
  timer.it_interval.tv_usec = 250000;
  /* Start a virtual timer.  It counts down whenever this process is
     executing.  */
  setitimer (ITIMER_VIRTUAL, &timer, NULL);

  /* Do busy work.  */
  while (1);
}
```

8.14 *sysinfo*: Obtaining System Statistics

The sysinfo system call fills a structure with system statistics. Its only argument is a pointer to a struct sysinfo. Some of the more interesting fields of struct sysinfo that are filled include these:

- uptime—Time elapsed since the system booted, in seconds
- totalram—Total available physical RAM
- freeram—Free physical RAM
- procs—Number of processes on the system

See the sysinfo man page for a full description of structsysinfo. Include <linux/kernel.h>, <linux/sys.h>, and <sys/sysinfo.h> if you use sysinfo.

The program in Listing 8.12 prints some statistics about the current system.

Listing 8.12   (*sysinfo.c*) **Print System Statistics**

```
#include <linux/kernel.h>
#include <linux/sys.h>
#include <stdio.h>
#include <sys/sysinfo.h>

int main ()
{
  /* Conversion constants.  */
  const long minute = 60;
  const long hour = minute * 60;
  const long day = hour * 24;
  const double megabyte = 1024 * 1024;
  /* Obtain system statistics.  */
  struct sysinfo si;
  sysinfo (&si);
  /* Summarize interesting values.  */
  printf ("system uptime : %ld days, %ld:%02ld:%02ld\n",
          si.uptime / day, (si.uptime % day) / hour,
          (si.uptime % hour) / minute, si.uptime % minute);
  printf ("total RAM     : %5.1f MB\n", si.totalram / megabyte);
  printf ("free RAM      : %5.1f MB\n", si.freeram / megabyte);
  printf ("process count : %d\n", si.procs);
  return 0;
}
```

8.15   *uname*

The uname system call fills a structure with various system information, including the computer's network name and domain name, and the operating system version it's running. Pass uname a single argument, a pointer to a struct utsname object. Include <sys/utsname.h> if you use uname.

The call to uname fills in these fields:

- sysname—The name of the operating system (such as Linux).

- release, version—The Linux kernel release number and version level.

- machine—Some information about the hardware platform running Linux. For x86 Linux, this is i386 or i686, depending on the processor.

- node—The computer's unqualified hostname.

- __domain—The computer's domain name.

Each of these fields is a character string.

The small program in Listing 8.13 prints the Linux release and version number and the hardware information.

Listing 8.13   (*print-uname*) **Print Linux Version Number and Hardware Information**

```c
#include <stdio.h>
#include <sys/utsname.h>

int main ()
{
  struct utsname u;
  uname (&u);
  printf ("%s release %s (version %s) on %s\n", u.sysname, u.release,
          u.version, u.machine);
  return 0;
}
```

9

Inline Assembly Code

T ODAY, FEW PROGRAMMERS USE ASSEMBLY LANGUAGE. Higher-level languages such as C and C++ run on nearly all architectures and yield higher productivity when writing and maintaining code. For occasions when programmers need to use assembly instructions in their programs, the GNU Compiler Collection permits programmers to add architecture-dependent assembly language instructions to their programs.

GCC's inline assembly statements should not be used indiscriminately. Assembly language instructions are architecture-dependent, so, for example, programs using x86 instructions cannot be compiled on PowerPC computers. To use them, you'll require a facility in the assembly language for your architecture. However, inline assembly statements permit you to access hardware directly and can also yield faster code.

An `asm` instruction allows you to insert assembly instructions into C and C++ programs. For example, this instruction

```
asm ("fsin" : "=t" (answer) : "0" (angle));
```

is an x86-specific way of coding this C statement:[1]

```
answer = sin (angle);
```

1. The expression `sin (angle)` is usually implemented as a function call into the math library, but if you specify the `-01` or higher optimization flag, GCC is smart enough to replace the function call with a single `fsin` assembly instruction.

Observe that unlike ordinary assembly code instructions, `asm` statements permit you to specify input and output operands using C syntax.

To read more about the x86 instruction set, which we will use in this chapter, see `http://developer.intel.com/design/pentiumii/manuals/` and `http://www.x86-64.org/documentation`.

9.1   When to Use Assembly Code

Although `asm` statements can be abused, they allow your programs to access the computer hardware directly, and they can produce programs that execute quickly. You can use them when writing operating system code that directly needs to interact with hardware. For example, `/usr/include/asm/io.h` contains assembly instructions to access input/output ports directly. The Linux source code file `/usr/src/linux/arch/i386/kernel/process.s` provides another example, using `hlt` in idle loop code. See other Linux source code files in `/usr/src/linux/arch/` and `/usr/src/linux/drivers/`.

Assembly instructions can also speed the innermost loop of computer programs. For example, if the majority of a program's running time is computing the sine and cosine of the same angles, this innermost loop could be recoded using the `fsincos` x86 instruction.[2] See, for example, `/usr/include/bits/mathinline.h`, which wraps up into macros some inline assembly sequences that speed transcendental function computation.

You should use inline assembly to speed up code only as a last resort. Current compilers are quite sophisticated and know a lot about the details of the processors for which they generate code. Therefore, compilers can often choose code sequences that may seem unintuitive or roundabout but that actually execute faster than other instruction sequences. Unless you understand the instruction set and scheduling attributes of your target processor very well, you're probably better off letting the compiler's optimizers generate assembly code for you for most operations.

Occasionally, one or two assembly instructions can replace several lines of higher-level language code. For example, determining the position of the most significant nonzero bit of a nonzero integer using the C programming languages requires a loop or floating-point computations. Many architectures, including the x86, have a single assembly instruction (`bsr`) to compute this bit position. We'll demonstrate the use of one of these in Section 9.4, "Example."

2. Algorithmic or data structure changes may be more effective in reducing a program's running time than using assembly instructions.

9.2 Simple Inline Assembly

Here we introduce the syntax of `asm` assembler instructions with an x86 example to shift a value 8 bits to the right:

```
asm ("shrl $8, %0" : "=r" (answer) : "r" (operand) : "cc");
```

The keyword `asm` is followed by a parenthetic expression consisting of sections separated by colons. The first section contains an assembler instruction and its operands. In this example, `shrl` right-shifts the bits in its first operand. Its first operand is represented by `%0`. Its second operand is the immediate constant `$8`.

The second section specifies the outputs. The instruction's one output will be placed in the C variable `answer`, which must be an lvalue. The string `"=r"` contains an equals sign indicating an output operand and an `r` indicating that `answer` is stored in a register.

The third section specifies the inputs. The C variable `operand` specifies the value to shift. The string `"r"` indicates that it is stored in a register but omits an equals sign because it is an input operand, not an output operand.

The fourth section indicates that the instruction changes the value in the condition code `cc` register.

9.2.1 Converting an *asm* to Assembly Instructions

GCC's treatment of `asm` statements is very simple. It produces assembly instructions to deal with the `asm`'s operands, and it replaces the `asm` statement with the instruction that you specify. It does not analyze the instruction in any way.

For example, GCC converts this program fragment

```
double foo, bar;
asm ("mycool_asm %1, %0" : "=r" (bar) : "r" (foo));
```

to these x86 assembly instructions:

```
        movl -8(%ebp),%edx
        movl -4(%ebp),%ecx
#APP
        mycool_asm %edx, %edx
#NO_APP
        movl %edx,-16(%ebp)
        movl %ecx,-12(%ebp)
```

Remember that `foo` and `bar` each require two words of stack storage on a 32-bit x86 architecture. The register `ebp` points to data on the stack.

The first two instructions copy `foo` into registers EDX and ECX on which `mycool_asm` operates. The compiler decides to use the same registers to store the answer, which is copied into `bar` by the final two instructions. It chooses appropriate registers, even reusing the same registers, and copies operands to and from the proper locations automatically.

9.3   Extended Assembly Syntax

In the subsections that follow, we describe the syntax rules for asm statements. Their sections are separated by colons.

We will refer to this illustrative asm statement, which computes the Boolean expression x > y:

```
asm ("fucomip %%st(1), %%st; seta %%al" :
     "=a" (result) : "u" (y), "t" (x) : "cc", "st");
```

First, fucomip compares its two operands x and y, and stores values indicating the result into the condition code register. Then seta converts these values into a 0 or 1 result.

9.3.1   Assembler Instructions

The first section contains the assembler instructions, enclosed in quotation marks. The example asm contains two assembly instructions, fucomip and seta, separated by semicolons. If the assembler does not permit semicolons, use newline characters (\n) to separate instructions.

The compiler ignores the contents of this first section, except that one level of percentage signs is removed, so %% changes to %. The meaning of %%st(1) and other such terms is architecture-dependent.

GCC will complain if you specify the -traditional option or the -ansi option when compiling a program containing asm statements. To avoid producing these errors, such as in header files, use the alternative keyword __asm__.

9.3.2   Outputs

The second section specifies the instructions' output operands using C syntax. Each operand is specified by an operand constraint string followed by a C expression in parentheses. For output operands, which must be lvalues, the constraint string should begin with an equals sign. The compiler checks that the C expression for each output operand is in fact an lvalue.

Letters specifying registers for a particular architecture can be found in the GCC source code, in the REG_CLASS_FROM_LETTER macro. For example, the gcc/config/i386/i386.h configuration file in GCC lists the register letters for the x86 architecture.[3] Table 9.1 summarizes these.

---

3. You'll need to have some familiarity with GCC's internals to make sense of this file.

Table 9.1   **Register Letters for the Intel x86 Architecture**

Register Letter	Registers That GCC May Use
R	General register (EAX, EBX, ECX, EDX, ESI, EDI, EBP, ESP)
q	General register for data (EAX, EBX, ECX, EDX)
f	Floating-point register
t	Top floating-point register
u	Second-from-top floating-point register
a	EAX register
b	EBX register
c	ECX register
d	EDX register
x	SSE register (Streaming SIMD Extension register)
y	MMX multimedia registers
A	An 8-byte value formed from EAX and EDX
D	Destination pointer for string operations (EDI)
S	Source pointer for string operations (ESI)

Multiple operands in an `asm` statement, each specified by a constraint string and a C expression, are separated by commas, as illustrated in the example `asm`'s input section. You may specify up to 10 operands, denoted `%0`, `%1`, ..., `%9`, in the output and input sections. If there are no output operands but there are input operands or clobbered registers, leave the output section empty or mark it with a comment like `/* no outputs */`.

9.3.3   Inputs

The third section specifies the input operands for the assembler instructions. The constraint string for an input operand should not have an equals sign, which indicates an lvalue. Otherwise, an input operand's syntax is the same as for output operands.

To indicate that a register is both read from and written to in the same `asm`, use an input constraint string of the output operand's number. For example, to indicate that an input register is the same as the first output register number, use `0`. Output operands are numbered left to right, starting with 0. Merely specifying the same C expression for an output operand and an input operand does not guarantee that the two values will be placed in the same register.

This input section can be omitted if there are no input operands and the subsequent clobber section is empty.

9.3.4 Clobbers

If an instruction modifies the values of one or more registers as a side effect, specify the clobbered registers in the `asm`'s fourth section. For example, the `fucomip` instruction modifies the condition code register, which is denoted `cc`. Separate strings representing clobbered registers with commas. If the instruction can modify an arbitrary memory location, specify `memory`. Using the clobber information, the compiler determines which values must be reloaded after the `asm` executes. If you don't specify this information correctly, GCC may assume incorrectly that registers still contain values that have, in fact, been overwritten, which will affect your program's correctness.

9.4 Example

The x86 architecture includes instructions that determine the positions of the least significant set bit and the most significant set bit in a word. The processor can execute these instructions quite efficiently. In contrast, implementing the same operation in C requires a loop and a bit shift.

For example, the `bsrl` assembly instruction computes the position of the most significant bit set in its first operand, and places the bit position (counting from 0, the least significant bit) into its second operand. To place the bit position for `number` into `position`, we could use this `asm` statement:

```
asm ("bsrl %1, %0" : "=r" (position) : "r" (number));
```

One way you could implement the same operation in C is using this loop:

```
long i;
for (i = (number >> 1), position = 0; i != 0; ++position)
  i >>= 1;
```

To test the relative speeds of these two versions, we'll place them in a loop that computes the bit positions for a large number of values. Listing 9.1 does this using the C loop implementation. The program loops over integers, from 1 up to the value specified on the command line. For each value of `number`, it computes the most significant bit that is set. Listing 9.2 does the same thing using the inline assembly instruction. Note that in both versions, we assign the computed bit position to a volatile variable `result`. This is to coerce the compiler's optimizer so that it does not eliminate the entire bit position computation; if the result is not used or stored in memory, the optimizer eliminates the computation as "dead code."

Listing 9.1 **(bit-pos-loop.c) Find Bit Position Using a Loop**

```
#include <stdio.h>
#include <stdlib.h>

int main (int argc, char* argv[])
{
  long max = atoi (argv[1]);
  long number;
```

```
    long i;
    unsigned position;
    volatile unsigned result;

    /* Repeat the operation for a large number of values.  */
    for (number = 1; number <= max; ++number) {
      /* Repeatedly shift the number to the right, until the result is
         zero.  Keep count of the number of shifts this requires.  */
      for (i = (number >> 1), position = 0; i != 0; ++position)
        i >>= 1;
      /* The position of the most significant set bit is the number of
         shifts we needed after the first one.  */
      result = position;
    }

    return 0;
}
```

Listing 9.2   (*bit-pos-asm.c*) **Find Bit Position Using** *bsrl*

```
#include <stdio.h>
#include <stdlib.h>

int main (int argc, char* argv[])
{
  long max = atoi (argv[1]);
  long number;
  unsigned position;
  volatile unsigned result;

  /* Repeat the operation for a large number of values.  */
  for (number = 1; number <= max; ++number) {
    /* Compute the position of the most significant set bit using the
       bsrl assembly instruction.  */
    asm ("bsrl %1, %0" : "=r" (position) : "r" (number));
    result = position;
  }

  return 0;
}
```

We'll compile both versions with full optimization:

```
% cc -O2 -o bit-pos-loop bit-pos-loop.c
% cc -O2 -o bit-pos-asm bit-pos-asm.c
```

Now let's run each using the `time` command to measure execution time. We'll specify a large value as the command-line argument, to make sure that each version takes at least a few seconds to run.

```
% time ./bit-pos-loop 250000000
19.51user 0.00system 0:20.40elapsed 95%CPU (0avgtext+0avgdata
0maxresident)k0inputs+0outputs (73major+11minor)pagefaults 0swaps
% time ./bit-pos-asm 250000000
3.19user 0.00system 0:03.32elapsed 95%CPU (0avgtext+0avgdata
0maxresident)k0inputs+0outputs (73major+11minor)pagefaults 0swaps
```

Notice that the version that uses inline assembly executes a great deal faster (your results for this example may vary).

9.5   Optimization Issues

GCC's optimizer attempts to rearrange and rewrite programs' code to minimize execution time even in the presence of asm expressions. If the optimizer determines that an asm's output values are not used, the instruction will be omitted unless the keyword volatile occurs between asm and its arguments. (As a special case, GCC will not move an asm without any output operands outside a loop.) Any asm can be moved in ways that are difficult to predict, even across jumps. The only way to guarantee a particular assembly instruction ordering is to include all the instructions in the same asm.

Using asms can restrict the optimizer's effectiveness because the compiler does not know the asms' semantics. GCC is forced to make conservative guesses that may prevent some optimizations. *Caveat emptor!*

9.6   Maintenance and Portability Issues

If you decide to use nonportable, architecture-dependent asm statements, encapsulating these statements within macros or functions can aid in maintenance and porting. Placing all these macros in one file and documenting them will ease porting to a different architecture, something that occurs with surprising frequency even for "throwaway" programs. Thus, the programmer will need to rewrite only one file for the different architecture.

For example, most asm statements in the Linux source code are grouped into /usr/src/linux/include/asm and /usr/src/linux/include/asm-i386 header files, and /usr/src/linux/arch/i386/ and /usr/src/linux/drivers/ source files.

10

Security

M UCH OF THE POWER OF A GNU/LINUX SYSTEM COMES FROM its support for multiple users and for networking. Many people can use the system at once, and they can connect to the system from remote locations. Unfortunately, with this power comes risk, especially for systems connected to the Internet. Under some circumstances, a remote "hacker" can connect to the system and read, modify, or remove files that are stored on the machine. Or, two users on the same machine can read, modify, or remove each other's files when they should not be allowed to do so. When this happens, the system's security is said to have been *compromised*.

The Linux kernel provides a variety of facilities to ensure that these events do not take place. But to avoid security breaches, ordinary applications must be careful as well. For example, imagine that you are developing accounting software. Although you might want all users to be able to file expense reports with the system, you wouldn't want all users to be able to *approve* those reports. You might want users to be able to view their own payroll information, but you certainly wouldn't want them to be able to view everyone else's payroll information. You might want managers to be able to view the salaries of employees in their departments, but you wouldn't want them to view the salaries of employees in other departments.

To enforce these kinds of controls, you have to be very careful. It's amazingly easy to make a mistake that allows users to do something you didn't intend them to be able to do. The best approach is to enlist the help of security experts. Still, every application developer ought to understand the basics.

10.1 Users and Groups

Each Linux user is assigned a unique number, called a *user ID*, or *UID*. Of course, when you log in, you use a username rather than a user ID. The system converts your username to a particular user ID, and from then on it's only the user ID that counts.

You can actually have more than one username for the same user ID. As far as the system is concerned, the user IDs, not the usernames, matter. There's no way to give one username more power than another if they both correspond to the same user ID.

You can control access to a file or other resource by associating it with a particular user ID. Then only the user corresponding to that user ID can access the resource. For example, you can create a file that only you can read, or a directory in which only you can create new files. That's good enough for many simple cases.

Sometimes, however, you want to share a resource among multiple users. For example, if you're a manager, you might want to create a file that any manager can read but that ordinary employees cannot. Linux doesn't allow you to associate multiple user IDs with a file, so you can't just create a list of all the people to whom you want to give access and attach them all to the file.

You can, however, create a *group*. Each group is assigned a unique number, called a *group ID*, or *GID*. Every group contains one or more user IDs. A single user ID can be a member of lots of groups, but groups can't contain other groups; they can contain only users. Like users, groups have names. Also like usernames, however, the group names don't really matter; the system always uses the group ID internally.

Continuing our example, you could create a managers group and put the user IDs for all the managers in this group. You could then create a file that can be read by anyone in the managers group but not by people who aren't in the group. In general, you can associate only one group with a resource. There's no way to specify that users can access a file only if they're in either group 7 or group 42, for example.

If you're curious to see what your user ID is and what groups you are in, you can use the id command. For example, the output might look like this:

```
% id
uid=501(mitchell) gid=501(mitchell) groups=501(mitchell),503(csl)
```

The first part shows you that the user ID for the user who ran the command was 501. The command also figures out what the corresponding username is and displays that in parentheses. The command shows that user ID 501 is actually in two groups: group 501 (called mitchell) and group 503 (called csl). You're probably wondering why group 501 appears twice: once in the gid field and once in the groups field. We'll explain this later.

10.1.1   The Superuser

One user account is very special.[1] This user has user ID 0 and usually has the username root. It is also sometimes referred to as the *superuser* account. The root user can do just about anything: read any file, remove any file, add new users, turn off network access, and so forth. Lots of special operations can be performed only by processes running with root privilege—that is, running as user root.

The trouble with this design is that a lot of programs need to be run by root because a lot of programs need to perform one of these special operations. If any of these programs misbehaves, chaos can result. There's no effective way to contain a program when it's run by root; it can do *anything*. Programs run by root must be written very carefully.

10.2   Process User IDs and Process Group IDs

Until now, we've talked about commands being executed by a particular user. That's not quite accurate because the computer never really knows which user is using it. If Eve learns Alice's username and password, then Eve can log in as Alice, and the computer will let Eve do everything that Alice can do. The system knows only which user ID is in use, not which user is typing the commands. If Alice can't be trusted to keep her password to herself, for example, then nothing you do as an application developer will prevent Eve from accessing Alice's files. The responsibility for system security is shared among the application developer, the users of the system, and the administrators of the system.

Every process has an associated user ID and group ID. When you invoke a command, it typically runs in a process whose user and group IDs are the same as your user and group IDs. When we say that a user performs an operation, we really mean that a process with the corresponding user ID performs that operation. When the process makes a system call, the kernel decides whether to allow the operation to proceed. It makes that determination by examining the permissions associated with the resources that the process is trying to access and by checking the user ID and group ID associated with the process trying to perform the action.

Now you know what that middle field printed by the id command is all about. It's showing the group ID of the current process. Even though user 501 is in multiple groups, the current process can have only one group ID. In the example shown previously, the current group ID is 501.

If you have to manipulate user IDs and group IDs in your program (and you will, if you're writing programs that deal with security), then you should use the uid_t and gid_t types defined in <sys/types.h>. Even though user IDs and group IDs are essentially just integers, avoid making any assumptions about how many bits are used in these types or perform arithmetic operations on them. Just treat them as opaque handles for user and group identity.

---

1. The fact that there is only one special user gave AT&T the name for its UNIX operating system. In contrast, an earlier operating system that had multiple special users was called MULTICS. GNU/Linux, of course, is mostly compatible with UNIX.

To get the user ID and group ID for the current process, you can use the `geteuid` and `getegid` functions, declared in `<unistd.h>`. These functions don't take any parameters, and they always work; you don't have to check for errors. Listing 10.1 shows a simple program that provides a subset of the functionality provide by the `id` command:

Listing 10.1   **(*simpleid.c*) Print User and Group IDs**

```
#include <sys/types.h>
#include <unistd.h>
#include <stdio.h>

int main()
{
  uid_t uid = geteuid ();
  gid_t gid = getegid ();
  printf ("uid=%d gid=%d\n", (int) uid, (int) gid);
  return 0;
}
```

When this program is run (by the same user who ran the real `id` program) the output is as follows:

```
% ./simpleid
uid=501 gid=501
```

10.3   File System Permissions

A good way to see users and groups in action is to look at file system permissions. By examining how the system associates permissions with each file and then seeing how the kernel checks to see who is allowed to access which files, the concepts of user ID and group ID should become clearer.

Each file has exactly one *owning user* and exactly one *owning group*. When you create a new file, the file is owned by the user and group of the creating process.[2]

The basic things that you can do with files, as far as Linux is concerned, are *read* from them, *write* to them, and *execute* them. (Note that creating a file and removing a file are not considered things you can do with the file; they're considered things you can do with the directory containing the file. We'll get to this a little later.) If you can't read a file, Linux won't let you examine the file's contents. If you can't write a file, you can't change its contents. If there's a program file for which you do not have execute permission, you cannot run the program.

---

2. Actually, there are some rare exceptions, involving *sticky bits*, discussed later in Section 10.3.2, "Sticky Bits."

Linux enables you to designate which of these three actions—reading, writing, and executing—can be performed by the owning user, owning group, and everybody else. For example, you could say that the owning user can do anything she wants with the file, that anyone in the owning group can read and execute the file (but not write to it), and that nobody else can access the file at all.

You can view these *permission bits* interactively with the `ls` command by using the `-l` or `-o` options and programmatically with the `stat` system call. You can set the *permission bits* interactively with the `chmod` program[3] or programmatically with the system call of the same name. To look at the permissions on a file named `hello`, use `ls -l hello`. Here's how the output might look:

```
% ls -l hello
-rwxr-x---    1 samuel   csl          11734 Jan 22 16:29 hello
```

The `samuel` and `csl` fields indicate that the owning user is `samuel` and that the owning group is `csl`.

The string of characters at the beginning of the line indicates the permissions associated with the file. The first dash indicates that this is a normal file. It would be `d` for a directory, or it can be other letters for special kinds of files such as devices (see Chapter 6, "Devices") or named pipes (see Chapter 5, "Interprocess Communication," Section 5.4, "Pipes"). The next three characters show permissions for the owning user; they indicate that `samuel` can read, write, and execute the file. The next three characters show permissions for members of the `csl` group; these members are allowed only to read and execute the file. The last three characters show permissions for everyone else; these users are not allowed to do anything with `hello`.

Let's see how this works. First, let's try to access the file as the user `nobody`, who is not in the `csl` group:

```
% id
uid=99(nobody) gid=99(nobody) groups=99(nobody)
% cat hello
cat: hello: Permission denied
% echo hi > hello
sh: ./hello: Permission denied
% ./hello
sh: ./hello: Permission denied
```

We can't read the file, which is why `cat` fails; we can't write to the file, which is why `echo` fails; and we can't run the file, which is why `./hello` fails.

---

3. You'll sometimes see the permission bits for a file referred to as the file's *mode*. The name of the `chmod` command is short for "change mode."

Things are better if we are accessing the file as `mitchell`, who is a member of the `csl` group:

```
% id
uid=501(mitchell) gid=501(mitchell) groups=501(mitchell),503(csl)
% cat hello
#!/bin/bash
echo "Hello, world."
% ./hello
Hello, world.
% echo hi > hello
bash: ./hello: Permission denied
```

We can list the contents of the file, and we can run it (it's a simple shell script), but we still can't write to it.

If we run as the owner (`samuel`), we can even overwrite the file:

```
% id
uid=502(samuel) gid=502(samuel) groups=502(samuel),503(csl)
% echo hi > hello
% cat hello
hi
```

You can change the permissions associated with a file only if you are the file's owner (or the superuser). For example, if you now want to allow everyone to execute the file, you can do this:

```
% chmod o+x hello
% ls -l hello
-rwxr-x--x    1 samuel    csl          3 Jan 22 16:38 hello
```

Note that there's now an `x` at the end of the first string of characters. The `o+x` bit means that you want to add the execute permission for other people (not the file's owner or members of its owning group). You could use `g-w` instead, to remove the write permission from the group. See the man page in section 1 for `chmod` for details about this syntax:

```
% man 1 chmod
```

Programmatically, you can use the `stat` system call to find the permissions associated with a file. This function takes two parameters: the name of the file you want to find out about, and the address of a data structure that is filled in with information about the file. See Appendix B, "Low-Level I/O," Section B.2, "stat," for a discussion of other information that you can obtain with `stat`. Listing 10.2 shows an example of using `stat` to obtain file permissions.

Listing 10.2   *(stat-perm.c)* **Determine File Owner's Write Permission**

```
#include <stdio.h>
#include <sys/stat.h>

int main (int argc, char* argv[])
{
  const char* const filename = argv[1];
  struct stat buf;
```

```
    /* Get file information.  */
    stat (filename, &buf);
    /* If the permissions are set such that the file's owner can write
       to it, print a message.  */
    if (buf.st_mode & S_IWUSR)
      printf ("Owning user can write `%s'.\n", filename);
    return 0;
}
```

If you run this program on our `hello` program, it says:

```
% ./stat-perm hello
Owning user can write 'hello'.
```

The `S_IWUSR` constant corresponds to write permission for the owning user. There are other constants for all the other bits. For example, `S_IRGRP` is read permission for the owning group, and `S_IXOTH` is execute permission for users who are neither the owning user nor a member of the owning group. If you store permissions in a variable, use the typedef `mode_t` for that variable. Like most system calls, `stat` will return -1 and set `errno` if it can't obtain information about the file.

You can use the `chmod` function to change the permission bits on an existing file. You call `chmod` with the name of the file you want to change and the permission bits you want set, presented as the bitwise or of the various permission constants mentioned previously. For example, this next line would make `hello` readable and executable by its owning user but would disable all other permissions associated with `hello`:

```
chmod ("hello", S_IRUSR | S_IXUSR);
```

The same permission bits apply to directories, but they have different meanings. If a user is allowed to read from a directory, the user is allowed to see the list of files that are present in that directory. If a user is allowed to write to a directory, the user is allowed to add or remove files from the directory. Note that a user may remove files from a directory if she is allowed to write to the directory, *even if she does not have permission to modify the file she is removing.* If a user is allowed to execute a directory, the user is allowed to enter that directory and access the files therein. Without execute access to a directory, a user is not allowed to access the files in that directory independent of the permissions on the files themselves.

To summarize, let's review how the kernel decides whether to allow a process to access a particular file. It checks to see whether the accessing user is the owning user, a member of the owning group, or someone else. The category into which the accessing user falls is used to determine which set of read/write/execute bits are checked. Then the kernel checks the operation that is being performed against the permission bits that apply to this user.[4]

---

4. The kernel may also deny access to a file if a component directory in its file path is inaccessible. For instance, if a process may not access the directory `/tmp/private/`, it may not read `/tmp/private/data`, even if the permissions on the latter are set to allow the access.

There is one important exception: Processes running as root (those with user ID 0) are always allowed to access any file, regardless of the permissions associated with it.

10.3.1   Security Hole: Programs Without Execute Permissions

Here's a first example of where security gets very tricky. You might think that if you disallow execution of a program, then nobody can run it. After all, that's what it means to disallow execution. But a malicious user can make a copy of the program, change the permissions to make it executable, and then run the copy! If you rely on users not being able to run programs that aren't executable but then don't prevent them from copying the programs, you have a *security hole*—a means by which users can perform some action that you didn't intend.

10.3.2   Sticky Bits

In addition to read, write, and execute permissions, there is a magic bit called the *sticky bit*.[5] This bit applies only to directories.

A directory that has the sticky bit set allows you to delete a file only if you are the owner of the file. As mentioned previously, you can ordinarily delete a file if you have write access to the directory that contains it, even if you are not the file's owner. When the sticky bit is set, you *still* must have write access to the directory, but you must also be the owner of the file that you want to delete.

A few directories on the typical GNU/Linux system have the sticky bit set. For example, the /tmp directory, in which any user can place temporary files, has the sticky bit set. This directory is specifically designed to be used by all users, so the directory must be writable by everyone. But it would be bad if one user could delete another user's files, so the sticky bit is set on the directory. Then only the owning user (or root, of course) can remove a file.

You can see the sticky bit is set because of the t at the end of the permission bits when you run ls on /tmp:

```
% ls -ld /tmp
drwxrwxrwt   12 root      root         2048 Jan 24 17:51 /tmp
```

The corresponding constant to use with stat and chmod is S_ISVTX.

If your program creates directories that behave like /tmp, in that lots of people put things there but shouldn't be able to remove each other's files, then you should set the sticky bit on the directory. You can set the sticky bit on a directory with the chmod command by invoking the following:

```
% chmod o+t directory
```

---

5. This name is anachronistic; it goes back to a time when setting the sticky bit caused a program to be retained in main memory even when it was done executing. The pages allocated to the program were "stuck" in memory.

To set the sticky bit programmatically, call chmod with the S_ISVTX mode flag. For example, to set the sticky bit of the directory specified by dir_path to those of the /tmp and give full read, write, and execute permissions to all users, use this call:

```
chmod (dir_path, S_IRWXU | S_IRWXG | S_IRWXO | S_ISVTX);
```

10.4   Real and Effective IDs

Until now, we've talked about the user ID and group ID associated with a process as if there were only one such user ID and one such group ID. But, actually, it's not quite that simple.

Every process really has two user IDs: the *effective user ID* and the *real user ID*. (Of course, there's also an *effective group ID* and *real group ID*. Just about everything that's true about user IDs is also true about group IDs.) Most of the time, the kernel checks only the effective user ID. For example, if a process tries to open a file, the kernel checks the effective user ID when deciding whether to let the process access the file.

The geteuid and getegid functions described previously return the effective user ID and the effective group ID. Corresponding getuid and getgid functions return the real user ID and real group ID.

If the kernel cares about only the effective user ID, it doesn't seem like there's much point in having a distinction between a real user ID and an effective user ID. However, there is one very important case in which the real user ID matters. If you want to change the effective user ID of an already running process, the kernel looks at the real user ID as well as the effective user ID.

Before looking at *how* you can change the effective user ID of a process, let's examine *why* you would want to do such a thing by looking back at our accounting package. Suppose that there's a server process that might need to look at any file on the system, regardless of the user who created it. Such a process must run as root because only root can be guaranteed to be capable of looking at any file. But now suppose that a request comes in from a particular user (say, mitchell) to access some file. The server process could carefully examine the permissions associated with the files in question and try to decide whether mitchell should be allowed to access those files. But that would mean duplicating all the processing that the kernel would normally do to check file access permissions. Reimplementing that logic would be complex, error-prone, and tedious.

A better approach is simply to temporarily change the effective user ID of the process from root to mitchell and then try to perform the operations required. If mitchell is not allowed to access the data, the kernel will prevent the process from doing so and will return appropriate indications of error. After all the operations taken on behalf of mitchell are complete, the process can restore its original effective user ID to root.

Programs that authenticate users when they log in take advantage of the capability to change user IDs as well. These login programs run as `root`. When the user enters a username and password, the login program verifies the username and password in the system password database. Then the login program changes both the effective user ID and the real ID to be that of the user. Finally, the login program calls `exec` to start the user's shell, leaving the user running a shell whose effective user ID and real user ID are that of the user.

The function used to change the user IDs for a process is `setreuid`. (There is, of course, a corresponding `setregid` function as well.) This function takes two arguments. The first argument is the desired real user ID; the second is the desired effective user ID. For example, here's how you would exchange the effective and real user IDs:

```
setreuid (geteuid(), getuid ());
```

Obviously, the kernel won't let just any process change its user IDs. If a process were allowed to change its effective user ID at will, then any user could easily impersonate any other user, simply by changing the effective user ID of one of his processes. The kernel will let a process running with an effective user ID of 0 change its user IDs as it sees fit. (Again, notice how much power a process running as `root` has! A process whose effective user ID is 0 can do absolutely anything it pleases.) Any other process, however, can do only one of the following things:

- Set its effective user ID to be the same as its real user ID
- Set its real user ID to be the same as its effective user ID
- Swap the two user IDs

The first alternative would be used by our accounting process when it has finished accessing files as `mitchell` and wants to return to being `root`. The second alternative could be used by a login program after it has set the effective user ID to that of the user who just logged in. Setting the real user ID ensures that the user will never be able go back to being `root`. Swapping the two user IDs is almost a historical artifact; modern programs rarely use this functionality.

You can pass -1 to either argument to `setreuid` if you want to leave that user ID alone. There's also a convenience function called `seteuid`. This function sets the effective user ID, but it doesn't modify the real user ID. The following two statements both do exactly the same thing:

```
seteuid (id);
setreuid (-1, id);
```

10.4.1 Setuid Programs

Using the previous techniques, you know how to make a `root` process impersonate another process temporarily and then return to being `root`. You also know how to make a `root` process drop all its special privileges by setting both its real user ID and its effective user ID.

Here's a puzzle: Can you, running as a non-`root` user, ever become `root`? That doesn't seem possible, using the previous techniques, but here's proof that it can be done:

```
% whoami
mitchell
% su
Password: ...
% whoami
root
```

The `whoami` command is just like `id`, except that it shows only the effective user ID, not all the other information. The `su` command enables you to become the superuser if you know the `root` password.

How does `su` work? Because we know that the shell was originally running with both its real user ID and its effective user ID set to `mitchell`, `setreuid` won't allow us to change either user ID.

The trick is that the `su` program is a *setuid* program. That means that when it is run, the effective user ID of the process will be that of the file's owner rather than the effective user ID of the process that performed the `exec` call. (The real user ID will still be that of the executing user.) To create a setuid program, you use `chmod +s` at the command line, or use the `S_ISUID` flag if calling `chmod` programmatically.[6]

For example, consider the program in Listing 10.3.

Listing 10.3 (*setuid-test.c*) **Setuid Demonstration Program**

```
#include <stdio.h>
#include <unistd.h>

int main ()
{
  printf ("uid=%d euid=%d\n", (int) getuid (), (int) geteuid ());
  return 0;
}
```

Now suppose that this program is setuid and owned by `root`. In that case, the `ls` output will look like this:

```
-rwsrws--x   1 root     root         11931 Jan 24 18:25 setuid-test
```

The `s` bits indicate that the file is not only executable (as an `x` bit would indicate) but also setuid and setgid. When we use this program, we get output like this:

```
% whoami
mitchell
% ./setuid-test
uid=501 euid=0
```

6. Of course, there is a similar notion of a setgid program. When run, its effective group ID is the same as that of the group owner of the file. Most setuid programs are also setgid programs.

Note that the effective user ID is set to 0 when the program is run.

You can use the chmod command with the u+s or g+s arguments to set the setuid and setgid bits on an executable file, respectively—for example:

```
% ls -l program
-rwxr-xr-x    1 samuel   csl              0 Jan 30 23:38 program
% chmod g+s program
% ls -l program
-rwxr-sr-x    1 samuel   csl              0 Jan 30 23:38 program
% chmod u+s program
% ls -l program
-rwsr-sr-x    1 samuel   csl              0 Jan 30 23:38 program
```

You can also use the chmod call with the S_ISUID or S_ISGID mode flags.

su is capable of changing the effective user ID through this mechanism. It runs initially with an effective user ID of 0. Then it prompts you for a password. If the password matches the root password, it sets its real user ID to be root as well and then starts a new shell. Otherwise, it exits, unceremoniously leaving you as a non-privileged user.

Take a look at the permissions on the su program:

```
% ls -l /bin/su
-rwsr-xr-x    1 root     root        14188 Mar  7 2000 /bin/su
```

Notice that it's owned by root and that the setuid bit is set.

Note that su doesn't actually change the user ID of the shell from which it was run. Instead, it starts a new shell process with the new user ID. The original shell is blocked until the new shell completes and su exits.

10.5   Authenticating Users

Often, if you have a setuid program, you don't want to offer its services to everyone. For example, the su program lets you become root only if you know the root password. The program makes you prove that you are entitled to become root before going ahead with its actions. This process is called *authentication*—the su program is checking to see that you are authentic.

If you're administering a very secure system, you probably don't want to let people log in just by typing an ordinary password. Users tend to write down passwords, and black hats tend to find them. Users tend to pick passwords that involve their birthdays, the names of their pets, and so forth.[7] Passwords just aren't all that secure.

---

7. It has been found that system administrators tend to pick the word *god* as their password more often than any other password. (Make of that what you will.) So, if you ever need root access on a machine and the sysadmin isn't around, a little divine inspiration might be just what you need.

For example, many organizations now require the use of special "one-time" passwords that are generated by special electronic ID cards that users keep with them. The same password can't be used twice, and you can't get a valid password out of the ID card without entering a PIN. So, an attacker must obtain both the physical card and the PIN to break in. In a really secure facility, retinal scans or other kinds of biometric testing are used.

If you're writing a program that must perform authentication, you should allow the system administrator to use whatever means of authentication is appropriate for that installation. GNU/Linux comes with a very useful library that makes this very easy. This facility, called *Pluggable Authentication Modules*, or *PAM*, makes it easy to write applications that authenticate their users as the system administrator sees fit.

It's easiest to see how PAM works by looking at a simple PAM application. Listing 10.4 illustrates the use of PAM.

Listing 10.4   (*pam.c*) **PAM Example**

```
#include <security/pam_appl.h>
#include <security/pam_misc.h>
#include <stdio.h>

int main ()
{
  pam_handle_t* pamh;
  struct pam_conv pamc;

  /* Set up the PAM conversation.  */
  pamc.conv = &misc_conv;
  pamc.appdata_ptr = NULL;
  /* Start a new authentication session.  */
  pam_start ("su", getenv ("USER"), &pamc, &pamh);
  /* Authenticate the user.  */
  if (pam_authenticate (pamh, 0) != PAM_SUCCESS)
    fprintf (stderr, "Authentication failed!\n");
  else
    fprintf (stderr, "Authentication OK.\n");
  /* All done.  */
  pam_end (pamh, 0);
  return 0;
}
```

To compile this program, you have to link it with two libraries: the `libpam` library and a helper library called `libpam_misc`:

```
% gcc -o pam pam.c -lpam -lpam_misc
```

This program starts off by building up a PAM *conversation object*. This object is used by the PAM library whenever it needs to prompt the user for information. The `misc_conv` function used in this example is a standard conversation function that uses the terminal for input and output. You could write your own function that pops up a dialog box, or that uses speech for input and output, or that provides even more exotic input and output methods.

The program then calls `pam_start`. This function initializes the PAM library. The first argument is a service name. You should use a name that uniquely identifies your application. For example, if your application is named whizbang, you should probably use that for the service name, too. However, the program probably won't work until the system administrator explicitly configures the system to work with your service. So, in this example, we use the su service, which says that our program should authenticate users in the same way that the su command does. You should *not* use this technique in a real program. Pick a real service name, and have your installation scripts help the system administrator to set up a correct PAM configuration for your application.

The second argument is the name of the user whom you want to authenticate. In this example, we use the value of the USER environment variable. (Normally, this is the username that corresponds to the effective user ID of the current process, but that's not always the case.) In most real programs, you would prompt for a username at this point. The third argument indicates the PAM conversation, discussed previously. The call to `pam_start` fills in the handle provided as the fourth argument. Pass this handle to subsequent calls to PAM library routines.

Next, the program calls `pam_authenticate`. The second argument enables you to pass various flags; the value 0 means to use the default options. The return value from this function indicates whether authentication succeeded.

Finally, the programs calls `pam_end` to clean up any allocated data structures.

Let's assume that the valid password for the current user is "password" (an exceptionally poor password). Then, running this program with the correct password produces the expected:

```
% ./pam
Password: password

Authentication OK.
```

If you run this program in a terminal, the password probably won't actually appear when you type it in; it's hidden to prevent others from peeking at your password over your shoulder as you type.

However, if a hacker tries to use the wrong password, the PAM library will correctly indicate failure:

```
% ./pam
Password: badguess

Authentication failed!
```

The basics covered here are enough for most simple programs. Full documentation about how PAM works is available in /usr/doc/pam on most GNU/Linux systems.

10.6 More Security Holes

Although this chapter will point out a few common security holes, you should by no means rely on this book to cover all possible security holes. A great many have already been discovered, and many more are out there waiting to be found. If you are trying to write secure code, there is really no substitute for having a security expert audit your code.

10.6.1 Buffer Overruns

Almost every major Internet application daemon, including the sendmail daemon, the finger daemon, the talk daemon, and others, has at one point been compromised through a *buffer overrun*.

If you are writing any code that will ever be run as root, you absolutely must be aware of this particular kind of security hole. If you are writing a program that performs any kind of interprocess communication, you should definitely be aware of this kind of security hole. If you are writing a program that reads files (or *might* read files) that are not owned by the user executing the program, you should be aware of this kind of security hole. That last criterion applies to almost every program. Fundamentally, if you're going to write GNU/Linux software, you ought to know about buffer overruns.

The idea behind a buffer overrun attack is to trick a program into executing code that it did not intend to execute. The usual mechanism for achieving this feat is to overwrite some portion of the program's process stack. The program's stack contains, among other things, the memory location to which the program will transfer control when the current function returns. Therefore, if you can put the code that you want to have executed into memory somewhere and then change the return address to point to that piece of memory, you can cause the program to execute anything. When the program returns from the function it is executing, it will jump to the new code and execute whatever is there, running with the privileges of the current process. Clearly, if the current process is running as root, this would be a disaster. If the process is running as another user, it's a disaster "only" for that user—and anybody else who depends on the contents of files owned by that user, and so forth.

If the program is running as a daemon and listening for incoming network connections, the situation is even worse. A daemon typically runs as root. If it contains buffer overrun bugs, anyone who can connect via the network to a computer running the daemon can seize control of the computer by sending a malignant sequence of data to the daemon over the network. A program that does not engage in network communications is much safer because only users who are already able to log in to the computer running the program are able to attack it.

The buggy versions of `finger`, `talk`, and `sendmail` all shared a common flaw. Each used a fixed-length string buffer, which implied a constant upper limit on the size of the string but then allowed network clients to provide strings that overflowed the buffer. For example, they contained code similar to this:

```
#include <stdio.h>

int main ()
{
  /* Nobody in their right mind would have more than 32 characters in
     their username.  Plus, I think UNIX allows only 8-character
     usernames.  So, this should be plenty of space.  */
  char username[32];
  /* Prompt the user for the username.  */
  printf ("Enter your username: ");
  /* Read a line of input.  */
  gets (username);
  /* Do other things here...  */

  return 0;
}
```

The combination of the 32-character buffer with the `gets` function permits a buffer overrun. The `gets` function reads user input up until the next newline character and stores the entire result in the `username` buffer. The comments in the code are correct in that people generally have short usernames, so no well-meaning user is likely to type in more than 32 characters. But when you're writing secure software, you must consider what a malicious attacker might do. In this case, the attacker might deliberately type in a very long username. Local variables such as `username` are stored on the stack, so by exceeding the array bounds, it's possible to put arbitrary bytes onto the stack beyond the area reserved for the `username` variable. The username will overrun the buffer and overwrite parts of the surrounding stack, allowing the kind of attack described previously.

Fortunately, it's relatively easy to prevent buffer overruns. When reading strings, you should always use a function, such as `getline`, that either dynamically allocates a sufficiently large buffer or stops reading input if the buffer is full. For example, you could use this:

```
char* username = getline (NULL, 0, stdin);
```

This call automatically uses `malloc` to allocate a buffer big enough to hold the line and returns it to you. You have to remember to call `free` to deallocate the buffer, of course, to avoid leaking memory.

Your life will be even easier if you use C++ or another language that provides simple primitives for reading input. In C++, for example, you can simply use this:

```
string username;
getline (cin, username);
```

The username string will automatically be deallocated as well; you don't have to remember to free it.[8]

Of course, buffer overruns can occur with any statically sized array, not just with strings. If you want to write secure code, you should never write into a data structure, on the stack or elsewhere, without verifying that you're not going to write beyond its region of memory.

10.6.2   Race Conditions in */tmp*

Another very common problem involves the creation of files with predictable names, typically in the /tmp directory. Suppose that your program prog, running as root, always creates a temporary file called /tmp/prog and writes some vital information there. A malicious user can create a symbolic link from /tmp/prog to any other file on the system. When your program goes to create the file, the open system call will succeed. However, the data that you write will not go to /tmp/prog; instead, it will be written to some arbitrary file of the attacker's choosing.

This kind of attack is said to exploit a *race condition*. There is implicitly a race between you and the attacker. Whoever manages to create the file first wins.

This attack is often used to destroy important parts of the file system. By creating the appropriate links, the attacker can trick a program running as root that is supposed to write a temporary file into overwriting an important system file instead. For example, by making a symbolic link to /etc/passwd, the attacker can wipe out the system's password database. There are also ways in which a malicious user can obtain root access using this technique.

One attempt at avoiding this attack is to use a randomized name for the file. For example, you could read from /dev/random to get some bits to use in the name of the file. This certainly makes it harder for a malicious user to guess the filename, but it doesn't make it impossible. The attacker might just create a large number of symbolic links, using many potential names. Even if she has to try 10,000 times before wining the race condition, that one time could be disastrous.

Another approach is to use the O_EXCL flag when calling open. This flag causes open to fail if the file already exists. Unfortunately, if you're using the Network File System (NFS), or if anyone who's using your program might ever be using NFS, that's not a sufficiently robust approach because O_EXCL is not reliable when NFS is in use. You can't ever really know for sure whether your code will be used on a system that uses NFS, so if you're highly paranoid, don't rely on using O_EXCL.

In Chapter 2, "Writing Good GNU/Linux Software," Section 2.1.7, "Using Temporary Files," we showed how to use mkstemp to create temporary files. Unfortunately, what mkstemp does on Linux is open the file with O_EXCL after trying to pick a name that is hard to guess. In other words, using mkstemp is still insecure if /tmp is mounted over NFS.[9] So, using mkstemp is better than nothing, but it's not fully secure.

---

8. Some programmers believe that C++ is a horrible and overly complex language. Their arguments about multiple inheritance and other such complications have some merit, but it is easier to write code that avoids buffer overruns and other similar problems in C++ than in C.

9. Obviously, if you're also a system administrator, you shouldn't mount /tmp over NFS.

One approach that works is to call lstat on the newly created file (lstat is discussed in Section B.2, "stat"). The lstat function is like stat, except that if the file referred to is a symbolic link, lstat tells you about the link, not the file to which it refers. If lstat tells you that your new file is an ordinary file, not a symbolic link, and that it is owned by you, then you should be okay.

Listing 10.5 presents a function that tries to securely open a file in /tmp. The authors of this book have not had it audited professionally, nor are we professional security experts, so there's a good chance that it has a weakness, too. We do not recommend that you use this code without getting an audit, but it should at least convince you that writing secure code is tricky. To help dissuade you, we've deliberately made the interface difficult to use in real programs. Error checking is an important part of writing secure software, so we've included error-checking logic in this example.

Listing 10.5   (*temp-file.c*) **Create a Temporary File**

```
#include <fcntl.h>
#include <stdlib.h>
#include <sys/stat.h>
#include <unistd.h>

/* Returns the file descriptor for a newly created temporary file.
   The temporary file will be readable and writable by the effective
   user ID of the current process but will not be readable or
   writable by anybody else.

   Returns -1 if the temporary file could not be created.  */

int secure_temp_file ()
{
  /* This file descriptor points to /dev/random and allows us to get
     a good source of random bits.  */
  static int random_fd = -1;
  /* A random integer.  */
  unsigned int random;
  /* A buffer, used to convert from a numeric to a string
     representation of random.  This buffer has fixed size, meaning
     that we potentially have a buffer overrun bug if the integers on
     this machine have a *lot* of bits.  */
  char filename[128];
  /* The file descriptor for the new temporary file.  */
  int fd;
  /* Information about the newly created file.  */
  struct stat stat_buf;

  /* If we haven't already opened /dev/random, do so now.  (This is
     not threadsafe.)  */
  if (random_fd == -1) {
```

```
        /* Open /dev/random.  Note that we're assuming that /dev/random
           really is a source of random bits, not a file full of zeros
           placed there by an attacker.  */
        random_fd = open ("/dev/random", O_RDONLY);
        /* If we couldn't open /dev/random, give up.  */
        if (random_fd == -1)
          return -1;
      }

      /* Read an integer from /dev/random.  */
      if (read (random_fd, &random, sizeof (random)) !=
          sizeof (random))
        return -1;
      /* Create a filename out of the random number.  */
      sprintf (filename, "/tmp/%u", random);
      /* Try to open the file.  */
      fd = open (filename,
                 /* Use O_EXECL, even though it doesn't work under NFS.  */
                 O_RDWR | O_CREAT | O_EXCL,
                 /* Make sure nobody else can read or write the file.  */
                 S_IRUSR | S_IWUSR);
      if (fd == -1)
        return -1;

      /* Call lstat on the file, to make sure that it is not a symbolic
         link.  */
      if (lstat (filename, &stat_buf) == -1)
        return -1;
      /* If the file is not a regular file, someone has tried to trick
         us.  */
      if (!S_ISREG (stat_buf.st_mode))
        return -1;
      /* If we don't own the file, someone else might remove it, read it,
         or change it while we're looking at it.  */
      if (stat_buf.st_uid != geteuid () || stat_buf.st_gid != getegid ())
        return -1;
      /* If there are any more permission bits set on the file,
         something's fishy.  */
      if ((stat_buf.st_mode & ~(S_IRUSR | S_IWUSR)) != 0)
        return -1;

      return fd;
    }
```

This function calls open to create the file and then calls lstat a few lines later to make sure that the file is not a symbolic link. If you're thinking carefully, you'll realize that there seems to be a race condition at this point. In particular, an attacker could remove the file and replace it with a symbolic link between the time we call open and the time we call lstat. That won't harm us directly because we already have an open file descriptor to the newly created file, but it will cause us to indicate an error to our caller. This attack doesn't create any direct harm, but it does make it impossible for our program to get its work done. Such an attack is called a *denial-of-service* (*DoS*) attack.

Fortunately, the sticky bit comes to the rescue. Because the sticky bit is set on /tmp, nobody else can remove files from that directory. Of course, root can still remove files from /tmp, but if the attacker has root privilege, there's nothing you can do to protect your program.

If you choose to assume competent system administration, then /tmp will not be mounted via NFS. And if the system administrator was foolish enough to mount /tmp over NFS, then there's a good chance that the sticky bit isn't set, either. So, for most practical purposes, we think it's safe to use mkstemp. But you should be aware of these issues, and you should definitely not rely on O_EXCL to work correctly if the directory in use is not /tmp—nor you should rely on the sticky bit being set anywhere else.

10.6.3 Using *system* or *popen*

The third common security hole that every programmer should bear in mind involves using the shell to execute other programs. As a toy example, let's consider a dictionary server. This program is designed to accept connections via the Internet. Each client sends a word, and the server tells it whether that is a valid English word. Because every GNU/Linux system comes with a list of about 45,000 English words in /usr/dict/words, an easy way to build this server is to invoke the grep program, like this:

```
% grep -x word /usr/dict/words
```

Here, *word* is the word that the user is curious about. The exit code from grep will tell you whether that word appears in /usr/dict/words.[10]

Listing 10.6 shows how you might try to code the part of the server that invokes grep:

Listing 10.6 (*grep-dictionary.c*) **Search for a Word in the Dictionary**

```
#include <stdio.h>
#include <stdlib.h>

/* Returns a nonzero value if and only if the WORD appears in
   /usr/dict/words.  */

int grep_for_word (const char* word)
{
  size_t length;
  char* buffer;
  int exit_code;
```

10. If you don't know about grep, you should look at the manual pages. It's an incredibly useful program.

```
/* Build up the string 'grep -x WORD /usr/dict/words'.  Allocate the
   string dynamically to avoid buffer overruns.  */
length =
  strlen ("grep -x ") + strlen (word) + strlen (" /usr/dict/words") + 1;
buffer = (char*) malloc (length);
sprintf (buffer, "grep -x %s /usr/dict/words", word);

/* Run the command.  */
exit_code = system (buffer);
/* Free the buffer.  */
free (buffer);
/* If grep returned 0, then the word was present in the
   dictionary.  */
return exit_code == 0;
}
```

Note that by calculating the number of characters we need and then allocating the buffer dynamically, we're sure to be safe from buffer overruns.

Unfortunately, the use of the system function (described in Chapter 3, "Processes," Section 3.2.1, "Using system") is unsafe. This function invokes the standard system shell to run the command and then returns the exit value. But what happens if a malicious hacker sends a "word" that is actually the following line or a similar string?

```
foo /dev/null; rm -rf /
```

In that case, the server will execute this command:

```
grep -x foo /dev/null; rm -rf / /usr/dict/words
```

Now the problem is obvious. The user has turned one command, ostensibly the invocation of grep, into two commands because the shell treats a semicolon as a command separator. The first command is still a harmless invocation of grep, but the second removes all files on the entire system! Even if the server is not running as root, all the files that can be removed by the user running the server will be removed. The same problem can arise with popen (described in Section 5.4.4, "popen and pclose"), which creates a pipe between the parent and child process but still uses the shell to run the command.

There are two ways to avoid these problems. One is to use the exec family of functions instead of system or popen. That solution avoids the problem because characters that the shell treats specially (such as the semicolon in the previous command) are not treated specially when they appear in the argument list to an exec call. Of course, you give up the convenience of system and popen.

The other alternative is to validate the string to make sure that it is benign. In the dictionary server example, you would make sure that the word provided contains only alphabetic characters, using the `isalpha` function. If it doesn't contain any other characters, there's no way to trick the shell into executing a second command. Don't implement the check by looking for dangerous and unexpected characters; it's always safer to explicitly check for the characters that you know are safe rather than try to anticipate all the characters that might cause trouble.

11

A Sample GNU/Linux Application

THIS CHAPTER IS WHERE IT ALL COMES TOGETHER. WE'LL DESCRIBE and implement a complete GNU/Linux program that incorporates many of the techniques described in this book. The program provides information about the system it's running on via a Web interface.

The program is a complete demonstration of some of the methods we've described for GNU/Linux programming and illustrated in shorter programs. This program is written more like "real-world" code, unlike most of the code listings that we presented in previous chapters. It can serve as a jumping-off point for your own GNU/Linux programs.

11.1 Overview

The example program is part of a system for monitoring a running GNU/Linux system. It includes these features:

- The program incorporates a minimal Web server. Local or remote clients access system information by requesting Web pages from the server via HTTP.

- The program does not serve static HTML pages. Instead, the pages are generated on the fly by modules, each of which provides a page summarizing one aspect of the system's state.

- Modules are not linked statically into the server executable. Instead, they are loaded dynamically from shared libraries. Modules can be added, removed, or replaced while the server is running.

- The server services each connection in a child process. This enables the server to remain responsive even when individual requests take a while to complete, and it shields the server from failures in modules.

- The server does not require superuser privilege to run (as long as it is not run on a privileged port). However, this limits the system information that it can collect.

We provide four sample modules that demonstrate how modules might be written. They further illustrate some of the techniques for gathering system information presented previously in this book. The `time` module demonstrates using the `gettimeofday` system call. The `issue` module demonstrates low-level I/O and the `sendfile` system call. The `diskfree` module demonstrates the use of `fork`, `exec`, and `dup2` by running a command in a child process. The `processes` module demonstrates the use of the `/proc` file system and various system calls.

11.1.1 Caveats

This program has many of the features you'd expect in an application program, such as command-line parsing and error checking. At the same time, we've made some simplifications to improve readability and to focus on the GNU/Linux-specific topics discussed in this book. Bear in mind these caveats as you examine the code.

- We don't attempt to provide a full implementation of HTTP. Instead, we implement just enough for the server to interact with Web clients. A real-world program either would provide a more complete HTTP implementation or would interface with one of the various excellent Web server implementations[1] available instead of providing HTTP services directly.

- Similarly, we don't aim for full compliance with HTML specifications (see `http://www.w3.org/MarkUp/`). We generate simple HTML output that can be handled by popular Web browsers.

- The server is not tuned for high performance or minimum resource usage. In particular, we intentionally omit some of the network configuration code that you would expect in a Web server. This topic is outside the scope of this book. See one of the many excellent references on network application development, such as *UNIX Network Programming, Volume 1: Networking APIs—Sockets and XTI*, by W. Richard Stevens (Prentice Hall, 1997), for more information.

---

1. The most popular open source Web server for GNU/Linux is the Apache server, available from `http://www.apache.org`.

- We make no attempt to regulate the resources (number of processes, memory use, and so on) consumed by the server or its modules. Many multiprocess Web server implementations service connections using a fixed pool of processes rather than creating a new child process for each connection.

- The server loads the shared library for a server module each time it is requested and then immediately unloads it when the request has been completed. A more efficient implementation would probably cache loaded modules.

HTTP

The *Hypertext Transport Protocol* (*HTTP*) is used for communication between Web clients and servers. The client connects to the server by establishing a connection to a well-known port (usually port 80 for Internet Web servers, but any port may be used). HTTP requests and headers are composed of plain text.

Once connected, the client sends a request to the server. A typical request is GET /page HTTP/1.0. The GET method indicates that the client is requesting that the server send it a Web page. The second element is the path to that page on the server. The third element is the protocol and version. Subsequent lines contain header fields, formatted similarly to email headers, which contain extra information about the client. The header ends with a blank line.

The server sends back a response indicating the result of processing the request. A typical response is HTTP/1.0 200 OK. The first element is the protocol version. The next two elements indicate the result; in this case, result 200 indicates that the request was processed successfully. Subsequent lines contain header fields, formatted similarly to email headers. The header ends with a blank line. The server may then send arbitrary data to satisfy the request.

Typically, the server responds to a page request by sending back HTML source for the Web page. In this case, the response headers will include Content-type: text/html, indicating that the result is HTML source. The HTML source follows immediately after the header.

See the HTTP specification at http://www.w3.org/Protocols/ for more information.

11.2 Implementation

All but the very smallest programs written in C require careful organization to preserve the modularity and maintainability of the source code. This program is divided into four main source files.

Each source file exports functions or variables that may be accessed by the other parts of the program. For simplicity, all exported functions and variables are declared in a single header file, server.h (see Listing 11.1), which is included by the other files. Functions that are intended for use within a single compilation unit only are declared static and are not declared in server.h.

Listing 11.1 (*server.h*) **Function and Variable Declarations**

```
#ifndef SERVER_H
#define SERVER_H

#include <netinet/in.h>
#include <sys/types.h>

/*** Symbols defined in common.c.  ***********************************/

/* The name of this program.  */
extern const char* program_name;

/* If nonzero, print verbose messages.  */
extern int verbose;

/* Like malloc, except aborts the program if allocation fails.  */
extern void* xmalloc (size_t size);

/* Like realloc, except aborts the program if allocation fails.  */
extern void* xrealloc (void* ptr, size_t size);

/* Like strdup, except aborts the program if allocation fails.  */
extern char* xstrdup (const char* s);

/* Print an error message for a failed call OPERATION, using the value
   of errno, and end the program.  */
extern void system_error (const char* operation);

/* Print an error message for failure involving CAUSE, including a
   descriptive MESSAGE, and end the program.  */
extern void error (const char* cause, const char* message);

/* Return the directory containing the running program's executable.
   The return value is a memory buffer that the caller must deallocate
   using free.  This function calls abort on failure.  */
extern char* get_self_executable_directory ();


/*** Symbols defined in module.c  ***********************************/

/* An instance of a loaded server module.  */
struct server_module {
  /* The shared library handle corresponding to the loaded module.  */
  void* handle;
  /* A name describing the module.  */
  const char* name;
  /* The function that generates the HTML results for this module.  */
  void (* generate_function) (int);
};
```

```
/* The directory from which modules are loaded.  */
extern char* module_dir;

/* Attempt to load a server module with the name MODULE_PATH.  If a
   server module exists with this path, loads the module and returns a
   server_module structure representing it.  Otherwise, returns NULL.  */
extern struct server_module* module_open (const char* module_path);

/* Close a server module and deallocate the MODULE object.  */
extern void module_close (struct server_module* module);


/*** Symbols defined in server.c.  ************************************/

/* Run the server on LOCAL_ADDRESS and PORT.  */
extern void server_run (struct in_addr local_address, uint16_t port);


#endif   /* SERVER_H */
```

11.2.1   Common Functions

common.c (see Listing 11.2) contains functions of general utility that are used throughout the program.

Listing 11.2   *(common.c)* **General Utility Functions**

```
#include <errno.h>
#include <stdio.h>
#include <stdlib.h>
#include <string.h>
#include <unistd.h>

#include "server.h"

const char* program_name;

int verbose;

void* xmalloc (size_t size)
{
  void* ptr = malloc (size);
  /* Abort if the allocation failed.  */
  if (ptr == NULL)
    abort ();
  else
    return ptr;
}
```

continues

Listing 11.2   **Continued**

```
void* xrealloc (void* ptr, size_t size)
{
  ptr = realloc (ptr, size);
  /* Abort if the allocation failed.  */
  if (ptr == NULL)
    abort ();
  else
    return ptr;
}

char* xstrdup (const char* s)
{
  char* copy = strdup (s);
  /* Abort if the allocation failed.  */
  if (copy == NULL)
    abort ();
  else
    return copy;
}

void system_error (const char* operation)
{
  /* Generate an error message for errno.  */
  error (operation, strerror (errno));
}

void error (const char* cause, const char* message)
{
  /* Print an error message to stderr.  */
  fprintf (stderr, "%s: error: (%s) %s\n", program_name, cause, message);
  /* End the program.  */
  exit (1);
}

char* get_self_executable_directory ()
{
  int rval;
  char link_target[1024];
  char* last_slash;
  size_t result_length;
  char* result;

  /* Read the target of the symbolic link /proc/self/exe.  */
  rval = readlink ("/proc/self/exe", link_target, sizeof (link_target));
  if (rval == -1)
    /* The call to readlink failed, so bail.  */
    abort ();
  else
```

```
    /* NUL-terminate the target.  */
    link_target[rval] = '\0';
  /* We want to trim the name of the executable file, to obtain the
     directory that contains it.  Find the rightmost slash.  */
  last_slash = strrchr (link_target, '/');
  if (last_slash == NULL || last_slash == link_target)
    /* Something strange is going on.  */
    abort ();
  /* Allocate a buffer to hold the resulting path.  */
  result_length = last_slash - link_target;
  result = (char*) xmalloc (result_length + 1);
  /* Copy the result.  */
  strncpy (result, link_target, result_length);
  result[result_length] = '\0';
  return result;
}
```

You could use these functions in other programs as well; the contents of this file might be included in a common code library that is shared among many projects:

- `xmalloc`, `xrealloc`, and `xstrdup` are error-checking versions of the C library functions `malloc`, `realloc`, and `strdup`, respectively. Unlike the standard versions, which return a null pointer if the allocation fails, these functions immediately abort the program when insufficient memory is available.

  Early detection of memory allocation failure is a good idea. Otherwise, failed allocations introduce null pointers at unexpected places into the program. Because allocation failures are not easy to reproduce, debugging such problems can be difficult. Allocation failures are usually catastrophic, so aborting the program is often an acceptable course of action.

- The `error` function is for reporting a fatal program error. It prints a message to `stderr` and ends the program. For errors caused by failed system calls or library calls, `system_error` generates part of the error message from the value of `errno` (see Section 2.2.3, "Error Codes from System Calls," in Chapter 2, "Writing Good GNU/Linux Software").

- `get_self_executable_directory` determines the directory containing the executable file being run in the current process. The directory path can be used to locate other components of the program, which are installed in the same place at runtime. This function works by examining the symbolic link `/proc/self/exe` in the `/proc` file system (see Section 7.2.1, "`/proc/self`," in Chapter 7, "The `/proc` File System").

In addition, `common.c` defines two useful global variables:

- The value of `program_name` is the name of the program being run, as specified in its argument list (see Section 2.1.1, "The Argument List," in Chapter 2). When the program is invoked from the shell, this is the path and name of the program as the user entered it.

- The variable `verbose` is nonzero if the program is running in verbose mode. In this case, various parts of the program print progress messages to `stdout`.

11.2.2   Loading Server Modules

`module.c` (see Listing 11.3) provides the implementation of dynamically loadable server modules. A loaded server module is represented by an instance of `struct server_module`, which is defined in `server.h`.

Listing 11.3   *(module.c)* **Server Module Loading and Unloading**

```c
#include <dlfcn.h>
#include <stdlib.h>
#include <stdio.h>
#include <string.h>

#include "server.h"

char* module_dir;

struct server_module* module_open (const char* module_name)
{
  char* module_path;
  void* handle;
  void (* module_generate) (int);
  struct server_module* module;

  /* Construct the full path of the module shared library we'll try to
     load.  */
  module_path =
    (char*) xmalloc (strlen (module_dir) + strlen (module_name) + 2);
  sprintf (module_path, "%s/%s", module_dir, module_name);

  /* Attempt to open MODULE_PATH as a shared library.  */
  handle = dlopen (module_path, RTLD_NOW);
  free (module_path);
  if (handle == NULL) {
    /* Failed; either this path doesn't exist or it isn't a shared
       library.  */
    return NULL;
  }

  /* Resolve the module_generate symbol from the shared library.  */
  module_generate = (void (*) (int)) dlsym (handle, "module_generate");
  /* Make sure the symbol was found.  */
  if (module_generate == NULL) {
```

```
  /* The symbol is missing.  While this is a shared library, it
     probably isn't a server module.  Close up and indicate failure.  */
  dlclose (handle);
  return NULL;
}

/* Allocate and initialize a server_module object.  */
module = (struct server_module*) xmalloc (sizeof (struct server_module));
module->handle = handle;
module->name = xstrdup (module_name);
module->generate_function = module_generate;
/* Return it, indicating success.  */
return module;
}

void module_close (struct server_module* module)
{
  /* Close the shared library.  */
  dlclose (module->handle);
  /* Deallocate the module name.  */
  free ((char*) module->name);
  /* Deallocate the module object.  */
  free (module);
}
```

Each module is a shared library file (see Section 2.3.2, "Shared Libraries," in Chapter 2) and must define and export a function named module_generate. This function generates an HTML Web page and writes it to the client socket file descriptor passed as its argument.

module.c contains two functions:

- module_open attempts to load a server module with a given name. The name normally ends with the .so extension because server modules are implemented as shared libraries. This function opens the shared library with dlopen and resolves a symbol named module_generate from the library with dlsym (see Section 2.3.6, "Dynamic Loading and Unloading," in Chapter 2). If the library can't be opened, or if module_generate isn't a name exported by the library, the call fails and module_open returns a null pointer. Otherwise, it allocates and returns a module object.

- module_close closes the shared library corresponding to the server module and deallocates the struct server_module object.

module.c also defines a global variable module_dir. This is the path of the directory in which module_open attempts to find shared libraries corresponding to server modules.

11.2.3   The Server

server.c (see Listing 11.4) is the implementation of the minimal HTTP server.

Listing 11.4   *(server.c)* **Server Implementation**

```
#include <arpa/inet.h>
#include <assert.h>
#include <errno.h>
#include <netinet/in.h>
#include <signal.h>
#include <stdio.h>
#include <string.h>
#include <sys/types.h>
#include <sys/socket.h>
#include <sys/wait.h>
#include <unistd.h>

#include "server.h"

/* HTTP response and header for a successful request.  */

static char* ok_response =
  "HTTP/1.0 200 OK\n"
  "Content-type: text/html\n"
  "\n";

/* HTTP response, header, and body, indicating that we didn't
   understand the request.  */

static char* bad_request_response =
  "HTTP/1.0 400 Bad Request\n"
  "Content-type: text/html\n"
  "\n"
  "<html>\n"
  " <body>\n"
  "  <h1>Bad Request</h1>\n"
  "  <p>This server did not understand your request.</p>\n"
  " </body>\n"
  "</html>\n";

/* HTTP response, header, and body template, indicating that the
   requested document was not found.  */

static char* not_found_response_template =
  "HTTP/1.0 404 Not Found\n"
  "Content-type: text/html\n"
  "\n"
  "<html>\n"
  " <body>\n"
  "  <h1>Not Found</h1>\n"
```

```
"  <p>The requested URL %s was not found on this server.</p>\n"
" </body>\n"
"</html>\n";

/* HTTP response, header, and body template, indicating that the
   method was not understood.  */

static char* bad_method_response_template =
  "HTTP/1.0 501 Method Not Implemented\n"
  "Content-type: text/html\n"
  "\n"
  "<html>\n"
  " <body>\n"
  "  <h1>Method Not Implemented</h1>\n"
  "  <p>The method %s is not implemented by this server.</p>\n"
  " </body>\n"
  "</html>\n";

/* Handler for SIGCHLD, to clean up child processes that have
   terminated.  */

static void clean_up_child_process (int signal_number)
{
  int status;
  wait (&status);
}

/* Process an HTTP "GET" request for PAGE, and send the results to the
   file descriptor CONNECTION_FD.  */

static void handle_get (int connection_fd, const char* page)
{
  struct server_module* module = NULL;

  /* Make sure the requested page begins with a slash and does not
     contain any additional slashes -- we don't support any
     subdirectories.  */
  if (*page == '/' && strchr (page + 1, '/') == NULL) {
    char module_file_name[64];

    /* The page name looks OK.  Construct the module name by appending
       ".so" to the page name.  */
    snprintf (module_file_name, sizeof (module_file_name),
              "%s.so", page + 1);
    /* Try to open the module.  */
    module = module_open (module_file_name);
  }

  if (module == NULL) {
    /* Either the requested page was malformed, or we couldn't open a
       module with the indicated name.  Either way, return the HTTP
       response 404, Not Found.  */
```

continues

Listing 11.4   **Continued**

```
      char response[1024];

      /* Generate the response message.  */
      snprintf (response, sizeof (response), not_found_response_template, page);
      /* Send it to the client.  */
      write (connection_fd, response, strlen (response));
    }
    else {
      /* The requested module was loaded successfully.  */

      /* Send the HTTP response indicating success, and the HTTP header
         for an HTML page.  */
      write (connection_fd, ok_response, strlen (ok_response));
      /* Invoke the module, which will generate HTML output and send it
         to the client file descriptor.  */
      (*module->generate_function) (connection_fd);
      /* We're done with the module.  */
      module_close (module);
    }
}

/* Handle a client connection on the file descriptor CONNECTION_FD.  */

static void handle_connection (int connection_fd)
{
  char buffer[256];
  ssize_t bytes_read;

  /* Read some data from the client.  */
  bytes_read = read (connection_fd, buffer, sizeof (buffer) - 1);
  if (bytes_read > 0) {
    char method[sizeof (buffer)];
    char url[sizeof (buffer)];
    char protocol[sizeof (buffer)];

    /* Some data was read successfully.  NUL-terminate the buffer so
       we can use string operations on it.  */
    buffer[bytes_read] = '\0';
    /* The first line the client sends is the HTTP request, which is
       composed of a method, the requested page, and the protocol
       version.  */
    sscanf (buffer, "%s %s %s", method, url, protocol);
    /* The client may send various header information following the
       request.  For this HTTP implementation, we don't care about it.
       However, we need to read any data the client tries to send.  Keep
       on reading data until we get to the end of the header, which is
       delimited by a blank line.  HTTP specifies CR/LF as the line
       delimiter.  */
    while (strstr (buffer, "\r\n\r\n") == NULL)
```

```
      bytes_read = read (connection_fd, buffer, sizeof (buffer));
      /* Make sure the last read didn't fail.  If it did, there's a
         problem with the connection, so give up.  */
      if (bytes_read == -1) {
        close (connection_fd);
        return;
      }
      /* Check the protocol field.  We understand HTTP versions 1.0 and
         1.1.  */
      if (strcmp (protocol, "HTTP/1.0") && strcmp (protocol, "HTTP/1.1")) {
        /* We don't understand this protocol.  Report a bad response.  */
        write (connection_fd, bad_request_response,
               sizeof (bad_request_response));
      }
      else if (strcmp (method, "GET")) {
        /* This server only implements the GET method.  The client
           specified some other method, so report the failure.  */
        char response[1024];

        snprintf (response, sizeof (response),
                  bad_method_response_template, method);
        write (connection_fd, response, strlen (response));
      }
      else
        /* A valid request.  Process it.  */
        handle_get (connection_fd, url);
    }
    else if (bytes_read == 0)
      /* The client closed the connection before sending any data.
         Nothing to do.  */
      ;
    else
      /* The call to read failed.  */
      system_error ("read");
}


void server_run (struct in_addr local_address, uint16_t port)
{
  struct sockaddr_in socket_address;
  int rval;
  struct sigaction sigchld_action;
  int server_socket;

  /* Install a handler for SIGCHLD that cleans up child processes that
     have terminated.  */
  memset (&sigchld_action, 0, sizeof (sigchld_action));
  sigchld_action.sa_handler = &clean_up_child_process;
  sigaction (SIGCHLD, &sigchld_action, NULL);
```

continues

Listing 11.4 **Continued**

```
/* Create a TCP socket.  */
server_socket = socket (PF_INET, SOCK_STREAM, 0);
if (server_socket == -1)
  system_error ("socket");
/* Construct a socket address structure for the local address on
   which we want to listen for connections.  */
memset (&socket_address, 0, sizeof (socket_address));
socket_address.sin_family = AF_INET;
socket_address.sin_port = port;
socket_address.sin_addr = local_address;
/* Bind the socket to that address.  */
rval = bind (server_socket, &socket_address, sizeof (socket_address));
if (rval != 0)
  system_error ("bind");
/*  Instruct the socket to accept connections.  */
rval = listen (server_socket, 10);
if (rval != 0)
  system_error ("listen");

if (verbose) {
  /* In verbose mode, display the local address and port number
     we're listening on.  */
  socklen_t address_length;

  /* Find the socket's local address.  */
  address_length = sizeof (socket_address);
  rval = getsockname (server_socket, &socket_address, &address_length);
  assert (rval == 0);
  /* Print a message.  The port number needs to be converted from
     network byte order (big endian) to host byte order.  */
  printf ("server listening on %s:%d\n",
          inet_ntoa (socket_address.sin_addr),
          (int) ntohs (socket_address.sin_port));
}

/* Loop forever, handling connections.  */
while (1) {
  struct sockaddr_in remote_address;
  socklen_t address_length;
  int connection;
  pid_t child_pid;

  /* Accept a connection.  This call blocks until a connection is
     ready.  */
  address_length = sizeof (remote_address);
  connection = accept (server_socket, &remote_address, &address_length);
  if (connection == -1) {
    /* The call to accept failed.  */
    if (errno == EINTR)
```

```
        /* The call was interrupted by a signal.  Try again.  */
        continue;
      else
        /* Something else went wrong.  */
        system_error ("accept");
  }

  /* We have a connection.  Print a message if we're running in
     verbose mode.  */
  if (verbose) {
    socklen_t address_length;

    /* Get the remote address of the connection.  */
    address_length = sizeof (socket_address);
    rval = getpeername (connection, &socket_address, &address_length);
    assert (rval == 0);
    /* Print a message.  */
    printf ("connection accepted from %s\n",
            inet_ntoa (socket_address.sin_addr));
  }

  /* Fork a child process to handle the connection.  */
  child_pid = fork ();
  if (child_pid == 0) {
    /* This is the child process.  It shouldn't use stdin or stdout,
       so close them.  */
    close (STDIN_FILENO);
    close (STDOUT_FILENO);
    /* Also this child process shouldn't do anything with the
       listening socket.  */
    close (server_socket);
    /* Handle a request from the connection.  We have our own copy
       of the connected socket descriptor.  */
    handle_connection (connection);
    /* All done; close the connection socket, and end the child
       process.  */
    close (connection);
    exit (0);
  }
  else if (child_pid > 0) {
    /* This is the parent process.  The child process handles the
       connection, so we don't need our copy of the connected socket
       descriptor.  Close it.  Then continue with the loop and
       accept another connection.  */
    close (connection);
  }
  else
    /* Call to fork failed.  */
    system_error ("fork");
  }
}
```

These are the functions in `server.c`:

- `server_run` is the main entry point for running the server. This function starts the server and begins accepting connections, and does not return unless a serious error occurs. The server uses a TCP stream server socket (see Section 5.5.3, "Servers," in Chapter 5, "Interprocess Communication").

  The first argument to `server_run` specifies the local address at which connections are accepted. A GNU/Linux computer may have multiple network addresses, and each address may be bound to a different network interface.[2] To restrict the server to accept connections from a particular interface, specify the corresponding network address. Specify the local address `INADDR_ANY` to accept connections for any local address.

  The second argument to `server_run` is the port number on which to accept connections. If the port number is already in use, or if it corresponds to a privileged port and the server is not being run with superuser privilege, the server fails. The special value 0 instructs Linux to select an unused port automatically. See the `inet` man page for more information about Internet-domain addresses and port numbers.

  The server handles each client connection in a child process created with `fork` (see Section 3.2.2, "Using `fork` and `exec`," in Chapter 3, "Processes"). The main (parent) process continues accepting new connections while existing ones are being serviced. The child process invokes `handle_connection` and then closes the connection socket and exits.

- `handle_connection` processes a single client connection, using the socket file descriptor passed as its argument. This function reads data from the socket and attempts to interpret this as an HTTP page request.

  The server processes only HTTP version 1.0 and version 1.1 requests. When faced with a different protocol or version, it responds by sending the HTTP result code 400 and the message `bad_request_response`. The server understands only the HTTP GET method. If the client requests any other method, the server responds by sending the HTTP result code 501 and the message `bad_method_response_template`.

- If the client sends a well-formed GET request, `handle_connection` calls `handle_get` to service it. This function attempts to load a server module with a name generated from the requested page. For example, if the client requests the page named information, it attempts to load a server module named `information.so`. If the module can't be loaded, `handle_get` sends the client the HTTP result code 404 and the message `not_found_response_template`.

2. Your computer might be configured to include such interfaces as `eth0`, an Ethernet card; `lo`, the local (loopback) network; or `ppp0`, a dial-up network connection.

If the client sends a page request that corresponds to a server module, `handle_get` sends a result code 200 header to the client, which indicates that the request was processed successfully and invokes the module's `module_generate` function. This function generates the HTML source for a Web page and sends it to the Web client.

- `server_run` installs `clean_up_child_process` as the signal handler for `SIGCHLD`. This function simply cleans up terminated child processes (see Section 3.4.4, "Cleaning Up Children Asynchronously," in Chapter 3).

11.2.4   The Main Program

`main.c` (see Listing 11.5) provides the `main` function for the server program. Its responsibility is to parse command-line options, detect and report command-line errors, and configure and run the server.

Listing 11.5   (*main.c*) **Main Server Program and Command-Line Parsing**

```
#include <assert.h>
#include <getopt.h>
#include <netdb.h>
#include <stdio.h>
#include <stdlib.h>
#include <string.h>
#include <sys/stat.h>
#include <unistd.h>

#include "server.h"

/* Description of long options for getopt_long.  */

static const struct option long_options[] = {
  { "address",        1, NULL, 'a' },
  { "help",           0, NULL, 'h' },
  { "module-dir",     1, NULL, 'm' },
  { "port",           1, NULL, 'p' },
  { "verbose",        0, NULL, 'v' },
};

/* Description of short options for getopt_long.  */

static const char* const short_options = "a:hm:p:v";

/* Usage summary text.  */

static const char* const usage_template =
  "Usage: %s [ options ]\n"
  "  -a, --address ADDR      Bind to local address (by default, bind\n"
  "                            to all local addresses).\n"
```

continues

Listing 11.5   **Continued**

```
"  -h, --help                  Print this information.\n"
"  -m, --module-dir DIR        Load modules from specified directory\n"
"                                (by default, use executable directory).\n"
"  -p, --port PORT             Bind to specified port.\n"
"  -v, --verbose               Print verbose messages.\n";

/* Print usage information and exit.  If IS_ERROR is nonzero, write to
   stderr and use an error exit code.  Otherwise, write to stdout and
   use a non-error termination code.  Does not return.  */

static void print_usage (int is_error)
{
  fprintf (is_error ? stderr : stdout, usage_template, program_name);
  exit (is_error ? 1 : 0);
}

int main (int argc, char* const argv[])
{
  struct in_addr local_address;
  uint16_t port;
  int next_option;

  /* Store the program name, which we'll use in error messages.  */
  program_name = argv[0];

  /* Set defaults for options.  Bind the server to all local addresses,
     and assign an unused port automatically.  */
  local_address.s_addr = INADDR_ANY;
  port = 0;
  /* Don't print verbose messages.  */
  verbose = 0;
  /* Load modules from the directory containing this executable.  */
  module_dir = get_self_executable_directory ();
  assert (module_dir != NULL);

  /* Parse options.  */
  do {
    next_option =
      getopt_long (argc, argv, short_options, long_options, NULL);
    switch (next_option) {
    case 'a':
      /* User specified -a or --address.  */
      {
        struct hostent* local_host_name;

        /* Look up the hostname the user specified.  */
        local_host_name = gethostbyname (optarg);
        if (local_host_name == NULL || local_host_name->h_length == 0)
```

```
                        /* Could not resolve the name.  */
                        error (optarg, "invalid host name");
                      else
                        /* Hostname is OK, so use it.  */
                        local_address.s_addr =
                          *((int*) (local_host_name->h_addr_list[0]));
                  }
                  break;

                case 'h':
                  /* User specified -h or --help.  */
                  print_usage (0);

                case 'm':
                  /* User specified -m or --module-dir.  */
                  {
                    struct stat dir_info;

                    /* Check that it exists.  */
                    if (access (optarg, F_OK) != 0)
                      error (optarg, "module directory does not exist");
                    /* Check that it is accessible.  */
                    if (access (optarg, R_OK | X_OK) != 0)
                      error (optarg, "module directory is not accessible");
                    /* Make sure that it is a directory.  */
                    if (stat (optarg, &dir_info) != 0 || !S_ISDIR (dir_info.st_mode))
                      error (optarg, "not a directory");
                    /* It looks OK, so use it.  */
                    module_dir = strdup (optarg);
                  }
                  break;

                case 'p':
                  /* User specified -p or --port.  */
                  {
                    long value;
                    char* end;

                    value = strtol (optarg, &end, 10);
                    if (*end != '\0')
                      /* The user specified nondigits in the port number.  */
                      print_usage (1);
                    /* The port number needs to be converted to network (big endian)
                       byte order.  */
                    port = (uint16_t) htons (value);
                  }
                  break;

                case 'v':
                  /* User specified -v or --verbose.  */
                  verbose = 1;
                  break;
```

continues

Listing 11.5 **Continued**

```
    case '?':
      /* User specified an unrecognized option.  */
      print_usage (1);

    case -1:
      /* Done with options.  */
      break;

    default:
      abort ();
    }
} while (next_option != -1);

/* This program takes no additional arguments.  Issue an error if the
   user specified any.  */
if (optind != argc)
  print_usage (1);

/* Print the module directory, if we're running verbose.  */
if (verbose)
  printf ("modules will be loaded from %s\n", module_dir);

/* Run the server.  */
server_run (local_address, port);

return 0;
}
```

main.c contains these functions:

- main invokes getopt_long (see Section 2.1.3, "Using getopt_long," in Chapter 2) to parse command-line options. It provides both long and short option forms, the former in the long_options array and the latter in the short_options string.

  The default value for the server port is 0 and for a local address is INADDR_ANY. These can be overridden by the --port (-p) and --address (-a) options, respectively. If the user specifies an address, main calls the library function gethostbyname to convert it to a numerical Internet address.[3]

  The default value for the directory from which to load server modules is the directory containing the server executable, as determined by get_self_executable_directory. The user may override this with the --module-dir (-m) option; main makes sure that the specified directory is accessible.

  By default, verbose messages are not printed. The user may enable them by specifying the --verbose (-v) option.

---

3. gethostbyname performs name resolution using DNS, if necessary.

- If the user specifies the `--help` (`-h`) option or specifies invalid options, `main` invokes `print_usage`, which prints a usage summary and exits.

11.3 Modules

We provide four modules to demonstrate the kind of functionality you could implement using this server implementation. Implementing your own server module is as simple as defining a `module_generate` function to return the appropriate HTML text.

11.3.1 Show Wall-Clock Time

The `time.so` module (see Listing 11.6) generates a simple page containing the server's local wall-clock time. This module's `module_generate` calls `gettimeofday` to obtain the current time (see Section 8.7, "gettimeofday: Wall-Clock Time," in Chapter 8, "Linux System Calls") and uses `localtime` and `strftime` to generate a text representation of it. This representation is embedded in the HTML template `page_template`.

Listing 11.6   (*time.c*) **Server Module to Show Wall-Clock Time**

```
#include <assert.h>
#include <stdio.h>
#include <sys/time.h>
#include <time.h>

#include "server.h"

/* A template for the HTML page this module generates.   */

static char* page_template =
  "<html>\n"
  " <head>\n"
  "  <meta http-equiv=\"refresh\" content=\"5\">\n"
  " </head>\n"
  " <body>\n"
  "  <p>The current time is %s.</p>\n"
  " </body>\n"
  "</html>\n";

void module_generate (int fd)
{
  struct timeval tv;
  struct tm* ptm;
  char time_string[40];
  FILE* fp;

  /* Obtain the time of day, and convert it to a tm struct.  */
  gettimeofday (&tv, NULL);
  ptm = localtime (&tv.tv_sec);
```

continues

Listing 11.6 **Continued**

```
      /* Format the date and time, down to a single second.  */
      strftime (time_string, sizeof (time_string), "%H:%M:%S", ptm);

      /* Create a stream corresponding to the client socket file
         descriptor.  */
      fp = fdopen (fd, "w");
      assert (fp != NULL);
      /* Generate the HTML output.  */
      fprintf (fp, page_template, time_string);
      /* All done; flush the stream.  */
      fflush (fp);
    }
```

This module uses standard C library I/O routines for convenience. The `fdopen` call generates a stream pointer (`FILE*`) corresponding to the client socket file descriptor (see Section B.4, "Relation to Standard C Library I/O Functions," in Appendix B, "Low-Level I/O"). The module writes to it using `fprintf` and flushes it using `fflush` to prevent the loss of buffered data when the socket is closed.

The HTML page returned by the `time.so` module includes a `<meta>` element in the page header that instructs clients to reload the page every 5 seconds. This way the client displays the current time.

11.3.2 Show the GNU/Linux Distribution

The `issue.so` module (see Listing 11.7) displays information about the GNU/Linux distribution running on the server. This information is traditionally stored in the file `/etc/issue`. This module sends the contents of this file, wrapped in a `<pre>` element of an HTML page.

Listing 11.7 **(*issue.c*) Server Module to Display GNU/Linux Distribution Information**

```
#include <fcntl.h>
#include <string.h>
#include <sys/sendfile.h>
#include <sys/stat.h>
#include <sys/types.h>
#include <unistd.h>

#include "server.h"

/* HTML source for the start of the page we generate.  */

static char* page_start =
  "<html>\n"
  " <body>\n"
```

```
  "  <pre>\n";

/* HTML source for the end of the page we generate.  */

static char* page_end =
  "  </pre>\n"
  " </body>\n"
  "</html>\n";

/* HTML source for the page indicating there was a problem opening
   /proc/issue.  */

static char* error_page =
  "<html>\n"
  " <body>\n"
  "  <p>Error: Could not open /proc/issue.</p>\n"
  " </body>\n"
  "</html>\n";

/* HTML source indicating an error.  */

static char* error_message = "Error reading /proc/issue.";

void module_generate (int fd)
{
  int input_fd;
  struct stat file_info;
  int rval;

  /* Open /etc/issue.  */
  input_fd = open ("/etc/issue", O_RDONLY);
  if (input_fd == -1)
    system_error ("open");
  /* Obtain file information about it.  */
  rval = fstat (input_fd, &file_info);

  if (rval == -1)
    /* Either we couldn't open the file or we couldn't read from it.  */
    write (fd, error_page, strlen (error_page));
  else {
    int rval;
    off_t offset = 0;

    /* Write the start of the page.  */
    write (fd, page_start, strlen (page_start));
    /* Copy from /proc/issue to the client socket.  */
    rval = sendfile (fd, input_fd, &offset, file_info.st_size);
    if (rval == -1)
      /* Something went wrong sending the contents of /proc/issue.
         Write an error message.  */
      write (fd, error_message, strlen (error_message));
```

continues

Listing 11.7   **Continued**

```
    /* End the page.   */
    write (fd, page_end, strlen (page_end));
  }

  close (input_fd);
}
```

The module first tries to open /etc/issue. If that file can't be opened, the module
sends an error page to the client. Otherwise, the module sends the start of the
HTML page, contained in page_start. Then it sends the contents of /etc/issue using
sendfile (see Section 8.12, "sendfile: Fast Data Transfers," in Chapter 8). Finally, it
sends the end of the HTML page, contained in page_end.

You can easily adapt this module to send the contents of another file. If the file
contains a complete HTML page, simply omit the code that sends the contents of
page_start and page_end. You could also adapt the main server implementation to
serve static files, in the manner of a traditional Web server. Using sendfile provides an
extra degree of efficiency.

11.3.3   Show Free Disk Space

The diskfree.so module (see Listing 11.8) generates a page displaying information
about free disk space on the file systems mounted on the server computer. This generated information is simply the output of invoking the df -h command. Like issue.so,
this module wraps the output in a <pre> element of an HTML page.

Listing 11.8   (*diskfree.c*) **Server Module to Display Information About Free Disk
Space**

```
#include <stdlib.h>
#include <string.h>
#include <sys/types.h>
#include <sys/wait.h>
#include <unistd.h>

#include "server.h"

/* HTML source for the start of the page we generate.   */

static char* page_start =
  "<html>\n"
  " <body>\n"
  "   <pre>\n";
```

```
/* HTML source for the end of the page we generate.  */

static char* page_end =
  "  </pre>\n"
  " </body>\n"
  "</html>\n";

void module_generate (int fd)
{
  pid_t child_pid;
  int rval;

  /* Write the start of the page.  */
  write (fd, page_start, strlen (page_start));
  /* Fork a child process.  */
  child_pid = fork ();
  if (child_pid == 0) {
    /* This is the child process.  */
    /* Set up an argument list for the invocation of df.  */
    char* argv[] = { "/bin/df", "-h", NULL };

    /* Duplicate stdout and stderr to send data to the client socket.  */
    rval = dup2 (fd, STDOUT_FILENO);
    if (rval == -1)
      system_error ("dup2");
    rval = dup2 (fd, STDERR_FILENO);
    if (rval == -1)
      system_error ("dup2");
    /* Run df to show the free space on mounted file systems.  */
    execv (argv[0], argv);
    /* A call to execv does not return unless an error occurred.  */
    system_error ("execv");
  }
  else if (child_pid > 0) {
    /* This is the parent process.  Wait for the child process to
       finish.  */
    rval = waitpid (child_pid, NULL, 0);
    if (rval == -1)
      system_error ("waitpid");
  }
  else
    /* The call to fork failed.  */
    system_error ("fork");
  /* Write the end of the page.  */
  write (fd, page_end, strlen (page_end));
}
```

While `issue.so` sends the contents of a file using `sendfile`, this module must invoke a command and redirect its output to the client. To do this, the module follows these steps:

1. First, the module creates a child process using `fork` (see Section 3.2.2, "Using `fork` and `exec`," in Chapter 3).

2. The child process copies the client socket file descriptor to file descriptors `STDOUT_FILENO` and `STDERR_FILENO`, which correspond to standard output and standard error (see Section 2.1.4, "Standard I/O," in Chapter 2). The file descriptors are copied using the `dup2` call (see Section 5.4.3, "Redirecting the Standard Input, Output, and Error Streams," in Chapter 5). All further output from the process to either of these streams is sent to the client socket.

3. The child process invokes the `df` command with the `-h` option by calling `execv` (see Section 3.2.2, "Using `fork` and `exec`," in Chapter 3).

4. The parent process waits for the child process to exit by calling `waitpid` (see Section 3.4.2, "The `wait` System Calls," in Chapter 3).

You could easily adapt this module to invoke a different command and redirect its output to the client.

11.3.4 Summarize Running Processes

The `processes.so` module (see Listing 11.9) is a more extensive server module implementation. It generates a page containing a table that summarizes the processes currently running on the server system. Each process is represented by a row in the table that lists the PID, the executable program name, the owning user and group names, and the resident set size.

Listing 11.9   (*processes.c*) **Server Module to Summarize Processes**

```
#include <assert.h>
#include <dirent.h>
#include <fcntl.h>
#include <grp.h>
#include <pwd.h>
#include <stdio.h>
#include <stdlib.h>
#include <string.h>
#include <sys/stat.h>
#include <sys/types.h>
#include <sys/uio.h>
#include <unistd.h>

#include "server.h"

/* Set *UID and *GID to the owning user ID and group ID, respectively,
   of process PID.  Return 0 on success, nonzero on failure.  */
```

```
static int get_uid_gid (pid_t pid, uid_t* uid, gid_t* gid)
{
  char dir_name[64];
  struct stat dir_info;
  int rval;

  /* Generate the name of the process's directory in /proc.  */
  snprintf (dir_name, sizeof (dir_name), "/proc/%d", (int) pid);
  /* Obtain information about the directory.  */
  rval = stat (dir_name, &dir_info);
  if (rval != 0)
    /* Couldn't find it; perhaps this process no longer exists.  */
    return 1;
  /* Make sure it's a directory; anything else is unexpected.  */
  assert (S_ISDIR (dir_info.st_mode));

  /* Extract the IDs we want.  */
  *uid = dir_info.st_uid;
  *gid = dir_info.st_gid;
  return 0;
}

/* Return the name of user UID.  The return value is a buffer that the
   caller must allocate with free.  UID must be a valid user ID.  */

static char* get_user_name (uid_t uid)
{
  struct passwd* entry;

  entry = getpwuid (uid);
  if (entry == NULL)
    system_error ("getpwuid");
  return xstrdup (entry->pw_name);
}

/* Return the name of group GID.  The return value is a buffer that the
   caller must allocate with free.  GID must be a valid group ID.  */

static char* get_group_name (gid_t gid)
{
  struct group* entry;

  entry = getgrgid (gid);
  if (entry == NULL)
    system_error ("getgrgid");
  return xstrdup (entry->gr_name);
}
```

continues

Listing 11.9   **Continued**

```
/* Return the name of the program running in process PID, or NULL on
   error.  The return value is a newly allocated buffer which the caller
   must deallocate with free.  */

static char* get_program_name (pid_t pid)
{
  char file_name[64];
  char status_info[256];
  int fd;
  int rval;
  char* open_paren;
  char* close_paren;
  char* result;

  /* Generate the name of the "stat" file in the process's /proc
     directory, and open it.  */
  snprintf (file_name, sizeof (file_name), "/proc/%d/stat", (int) pid);
  fd = open (file_name, O_RDONLY);
  if (fd == -1)
    /* Couldn't open the stat file for this process.  Perhaps the
       process no longer exists.  */
    return NULL;
  /* Read the contents.  */
  rval = read (fd, status_info, sizeof (status_info) - 1);
  close (fd);
  if (rval <= 0)
    /* Couldn't read, for some reason; bail.  */
    return NULL;
  /* NUL-terminate the file contents.  */
  status_info[rval] = '\0';

  /* The program name is the second element of the file contents and is
     surrounded by parentheses.  Find the positions of the parentheses
     in the file contents.  */
  open_paren = strchr (status_info, '(');
  close_paren = strchr (status_info, ')');
  if (open_paren == NULL
      || close_paren == NULL
      || close_paren < open_paren)
    /* Couldn't find them; bail.  */
    return NULL;
  /* Allocate memory for the result.  */
  result = (char*) xmalloc (close_paren - open_paren);
  /* Copy the program name into the result.  */
  strncpy (result, open_paren + 1, close_paren - open_paren - 1);
  /* strncpy doesn't NUL-terminate the result, so do it here.  */
  result[close_paren - open_paren - 1] = '\0';
  /* All done.  */
  return result;
}
```

```
/* Return the resident set size (RSS), in kilobytes, of process PID.
   Return -1 on failure.  */

static int get_rss (pid_t pid)
{
  char file_name[64];
  int fd;
  char mem_info[128];
  int rval;
  int rss;

  /* Generate the name of the process's "statm" entry in its /proc
     directory.  */
  snprintf (file_name, sizeof (file_name), "/proc/%d/statm", (int) pid);
  /* Open it.  */
  fd = open (file_name, O_RDONLY);
  if (fd == -1)
    /* Couldn't open it; perhaps this process no longer exists.  */
    return -1;
  /* Read the file's contents.  */
  rval = read (fd, mem_info, sizeof (mem_info) - 1);
  close (fd);
  if (rval <= 0)
    /* Couldn't read the contents; bail.  */
    return -1;
  /* NUL-terminate the contents.  */
  mem_info[rval] = '\0';
  /* Extract the RSS.  It's the second item.  */
  rval = sscanf (mem_info, "%*d %d", &rss);
  if (rval != 1)
    /* The contents of statm are formatted in a way we don't understand.  */
    return -1;

  /* The values in statm are in units of the system's page size.
     Convert the RSS to kilobytes.  */
  return rss * getpagesize () / 1024;
}

/* Generate an HTML table row for process PID.  The return value is a
   pointer to a buffer that the caller must deallocate with free, or
   NULL if an error occurs.  */

static char* format_process_info (pid_t pid)
{
  int rval;
  uid_t uid;
  gid_t gid;
  char* user_name;
  char* group_name;
  int rss;
  char* program_name;
```

continues

Listing 11.9   **Continued**

```
  size_t result_length;
  char* result;

  /* Obtain the process's user and group IDs.  */
  rval = get_uid_gid (pid, &uid, &gid);
  if (rval != 0)
    return NULL;
  /* Obtain the process's RSS.  */
  rss = get_rss (pid);
  if (rss == -1)
    return NULL;
  /* Obtain the process's program name.  */
  program_name = get_program_name (pid);
  if (program_name == NULL)
    return NULL;
  /* Convert user and group IDs to corresponding names.  */
  user_name = get_user_name (uid);
  group_name = get_group_name (gid);

  /* Compute the length of the string we'll need to hold the result, and
     allocate memory to hold it.  */
  result_length = strlen (program_name)
    + strlen (user_name) + strlen (group_name) + 128;
  result = (char*) xmalloc (result_length);
  /* Format the result.  */
  snprintf (result, result_length,
            "<tr><td align=\"right\">%d</td><td><tt>%s</tt></td><td>%s</td>"
            "<td>%s</td><td align=\"right\">%d</td></tr>\n",
            (int) pid, program_name, user_name, group_name, rss);
  /* Clean up.  */
  free (program_name);
  free (user_name);
  free (group_name);
  /* All done.  */
  return result;
}

/* HTML source for the start of the process listing page.  */

static char* page_start =
  "<html>\n"
  " <body>\n"
  "  <table cellpadding=\"4\" cellspacing=\"0\" border=\"1\">\n"
  "   <thead>\n"
  "    <tr>\n"
  "     <th>PID</th>\n"
  "     <th>Program</th>\n"
  "     <th>User</th>\n"
  "     <th>Group</th>\n"
```

```
"    <th>RSS (KB)</th>\n"
"    </tr>\n"
"   </thead>\n"
"   <tbody>\n";

/* HTML source for the end of the process listing page.  */

static char* page_end =
"   </tbody>\n"
"  </table>\n"
" </body>\n"
"</html>\n";

void module_generate (int fd)
{
  size_t i;
  DIR* proc_listing;

  /* Set up an iovec array.  We'll fill this with buffers that'll be
     part of our output, growing it dynamically as necessary.  */

  /* The number of elements in the array that we've used.  */
  size_t vec_length = 0;
  /* The allocated size of the array.  */
  size_t vec_size = 16;
  /* The array of iovcec elements.  */
  struct iovec* vec =
    (struct iovec*) xmalloc (vec_size * sizeof (struct iovec));

  /* The first buffer is the HTML source for the start of the page.  */
  vec[vec_length].iov_base = page_start;
  vec[vec_length].iov_len = strlen (page_start);
  ++vec_length;

  /* Start a directory listing for /proc.  */
  proc_listing = opendir ("/proc");
  if (proc_listing == NULL)
    system_error ("opendir");

  /* Loop over directory entries in /proc.  */
  while (1) {
    struct dirent* proc_entry;
    const char* name;
    pid_t pid;
    char* process_info;

    /* Get the next entry in /proc.  */
    proc_entry = readdir (proc_listing);
    if (proc_entry == NULL)
      /* We've hit the end of the listing.  */
      break;
```

continues

Listing 11.9 **Continued**

```
  /* If this entry is not composed purely of digits, it's not a
     process directory, so skip it.  */
  name = proc_entry->d_name;
  if (strspn (name, "0123456789") != strlen (name))
    continue;
  /* The name of the entry is the process ID.  */
  pid = (pid_t) atoi (name);
  /* Generate HTML for a table row describing this process.  */
  process_info = format_process_info (pid);
  if (process_info == NULL)
    /* Something went wrong.  The process may have vanished while we
       were looking at it.  Use a placeholder row instead.  */
    process_info = "<tr><td colspan=\"5\">ERROR</td></tr>";

  /* Make sure the iovec array is long enough to hold this buffer
     (plus one more because we'll add an extra element when we're done
     listing processes).  If not, grow it to twice its current size.  */
  if (vec_length == vec_size - 1) {
    vec_size *= 2;
    vec = xrealloc (vec, vec_size * sizeof (struct iovec));
  }
  /* Store this buffer as the next element of the array.  */
  vec[vec_length].iov_base = process_info;
  vec[vec_length].iov_len = strlen (process_info);
  ++vec_length;
}

/* End the directory listing operation.  */
closedir (proc_listing);

/* Add one last buffer with HTML that ends the page.  */
vec[vec_length].iov_base = page_end;
vec[vec_length].iov_len = strlen (page_end);
++vec_length;

/* Output the entire page to the client file descriptor all at once.  */
writev (fd, vec, vec_length);

/* Deallocate the buffers we created.  The first and last are static
   and should not be deallocated.  */
for (i = 1; i < vec_length - 1; ++i)
  free (vec[i].iov_base);
/* Deallocate the iovec array.  */
free (vec);
}
```

Gathering process data and formatting it as an HTML table is broken down into several simpler operations:

- `get_uid_gid` extracts the IDs of the owning user and group of a process. To do this, the function invokes `stat` (see Section B.2, "stat," in Appendix B) on the process's subdirectory in `/proc` (see Section 7.2, "Process Entries," in Chapter 7). The user and group that own this directory are identical to the process's owning user and group.

- `get_user_name` returns the username corresponding to a UID. This function simply calls the C library function `getpwuid`, which consults the system's `/etc/passwd` file and returns a copy of the result. `get_group_name` returns the group name corresponding to a GID. It uses the `getgrgid` call.

- `get_program_name` returns the name of the program running in a specified process. This information is extracted from the `stat` entry in the process's directory under `/proc` (see Section 7.2, "Process Entries," in Chapter 7). We use this entry rather than examining the `exe` symbolic link (see Section 7.2.4, "Process Executable," in Chapter 7) or `cmdline` entry (see Section 7.2.2, "Process Argument List," in Chapter 7) because the latter two are inaccessible if the process running the server isn't owned by the same user as the process being examined. Also, reading from `stat` doesn't force Linux to page the process under examination back into memory, if it happens to be swapped out.

- `get_rss` returns the resident set size of a process. This information is available as the second element in the contents of the process's `statm` entry (see Section 7.2.6, "Process Memory Statistics," in Chapter 7) in its `/proc` subdirectory.

- `format_process_info` generates a string containing HTML elements for a single table row, representing a single process. After calling the functions listed previously to obtain this information, it allocates a buffer and generates HTML using `snprintf`.

- `module_generate` generates the entire HTML page, including the table. The output consists of one string containing the start of the page and the table (in `page_start`), one string for each table row (generated by `format_process_info`), and one string containing the end of the table and the page (in `page_end`).

  `module_generate` determines the PIDs of the processes running on the system by examining the contents of `/proc`. It obtains a listing of this directory using `opendir` and `readdir` (see Section B.6, "Reading Directory Contents," in Appendix B). It scans the contents, looking for entries whose names are composed entirely of digits; these are taken to be process entries.

  Potentially a large number of strings must be written to the client socket—one each for the page start and end, plus one for each process. If we were to write each string to the client socket file descriptor with a separate call to `write`, this would generate unnecessary network traffic because each string may be sent in a separate network packet.

To optimize packing of data into packets, we use a single call to `writev` instead (see Section B.3, "Vector Reads and Writes," in Appendix B). To do this, we must construct an array of `struct iovec` objects, `vec`. However, because we do not know the number of processes beforehand, we must start with a small array and expand it as new processes are added. The variable `vec_length` contains the number of elements of `vec` that are used, while `vec_size` contains the allocated size of `vec`. When `vec_length` is about to exceed `vec_size`, we expand `vec` to twice its size by calling `xrealloc`. When we're done with the vector write, we must deallocate all of the dynamically allocated strings pointed to by `vec`, and then `vec` itself.

11.4   Using the Server

If we were planning to distribute this program in source form, maintain it on an ongoing basis, or port it to other platforms, we probably would want to package it using GNU Automake and GNU Autoconf, or a similar configuration automation system. Such tools are outside the scope of this book; for more information about them, consult *GNU Autoconf, Automake, and Libtool* (by Vaughan, Elliston, Tromey, and Taylor, published by New Riders, 2000).

11.4.1   The *Makefile*

Instead of using Autoconf or a similar tool, we provide a simple `Makefile` compatible with GNU Make[4] so that it's easy to compile and link the server and its modules. The `Makefile` is shown in Listing 11.10. See the info page for GNU Make for details of the file's syntax.

Listing 11.10   *(Makefile)* **GNU Make Configuration File for Server Example**

```
### Configuration.  ##################################################

# Default C compiler options.
CFLAGS              = -Wall -g
# C source files for the server.
SOURCES             = server.c module.c common.c main.c
# Corresponding object files.
OBJECTS             = $(SOURCES:.c=.o)
# Server module shared library files.
MODULES             = diskfree.so issue.so processes.so time.so


### Rules.  ##########################################################

# Phony targets don't correspond to files that are built; they're names
# for conceptual build targets.
.PHONY:       all clean
```

4. GNU Make comes installed on GNU/Linux systems.

```
# Default target: build everything.
all:            server $(MODULES)

# Clean up build products.
clean:
        rm -f $(OBJECTS) $(MODULES) server

# The main server program.  Link with -Wl,-export-dyanamic so
# dynamically loaded modules can bind symbols in the program.  Link in
# libdl, which contains calls for dynamic loading.
server:         $(OBJECTS)
        $(CC) $(CFLAGS) -Wl,-export-dynamic -o $@ $^ -ldl

# All object files in the server depend on server.h.  But use the
# default rule for building object files from source files.
$(OBJECTS):     server.h

# Rule for building module shared libraries from the corresponding
# source files.  Compile -fPIC and generate a shared object file.
$(MODULES): \
%.so:           %.c server.h
        $(CC) $(CFLAGS) -fPIC -shared -o $@ $<
```

The Makefile provides these targets:

- all (the default if you invoke make without arguments because it's the first target in the Makefile) includes the server executable and all the modules. The modules are listed in the variable MODULES.
- clean deletes any build products that are produced by the Makefile.
- server links the server executable. The source files listed in the variable SOURCES are compiled and linked in.
- The last rule is a generic pattern for compiling shared object files for server modules from the corresponding source files.

Note that source files for server modules are compiled with the -fPIC option because they are linked into shared libraries (see Section 2.3.2, "Shared Libraries," in Chapter 2).

Also observe that the server executable is linked with the -Wl,-export-dynamic compiler option. With this option, GCC passes the -export-dynamic option to the linker, which creates an executable file that also exports its external symbols as a shared library. This allows modules, which are dynamically loaded as shared libraries, to reference functions from common.c that are linked statically into the server executable.

11.4.2   Building the Server

Building the program is easy. From the directory containing the sources, simply invoke make:

```
% make
cc -Wall -g  -c -o server.o server.c
cc -Wall -g  -c -o module.o module.c
cc -Wall -g  -c -o common.o common.c
cc -Wall -g  -c -o main.o main.c
cc -Wall -g -Wl,-export-dynamic -o server server.o module.o common.o main.o -ldl
cc -Wall -g -fPIC -shared -o diskfree.so diskfree.c
cc -Wall -g -fPIC -shared -o issue.so issue.c
cc -Wall -g -fPIC -shared -o processes.so processes.c
cc -Wall -g -fPIC -shared -o time.so time.c
```

This builds the server program and the server module shared libraries.

```
% ls -l server *.so
-rwxr-xr-x  1 samuel   samuel    25769 Mar 11 01:15 diskfree.so
-rwxr-xr-x  1 samuel   samuel    31184 Mar 11 01:15 issue.so
-rwxr-xr-x  1 samuel   samuel    41579 Mar 11 01:15 processes.so
-rwxr-xr-x  1 samuel   samuel    71758 Mar 11 01:15 server
-rwxr-xr-x  1 samuel   samuel    13980 Mar 11 01:15 time.so
```

11.4.3   Running the Server

To run the server, simply invoke the server executable.

If you do not specify the server port number with the --port (-p) option, Linux will choose one for you; in this case, specify --verbose (-v) to make the server print out the port number in use.

If you do not specify an address with --address (-a), the server runs on all your computer's network addresses. If your computer is attached to a network, that means that others will be capable of accessing the server, provided that they know the correct port number to use and page to request. For security reasons, it's a good idea to specify the localhost address until you're confident that the server works correctly and is not releasing any information that you prefer to not make public. Binding to the localhost causes the server to bind to the local network device (designated "lo")—only programs running on the same computer can connect to it. If you specify a different address, it must be an address that corresponds to your computer:

```
% ./server --address localhost --port 4000
```

The server is now running. Open a browser window, and attempt to contact the server at this port number. Request a page whose name matches one of the modules. For instance, to invoke the diskfree.so module, use this URL:

```
http://localhost:4000/diskfree
```

Instead of 4000, enter the port number you specified (or the port number that Linux chose for you). Press Ctrl+C to kill the server when you're done.

If you didn't specify localhost as the server address, you can also connect to the server with a Web browser running on another computer by using your computer's hostname in the URL—for example:

```
http://host.domain.com:4000/diskfree
```

If you specify the --verbose (-v) option, the server prints some information at startup and displays the numerical Internet address of each client that connects to it. If you connect via the localhost address, the client address will always be 127.0.0.1.

If you experiment with writing your own server modules, you may place them in a different directory than the one containing the server module. In this case, specify that directory with the --module-dir (-m) option. The server will look in this directory for server modules instead.

If you forget the syntax of the command-line options, invoke server with the --help (-h) option.

```
% ./server --help
Usage: ./server [ options ]
  -a, --address ADDR        Bind to local address (by default, bind
                              to all local addresses).
  -h, --help                Print this information.
  -m, --module-dir DIR      Load modules from specified directory
                              (by default, use executable directory).
  -p, --port PORT           Bind to specified port.
  -v, --verbose             Print verbose messages.
```

11.5   Finishing Up

If you were really planning on releasing this program for general use, you'd need to write documentation for it as well. Many people don't realize that writing good documentation is just as difficult and time-consuming—and just as important—as writing good software. However, software documentation is a subject for another book, so we'll leave you with a few references of where to learn more about documenting GNU/Linux software.

You'd probably want to write a man page for the server program, for instance. This is the first place many users will look for information about a program. Man pages are formatted using a classic UNIX formatting system troff. To view the man page for troff, which describes the format of troff files, invoke the following:

```
% man troff
```

To learn about how GNU/Linux locates man pages, consult the man page for the man command itself by invoking this:

```
% man man
```

You might also want to write info pages, using the GNU Info system, for the server and its modules. Naturally, documentation about the info system comes in info format; to view it, invoke this line:

```
% info info
```

Many GNU/Linux programs come with documentation in plain text or HTML formats as well.

Happy GNU/Linux programming!

III

Appendixes

Other Development Tools

D EVELOPING CORRECT, FAST C OR C++ GNU/LINUX PROGRAMS requires more than just understanding the GNU/Linux operating system and its system calls. In this appendix, we discuss development tools to find runtime errors such as illegal use of dynamically allocated memory and to determine which parts of a program are taking most of the execution time. Analyzing a program's source code can reveal some of this information; by using these runtime tools and actually executing the program, you can find out much more.

A.1   Static Program Analysis

Some programming errors can be detected using static analysis tools that analyze the program's source code. If you invoke GCC with -Wall and -pedantic, the compiler issues warnings about risky or possibly erroneous programming constructions. By eliminating such constructions, you'll reduce the risk of program bugs, and you'll find it easier to compile your programs on different GNU/Linux variants and even on other operating systems.

Using various command options, you can cause GCC to issue warnings about many different types of questionable programming constructs. The -Wall option enables most of these checks. For example, the compiler will produce a warning about a comment that begins within another comment, about an incorrect return type specified for main, and about a non void function omitting a return statement. If you specify the -pedantic option, GCC emits warnings demanded by strict ANSI C and ISO C++ compliance. For example, use of the GNU asm extension causes a warning using this option. A few GNU extensions, such as using alternate keywords beginning with __ (two underscores), will not trigger warning messages. Although the GCC info pages deprecate use of this option, we recommend that you use it anyway and avoid most GNU language extensions because GCC extensions tend to change through time and frequently interact poorly with code optimization.

Listing A.1   (*hello.c*) **Hello World Program**

```
main ()
{
  printf ("Hello, world.\n");
}
```

Consider compiling the "Hello World" program shown in Listing A.1. Though GCC compiles the program without complaint, the source code does not obey ANSI C rules. If you enable warnings by compiling with the -Wall -pedantic, GCC reveals three questionable constructs.

```
% gcc -Wall -pedantic hello.c
hello.c:2: warning: return type defaults to 'int'
hello.c: In function 'main':
hello.c:3: warning: implicit declaration of function 'printf'
hello.c:4: warning: control reaches end of non-void function
```

These warnings indicate that the following problems occurred:

- The return type for main was not specified.
- The function printf is implicitly declared because <stdio.h> is not included.
- The function, implicitly declared to return an int, actually returns no value.

Analyzing a program's source code cannot find all programming mistakes and inefficiencies. In the next section, we present four tools to find mistakes in using dynamically allocated memory. In the subsequent section, we show how to analyze the program's execution time using the gprof profiler.

A.2   Finding Dynamic Memory Errors

When writing a program, you frequently can't know how much memory the program will need when it runs. For example, a line read from a file at runtime might have any finite length. C and C++ programs use `malloc`, `free`, and their variants to dynamically allocate memory while the program is running. The rules for dynamic memory use include these:

- The number of allocation calls (calls to `malloc`) must exactly match the number of deallocation calls (calls to `free`).

- Reads and writes to the allocated memory must occur within the memory, not outside its range.

- The allocated memory cannot be used before it is allocated or after it is deallocated.

Because dynamic memory allocation and deallocation occur at runtime, static program analysis rarely find violations. Instead, memory-checking tools run the program, collecting data to determine if any of these rules have been violated. The violations a tool may find include the following:

- Reading from memory before allocating it
- Writing to memory before allocating it
- Reading before the beginning of allocated memory
- Writing before the beginning of allocated memory
- Reading after the end of allocated memory
- Writing after the end of allocated memory
- Reading from memory after its deallocation
- Writing to memory after its deallocation
- Failing to deallocate allocated memory
- Deallocating the same memory twice
- Deallocating memory that is not allocated

It is also useful to warn about requesting an allocation with 0 bytes, which probably indicates programmer error.

Table A.1 indicates four different tools' diagnostic capabilities. Unfortunately, no single tool diagnoses all the memory use errors. Also, no tool claims to detect reading or writing before allocating memory, but doing so will probably cause a segmentation fault. Deallocating memory twice will probably also cause a segmentation fault. These tools diagnose only errors that actually occur while the program is running. If you run the program with inputs that cause no memory to be allocated, the tools will indicate no memory errors. To test a program thoroughly, you must run the program using different inputs to ensure that every possible path through the program occurs. Also, you may use only one tool at a time, so you'll have to repeat testing with several tools to get the best error checking.

Table A.1   **Capabilities of Dynamic Memory-Checking Tools (X Indicates Detection, and O Indicates Detection for Some Cases)**

Erroneous Behavior	*malloc* Checking	mtrace	ccmalloc	Electric Fence
Read before allocating memory				
Write before allocating memory				
Read before beginning of allocation				X
Write before beginning of allocation	O		O	X
Read after end of allocation				X
Write after end of allocation			X	X
Read after deallocation				X
Write after deallocation				X
Failure to deallocate memory		X	X	
Deallocating memory twice	X		X	
Deallocating nonallocated memory		X	X	
Zero-size memory allocation			X	X

In the sections that follow, we first describe how to use the more easily used `malloc` checking and `mtrace`, and then `ccmalloc` and Electric Fence.

A.2.1   A Program to Test Memory Allocation and Deallocation

We'll use the `malloc-use` program in Listing A.2 to illustrate memory allocation, deallocation, and use. To begin running it, specify the maximum number of allocated memory regions as its only command-line argument. For example, `malloc-use 12` creates an array A with 12 character pointers that do not point to anything. The program accepts five different commands:

- To allocate b bytes pointed to by array entry `A[i]`, enter `a i b`. The array index i can be any non-negative number smaller than the command-line argument. The number of bytes must be non-negative.
- To deallocate memory at array index i, enter `d i`.
- To read the pth character from the allocated memory at index i (as in `A[i][p]`), enter `r i p`. Here, p can have an integral value.
- To write a character to the pth position in the allocated memory at index i, enter `w i p`.
- When finished, enter `q`.

We'll present the program's code later, in Section A.2.7, and illustrate how to use it.

A.2.2 *malloc* Checking

The memory allocation functions provided by the GNU C library can detect writing before the beginning of an allocation and deallocating the same allocation twice. Defining the environment variable MALLOC_CHECK_ to the value 2 causes a program to halt when such an error is detected. (Note the environment variable's ending underscore.) There is no need to recompile the program.

We illustrate diagnosing a write to memory to a position just before the beginning of an allocation.

```
% export MALLOC_CHECK_=2
% ./malloc-use 12
Please enter a command: a 0 10
Please enter a command: w 0 -1
Please enter a command: d 0
Aborted (core dumped)
```

export turns on malloc checking. Specifying the value 2 causes the program to halt as soon as an error is detected.

Using malloc checking is advantageous because the program need not be recompiled, but its capability to diagnose errors is limited. Basically, it checks that the allocator data structures have not been corrupted. Thus, it can detect double deallocation of the same allocation. Also, writing just before the beginning of a memory allocation can usually be detected because the allocator stores the size of each memory allocation just before the allocated region. Thus, writing just before the allocated memory will corrupt this number. Unfortunately, consistency checking can occur only when your program calls allocation routines, not when it accesses memory, so many illegal reads and writes can occur before an error is detected. In the previous example, the illegal write was detected only when the allocated memory was deallocated.

A.2.3 Finding Memory Leaks Using *mtrace*

The mtrace tool helps diagnose the most common error when using dynamic memory: failure to match allocations and deallocations. There are four steps to using mtrace, which is available with the GNU C library:

1. Modify the source code to include <mcheck.h> and to invoke mtrace () as soon as the program starts, at the beginning of main. The call to mtrace turns on tracking of memory allocations and deallocations.

2. Specify the name of a file to store information about all memory allocations and deallocations:

   ```
   % export MALLOC_TRACE=memory.log
   ```

3. Run the program. All memory allocations and deallocations are stored in the logging file.

4. Using the `mtrace` command, analyze the memory allocations and deallocations to ensure that they match.

```
% mtrace my_program $MALLOC_TRACE
```

The messages produced by `mtrace` are relatively easy to understand. For example, for our `malloc-use` example, the output would look like this:

```
- 0000000000 Free 3 was never alloc'd malloc-use.c:39

Memory not freed:
-----------------
    Address     Size    Caller
 0x08049d48      0xc  at malloc-use.c:30
```

These messages indicate an attempt on line 39 of `malloc-use.c` to free memory that was never allocated, and an allocation of memory on line 30 that was never freed.

`mtrace` diagnoses errors by having the executable record all memory allocations and deallocations in the file specified by the `MALLOC_TRACE` environment variable. The executable must terminate normally for the data to be written. The `mtrace` command analyzes this file and lists unmatched allocations and deallocations.

A.2.4 Using *ccmalloc*

The `ccmalloc` library diagnoses dynamic memory errors by replacing `malloc` and `free` with code tracing their use. If the program terminates gracefully, it produces a report of memory leaks and other errors. The `ccmalloc` library was written by Armin Bierce.

You'll probably have to download and install the `ccmalloc` library yourself. Download it from `http://www.inf.ethz.ch/personal/biere/projects/ccmalloc/`, unpack the code, and run `configure`. Run `make` and `make install`, copy the `ccmalloc.cfg` file to the directory where you'll run the program you want to check, and rename the copy to `.ccmalloc`. Now you are ready to use the tool.

The program's object files must be linked with `ccmalloc`'s library and the dynamic linking library. Append `-lccmalloc -ldl` to your link command, for instance.

```
% gcc -g -Wall -pedantic malloc-use.o -o ccmalloc-use -lccmalloc -ldl
```

Execute the program to produce a report. For example, running our `malloc-use` program to allocate but not deallocate memory produces the following report:

```
% ./ccmalloc-use 12
file-name=a.out does not contain valid symbols
trying to find executable in current directory ...
using symbols from 'ccmalloc-use'
(to speed up this search specify 'file ccmalloc-use'
 in the startup file '.ccmalloc')
Please enter a command: a 0 12
Please enter a command: q
```

```
.---------------.
| ccmalloc report |
===========================================================
| total # of |   allocated | deallocated |    garbage |
+------------+-------------+-------------+-------------+
|     bytes |         60 |         48 |        12 |
+------------+-------------+-------------+-------------+
| allocations |          2 |          1 |         1 |
+------------+-------------+-------------+-------------+
| number of checks: 1                                  |
| number of counts: 3                                  |
| retrieving function names for addresses ... done.    |
| reading file info from gdb ... done.                 |
| sorting by number of not reclaimed bytes ... done.   |
| number of call chains: 1                             |
| number of ignored call chains: 0                     |
| number of reported call chains: 1                    |
| number of internal call chains: 1                    |
| number of library call chains: 0                     |
===========================================================
|
*100.0% = 12 Bytes of garbage allocated in 1 allocation
|   |
|   |        0x400389cb in <???>
|   |
|   |        0x08049198 in <main>
|   |                at malloc-use.c:89
|   |
|   |        0x08048fdc in <allocate>
|   |                at malloc-use.c:30
|   |
|   '-----> 0x08049647 in <malloc>
|                    at src/wrapper.c:284
|
'-----------------------------------------------------
```

The last few lines indicate the chain of function calls that allocated memory that was
not deallocated.

To use ccmalloc to diagnose writes before the beginning or after the end of the
allocated region, you'll have to modify the .ccmalloc file in the current directory. This
file is read when the program starts execution.

A.2.5   Electric Fence

Written by Bruce Perens, Electric Fence halts executing programs on the exact
line where a write or a read outside an allocation occurs. This is the only tool that
discovers illegal reads. It is included in most GNU/Linux distributions, but the source
code can be found at http://www.perens.com/FreeSoftware/.

As with `ccmalloc`, your program's object files must be linked with Electric Fence's library by appending `-lefence` to the linking command, for instance:

```
% gcc -g -Wall -pedantic malloc-use.o -o emalloc-use -lefence
```

As the program runs, allocated memory uses are checked for correctness. A violation causes a segmentation fault:

```
% ./emalloc-use 12
  Electric Fence 2.0.5 Copyright (C) 1987-1998 Bruce Perens.
Please enter a command: a 0 12
Please enter a command: r 0 12
Segmentation fault
```

Using a debugger, you can determine the context of the illegal action.

By default, Electric Fence diagnoses only accesses beyond the ends of allocations. To find accesses before the beginning of allocations *instead of* accesses beyond the end of allocations, use this code:

```
% export EF_PROTECT_BELOW=1
```

To find accesses to deallocated memory, set `EF_PROTECT_FREE` to 1. More capabilities are described in the `libefence` manual page.

Electric Fence diagnoses illegal memory accesses by storing each allocation on at least two memory pages. It places the allocation at the end of the first page; any access beyond the end of the allocation, on the second page, causes a segmentation fault. If you set `EF_PROTECT_BELOW` to 1, it places the allocation at the beginning of the second page instead. Because it allocates two memory pages per call to `malloc`, Electric Fence can use an enormous amount of memory. Use this library for debugging only.

A.2.6 Choosing Among the Different Memory-Debugging Tools

We have discussed four separate, incompatible tools to diagnose erroneous use of dynamic memory. How does a GNU/Linux programmer ensure that dynamic memory is correctly used? No tool guarantees diagnosing all errors, but using any of them does increase the probability of finding errors. To ease finding dynamically allocated memory errors, separately develop and test the code that deals with dynamic memory. This reduces the amount of code that you must search for errors. If you are using C++, write a class that handles all dynamic memory use. If you are using C, minimize the number of functions using allocation and deallocation. When testing this code, be sure to use only one tool at a one time because they are incompatible. When testing a program, be sure to vary how the program executes, to test the most commonly executed portions of the code.

Which of the four tools should you use? Because failing to match allocations and deallocations is the most common dynamic memory error, use `mtrace` during initial development. The program is available on all GNU/Linux systems and has been well tested. After ensuring that the number of allocations and deallocations match, use

Electric Fence to find illegal memory accesses. This will eliminate almost all memory errors. When using Electric Fence, you will need to be careful to not perform too many allocations and deallocations because each allocation requires at least two pages of memory. Using these two tools will reveal most memory errors.

A.2.7   Source Code for the Dynamic Memory Program

Listing A.2 shows the source code for a program illustrating dynamic memory allocation, deallocation, and use. See Section A.2.1, "A Program to Test Memory Allocation and Deallocation," for a description of how to use it.

Listing A.2   (*malloc-use.c*) **Dynamic Memory Allocation Checking Example**

```
/* Use C's dynamic memory allocation functions.  */

/* Invoke the program using one command-line argument specifying the
   size of an array.  This array consists of pointers to (possibly)
   allocated arrays.

   When the programming is running, select among the following
   commands:

   o allocate memory:    a <index> <memory-size>
   o deallocate memory: d <index>
   o read from memory:   r <index> <position-within-allocation>
   o write to memory:    w <index> <position-within-allocation>
   o quit:               q

   The user is responsible for obeying (or disobeying) the rules on dynamic
   memory use.  */

#ifdef MTRACE
#include <mcheck.h>
#endif /* MTRACE */
#include <stdio.h>
#include <stdlib.h>
#include <assert.h>

/* Allocate memory with the specified size, returning nonzero upon
   success.  */

void allocate (char** array, size_t size)
{
  *array = malloc (size);
}

/* Deallocate memory.  */

void deallocate (char** array)
```

continues

Listing A.2   **Continued**

```
{
  free ((void*) *array);
}

/* Read from a position in memory.  */

void read_from_memory (char* array, int position)
{
  char character = array[position];
}

/* Write to a position in memory.  */

void write_to_memory (char* array, int position)
{
  array[position] = 'a';
}

int main (int argc, char* argv[])
{
  char** array;
  unsigned array_size;
  char command[32];
  unsigned array_index;
  char command_letter;
  int size_or_position;
  int error = 0;

#ifdef MTRACE
  mtrace ();
#endif /* MTRACE */

  if (argc != 2) {
    fprintf (stderr, "%s: array-size\n", argv[0]);
    return 1;
  }

  array_size = strtoul (argv[1], 0, 0);
  array = (char **) calloc (array_size, sizeof (char *));
  assert (array != 0);

  /* Follow the user's commands.  */
  while (!error) {
    printf ("Please enter a command: ");
    command_letter = getchar ();
    assert (command_letter != EOF);
    switch (command_letter) {

    case 'a':
      fgets (command, sizeof (command), stdin);
      if (sscanf (command, "%u %i", &array_index, &size_or_position) == 2
          && array_index < array_size)
```

```
            allocate (&(array[array_index]), size_or_position);
          else
            error = 1;
          break;

      case 'd':
        fgets (command, sizeof (command), stdin);
        if (sscanf (command, "%u", &array_index) == 1
            && array_index < array_size)
          deallocate (&(array[array_index]));
        else
          error = 1;
        break;

      case 'r':
        fgets (command, sizeof (command), stdin);
        if (sscanf (command, "%u %i", &array_index, &size_or_position) == 2
            && array_index < array_size)
          read_from_memory (array[array_index], size_or_position);
        else
          error = 1;
        break;

      case 'w':
        fgets (command, sizeof (command), stdin);
        if (sscanf (command, "%u %i", &array_index, &size_or_position) == 2
            && array_index < array_size)
          write_to_memory (array[array_index], size_or_position);
        else
          error = 1;
        break;

      case 'q':
        free ((void *) array);
        return 0;

      default:
        error = 1;
      }
    }

    free ((void *) array);
    return 1;
  }
```

A.3   Profiling

Now that your program is (hopefully) correct, we turn to speeding its execution.
Using the profiler gprof, you can determine which functions require the most execution time. This can help you determine which parts of the program to optimize or
rewrite to execute more quickly. It can also help you find errors. For example, you
may find that a particular function is called many more times than you expect.

In this section, we describe how to use `gprof`. Rewriting code to run more quickly requires creativity and careful choice of algorithms.

Obtaining profiling information requires three steps:

1. Compile and link your program to enable profiling.

2. Execute your program to generate profiling data.

3. Use `gprof` to analyze and display the profiling data.

Before we illustrate these steps, we introduce a large enough program to make profiling interesting.

A.3.1   A Simple Calculator

To illustrate profiling, we'll use a simple calculator program. To ensure that the calculator takes a nontrivial amount of time, we'll use unary numbers for calculations, something we would definitely not want to do in a real-world program. Code for this program appears at the end of this chapter.

A *unary number* is represented by as many symbols as its value. For example, the number 1 is represented by "x," 2 by "xx," and 3 by "xxx." Instead of using x's, our program represents a non-negative number using a linked list with as many elements as the number's value. The `number.c` file contains routines to create the number 0, add 1 to a number, subtract 1 from a number, and add, subtract, and multiply numbers. Another function converts a string holding a non-negative decimal number to a unary number, and a function converts from a unary number to an `int`. Addition is implemented using repeated addition of 1s, while subtraction uses repeated removal of 1s. Multiplication is defined using repeated addition. The unary predicates `even` and `odd` each return the unary number for 1 if and only if its one operand is even or odd, respectively; otherwise they return the unary number for 0. The two predicates are mutually recursive. For example, a number is even if it is zero, or if one less than the number is odd.

The calculator accepts one-line postfix expressions[1] and prints each expression's value—for example:

```
% ./calculator
Please enter a postfix expression:
2 3 +
5
Please enter a postfix expression:
2 3 + 4 -
1
```

---

1. In *postfix* notation, a binary operator is placed after its operands instead of between them. So, for example, to multiply 6 and 8, you would use 6 8 ×. To multiply 6 and 8 and then add 5 to the result, you would use 6 8 × 5 +.

The calculator, defined in `calculator.c`, reads each expression, storing intermediate values on a stack of unary numbers, defined in `stack.c`. The stack stores its unary numbers in a linked list.

A.3.2 Collecting Profiling Information

The first step in profiling a program is to annotate its executable to collect profiling information. To do so, use the `-pg` compiler flag when both compiling the object files and linking. For example, consider this code:

```
% gcc -pg -c -o calculator.o calculator.c
% gcc -pg -c -o stack.o stack.c
% gcc -pg -c -o number.o number.c
% gcc -pg calculator.o stack.o number.o -o calculator
```

This enables collecting information about function calls and timing information. To collect line-by-line use information, also specify the debugging flag `-g`. To count basic block executions, such as the number of do-loop iterations, use `-a`.

The second step is to run the program. While it is running, profiling data is collected into a file named `gmon.out`, only for those portions of the code that are exercised. You must vary the program's input or commands to exercise the code sections that you want to profile. The program must terminate normally for the profiling file to be written.

A.3.3 Displaying Profiling Data

Given the name of an executable, `gprof` analyzes the `gmon.out` file to display information about how much time each function required. For example, consider the "flat" profiling data for computing $1787 \times 13 - 1918$ using our calculator program, which is produced by executing `gprof ./calculator`:

```
Flat profile:

Each sample counts as 0.01 seconds.
  %   cumulative   self              self     total
 time   seconds   seconds    calls  ms/call  ms/call  name
 26.07    1.76      1.76 20795463    0.00     0.00  decrement_number
 24.44    3.41      1.65     1787    0.92     1.72  add
 19.85    4.75      1.34 62413059    0.00     0.00  zerop
 15.11    5.77      1.02     1792    0.57     2.05  destroy_number
 14.37    6.74      0.97 20795463    0.00     0.00  add_one
  0.15    6.75      0.01     1788    0.01     0.01  copy_number
  0.00    6.75      0.00     1792    0.00     0.00  make_zero
  0.00    6.75      0.00       11    0.00     0.00  empty_stack
```

Computing the function `decrement_number` and all the functions it calls required 26.07% of the program's total execution time. It was called 20,795,463 times. Each individual execution required 0.0 seconds—namely, a time too small to measure. The `add` function was invoked 1,787 times, presumably to compute the product. Each call required 0.92 seconds. The `copy_number` function was invoked only 1,788 times, while it and the functions it calls required only 0.15% of the total execution time. Sometimes the `mcount` and `profil` functions used by profiling appear in the data.

In addition to the *flat profile data*, which indicates the total time spent within each function, `gprof` produces *call graph data* showing the time spent in each function and its children within the context of a function call chain:

```
index % time    self  children    called     name
                                              <spontaneous>
[1]    100.0    0.00    6.75                  main [1]
                0.00    6.75       2/2             apply_binary_function [2]
                0.00    0.00       1/1792          destroy_number [4]
                0.00    0.00       1/1             number_to_unsigned_int [10]
                0.00    0.00       3/3             string_to_number [12]
                0.00    0.00       3/5             push_stack [16]
                0.00    0.00       1/1             create_stack [18]
                0.00    0.00       1/11            empty_stack [14]
                0.00    0.00       1/5             pop_stack [15]
                0.00    0.00       1/1             clear_stack [17]
-----------------------------------------------------------------
                0.00    6.75       2/2             main [1]
[2]    100.0    0.00    6.75       2          apply_binary_function [2]
                0.00    6.74       1/1             product [3]
                0.00    0.01       4/1792          destroy_number [4]
                0.00    0.00       1/1             subtract [11]
                0.00    0.00       4/11            empty_stack [14]
                0.00    0.00       4/5             pop_stack [15]
                0.00    0.00       2/5             push_stack [16]
-----------------------------------------------------------------
                0.00    6.74       1/1             apply_binary_function [2]
[3]     99.8    0.00    6.74       1          product [3]
                1.02    2.65    1787/1792          destroy_number [4]
                1.65    1.43    1787/1787          add [5]
                0.00    0.00    1788/62413059      zerop [7]
                0.00    0.00       1/1792          make_zero [13]
```

The first frame shows that executing `main` and its children required 100% of the program's 6.75 seconds. It called `apply_binary_function` twice, which was called a total of two times throughout the entire program. Its caller was `<spontaneous>`; this indicates that the profiler was not capable of determining who called `main`. This first frame also shows that `string_to_number` called `push_stack` three times but was called five times throughout the program. The third frame shows that executing `product` and the functions it calls required 99.8% of the program's total execution time. It was invoked once by `apply_binary_function`.

The call graph data displays the total time spent executing a function and its children. If the function call graph is a tree, this number is easy to compute, but recursively defined functions must be treated specially. For example, the `even` function calls `odd`, which calls `even`. Each largest such call cycle is given its own number and is displayed individually in the call graph data. Consider this profiling data from determining whether $1787 \times 13 \times 3$ is even:

```
                0.00    0.02    1/1            main [1]
    [9]    0.1  0.00    0.02    1              apply_unary_function [9]
                0.01    0.00    1/1            even <cycle 1> [13]
                0.00    0.00    1/1806         destroy_number [5]
                0.00    0.00    1/13           empty_stack [17]
                0.00    0.00    1/6            pop_stack [18]
                0.00    0.00    1/6            push_stack [19]
    ------------------------------------------------
    [10]   0.1  0.01    0.00    1+69693        <cycle 1 as a whole> [10]
                0.00    0.00    34847            even <cycle 1> [13]
    ------------------------------------------------
                        34847                  even <cycle 1> [13]
    [11]   0.1  0.01    0.00    34847      odd <cycle 1> [11]
                0.00    0.00    34847/186997954   zerop [7]
                0.00    0.00    1/1806         make_zero [16]
                        34846                  even <cycle 1> [13]
```

The 1+69693 in the [10] frame indicates that cycle 1 was called once, while the functions in the cycle were called 69,693 times. The cycle called the even function. The next entry shows that odd was called 34,847 times by even.

In this section, we have briefly discussed only some of gprof's features. Its info pages contain information about other useful features:

- Use the -s option to sum the execution results from several different runs.
- Use the -c option to identify children that could have been called but were not.
- Use the -l option to display line-by-line profiling information.
- Use the -A option to display source code annotated with percentage execution numbers.

The info pages also provide more information about the interpretation of the analyzed data.

A.3.4 How *gprof* Collects Data

When a profiled executable runs, every time a function is called its count is also incremented. Also, gprof periodically interrupts the executable to determine the currently executing function. These samples determine function execution times. Because Linux's clock ticks are 0.01 seconds apart, these interruptions occur, at most, every 0.01 seconds. Thus, profiles for quickly executing programs or for quickly executing infrequently called functions may be inaccurate. To avoid these inaccuracies, run the executable for longer periods of time, or sum together profile data from several executions. Read about the -s option to sum profiling data in gprof's info pages.

A.3.5   Source Code for the Calculator Program

Listing A.3 presents a program that calculates the value of postfix expressions.

Listing A.3   (*calculator.c*) **Main Calculator Program**

```c
/* Calculate using unary numbers.  */

/* Enter one-line expressions using reverse postfix notation, e.g.,
     602 7 5 - 3 * +
   Nonnegative numbers are entered using decimal notation.  The
   operators "+", "-", and "*" are supported.  The unary operators
   "even" and "odd" return the number 1 if its one operand is even
   or odd, respectively.  Spaces must separate all words.  Negative
   numbers are not supported.  */

#include <stdio.h>
#include <stdlib.h>
#include <string.h>
#include <ctype.h>
#include "definitions.h"


/* Apply the binary function with operands obtained from the stack,
   pushing the answer on the stack.  Return nonzero upon success.  */

int apply_binary_function (number (*function) (number, number),
                           Stack* stack)
{
  number operand1, operand2;
  if (empty_stack (*stack))
    return 0;
  operand2 = pop_stack (stack);
  if (empty_stack (*stack))
    return 0;
  operand1 = pop_stack (stack);
  push_stack (stack, (*function) (operand1, operand2));
  destroy_number (operand1);
  destroy_number (operand2);
  return 1;
}

/* Apply the unary function with an operand obtained from the stack,
   pushing the answer on the stack.  Return nonzero upon success.  */

int apply_unary_function (number (*function) (number),
                          Stack* stack)
{
  number operand;
  if (empty_stack (*stack))
    return 0;
```

```
      operand = pop_stack (stack);
      push_stack (stack, (*function) (operand));
      destroy_number (operand);
      return 1;
    }


int main ()
{
   char command_line[1000];
   char* command_to_parse;
   char* token;
   Stack number_stack = create_stack ();

   while (1) {
     printf ("Please enter a postfix expression:\n");
     command_to_parse = fgets (command_line, sizeof (command_line), stdin);
     if (command_to_parse == NULL)
       return 0;

     token = strtok (command_to_parse, " \t\n");
     command_to_parse = 0;
     while (token != 0) {
       if (isdigit (token[0]))
         push_stack (&number_stack, string_to_number (token));
       else if (((strcmp (token, "+") == 0) &&
                 !apply_binary_function (&add, &number_stack)) ||
                ((strcmp (token, "-") == 0) &&
                 !apply_binary_function (&subtract, &number_stack)) ||
                ((strcmp (token, "*") == 0) &&
                 !apply_binary_function (&product, &number_stack)) ||
                ((strcmp (token, "even") == 0) &&
                 !apply_unary_function (&even, &number_stack)) ||
                ((strcmp (token, "odd") == 0) &&
                 !apply_unary_function (&odd, &number_stack)))
         return 1;
       token = strtok (command_to_parse, " \t\n");
     }
     if (empty_stack (number_stack))
       return 1;
     else {
       number answer = pop_stack (&number_stack);
       printf ("%u\n", number_to_unsigned_int (answer));
       destroy_number (answer);
       clear_stack (&number_stack);
     }
   }

   return 0;
}
```

The functions in Listing A.4 implement unary numbers using empty linked lists.

Listing A.4 *(number.c)* **Unary Number Implementation**

```c
/* Operate on unary numbers.  */

#include <assert.h>
#include <stdlib.h>
#include <limits.h>
#include "definitions.h"

/* Create a number representing zero.  */

number make_zero ()
{
  return 0;
}

/* Return nonzero if the number represents zero.  */

int zerop (number n)
{
  return n == 0;
}

/* Decrease a positive number by 1.  */

number decrement_number (number n)
{
  number answer;
  assert (!zerop (n));
  answer = n->one_less_;
  free (n);
  return answer;
}

/* Add 1 to a number.  */

number add_one (number n)
{
  number answer = malloc (sizeof (struct LinkedListNumber));
  answer->one_less_ = n;
  return answer;
}

/* Destroying a number.  */

void destroy_number (number n)
{
  while (!zerop (n))
    n = decrement_number (n);
```

```
}

/* Copy a number.  This function is needed only because of memory
   allocation.  */

number copy_number (number n)
{
  number answer = make_zero ();
  while (!zerop (n)) {
    answer = add_one (answer);
    n = n->one_less_;
  }
  return answer;
}

/* Add two numbers.  */

number add (number n1, number n2)
{
  number answer = copy_number (n2);
  number addend = n1;
  while (!zerop (addend)) {
    answer = add_one (answer);
    addend = addend->one_less_;
  }
  return answer;
}

/* Subtract a number from another.  */

number subtract (number n1, number n2)
{
  number answer = copy_number (n1);
  number subtrahend = n2;
  while (!zerop (subtrahend)) {
    assert (!zerop (answer));
    answer = decrement_number (answer);
    subtrahend = subtrahend->one_less_;
  }
  return answer;
}

/* Return the product of two numbers.  */

number product (number n1, number n2)
{
  number answer = make_zero ();
  number multiplicand = n1;
  while (!zerop (multiplicand)) {
    number answer2 = add (answer, n2);
    destroy_number (answer);
```

continues

Listing A.4   **Continued**

```
    answer = answer2;
    multiplicand = multiplicand->one_less_;
  }
  return answer;
}

/* Return nonzero if number is even.  */

number even (number n)
{
  if (zerop (n))
    return add_one (make_zero ());
  else
    return odd (n->one_less_);
}

/* Return nonzero if number is odd.  */

number odd (number n)
{
  if (zerop (n))
    return make_zero ();
  else
    return even (n->one_less_);
}

/* Convert a string representing a decimal integer into a "number".  */

number string_to_number (char * char_number)
{
  number answer = make_zero ();
  int num = strtoul (char_number, (char **) 0, 0);
  while (num != 0) {
    answer = add_one (answer);
    --num;
  }
  return answer;
}

/* Convert a "number" into an "unsigned int".  */

unsigned number_to_unsigned_int (number n)
{
  unsigned answer = 0;
  while (!zerop (n)) {
    n = n->one_less_;
    ++answer;
  }
  return answer;
}
```

The functions in Listing A.5 implement a stack of unary numbers using a linked list.

Listing A.5   (*stack.c*) **Unary Number Stack**
```
/* Provide a stack of "number"s.  */

#include <assert.h>
#include <stdlib.h>
#include "definitions.h"

/* Create an empty stack.  */

Stack create_stack ()
{
  return 0;
}

/* Return nonzero if the stack is empty.  */

int empty_stack (Stack stack)
{
  return stack == 0;
}

/* Remove the number at the top of a nonempty stack.  If the stack is
   empty, abort.  */

number pop_stack (Stack* stack)
{
  number answer;
  Stack rest_of_stack;

  assert (!empty_stack (*stack));
  answer = (*stack)->element_;
  rest_of_stack = (*stack)->next_;
  free (*stack);
  *stack = rest_of_stack;
  return answer;
}

/* Add a number to the beginning of a stack.  */

void push_stack (Stack* stack, number n)
{
  Stack new_stack = malloc (sizeof (struct StackElement));
  new_stack->element_ = n;
  new_stack->next_ = *stack;
  *stack = new_stack;
}

/* Remove all the stack's elements.  */
```

continues

Listing A.5   **Continued**

```
void clear_stack (Stack* stack)
{
  while (!empty_stack (*stack)) {
    number top = pop_stack (stack);
    destroy_number (top);
  }
}
```

Listing A.6 contains declarations for stacks and numbers.

Listing A.6   *(definitions.h)* **Header File for number.c and stack.c**

```
#ifndef DEFINITIONS_H
#define DEFINITIONS_H 1

/* Implement a number using a linked list.  */
struct LinkedListNumber
{
  struct LinkedListNumber*
                one_less_;
};
typedef struct LinkedListNumber* number;

/* Implement a stack of numbers as a linked list.  Use 0 to represent
   an empty stack.  */
struct StackElement
{
  number        element_;
  struct        StackElement* next_;
};
typedef struct StackElement* Stack;

/* Operate on the stack of numbers.  */
Stack create_stack ();
int empty_stack (Stack stack);
number pop_stack (Stack* stack);
void push_stack (Stack* stack, number n);
void clear_stack (Stack* stack);

/* Operations on numbers.  */
number make_zero ();
void destroy_number (number n);
number add (number n1, number n2);
number subtract (number n1, number n2);
number product (number n1, number n2);
number even (number n);
number odd (number n);
number string_to_number (char* char_number);
unsigned number_to_unsigned_int (number n);

#endif /* DEFINITIONS_H */
```

B

Low-Level I/O

C PROGRAMMERS ON GNU/LINUX HAVE TWO SETS OF INPUT/OUTPUT functions at their disposal. The standard C library provides I/O functions: printf, fopen, and so on.[1] The Linux kernel itself provides another set of I/O operations that operate at a lower level than the C library functions.

Because this book is for people who already know the C language, we'll assume that you have encountered and know how to use the C library I/O functions.

Often there are good reasons to use Linux's low-level I/O functions. Many of these are kernel system calls[2] and provide the most direct access to underlying system capabilities that is available to application programs. In fact, the standard C library I/O routines are implemented on top of the Linux low-level I/O system calls. Using the latter is usually the most efficient way to perform input and output operations—and is sometimes more convenient, too.

---

1. The C++ standard library provides *iostreams* with similar functionality. The standard C library is also available in the C++ language.

2. See Chapter 8, "Linux System Calls," for an explanation of the difference between a system call and an ordinary function call.

Throughout this book, we assume that you're familiar with the calls described in this appendix. You may already be familiar with them because they're nearly the same as those provided on other UNIX and UNIX-like operating systems (and on the Win32 platform as well). If you're not familiar with them, however, read on; you'll find the rest of the book much easier to understand if you familiarize yourself with this material first.

B.1   Reading and Writing Data

The first I/O function you likely encountered when you first learned the C language was printf. This formats a text string and then prints it to standard output. The generalized version, fprintf, can print the text to a stream other than standard output. A stream is represented by a FILE* pointer. You obtain a FILE* pointer by opening a file with fopen. When you're done, you can close it with fclose. In addition to fprintf, you can use such functions as fputc, fputs, and fwrite to write data to the stream, or fscanf, fgetc, fgets, and fread to read data.

With the Linux low-level I/O operations, you use a handle called a *file descriptor* instead of a FILE* pointer. A file descriptor is an integer value that refers to a particular instance of an open file in a single process. It can be open for reading, for writing, or for both reading and writing. A file descriptor doesn't have to refer to an open file; it can represent a connection with another system component that is capable of sending or receiving data. For example, a connection to a hardware device is represented by a file descriptor (see Chapter 6, "Devices"), as is an open socket (see Chapter 5, "Interprocess Communication," Section 5.5, "Sockets") or one end of a pipe (see Section 5.4, "Pipes").

Include the header files <fcntl.h>, <sys/types.h>, <sys/stat.h>, and <unistd.h> if you use any of the low-level I/O functions described here.

B.1.1   Opening a File

To open a file and produce a file descriptor that can access that file, use the open call. It takes as arguments the path name of the file to open, as a character string, and flags specifying how to open it. You can use open to create a new file; if you do, pass a third argument that specifies the access permissions to set for the new file.

If the second argument is O_RDONLY, the file is opened for reading only; an error will result if you subsequently try to write to the resulting file descriptor. Similarly, O_WRONLY causes the file descriptor to be write-only. Specifying O_RDWR produces a file descriptor that can be used both for reading and for writing. Note that not all files may be opened in all three modes. For instance, the permissions on a file might forbid a particular process from opening it for reading or for writing; a file on a read-only device such as a CD-ROM drive may not be opened for writing.

You can specify additional options by using the bitwise or of this value with one or more flags. These are the most commonly used values:

- Specify O_TRUNC to truncate the opened file, if it previously existed. Data written to the file descriptor will replace previous contents of the file.

- Specify O_APPEND to append to an existing file. Data written to the file descriptor will be added to the end of the file.

- Specify O_CREAT to create a new file. If the filename that you provide to open does not exist, a new file will be created, provided that the directory containing it exists and that the process has permission to create files in that directory. If the file already exists, it is opened instead.

- Specify O_EXCL with O_CREAT to force creation of a new file. If the file already exists, the open call will fail.

If you call open with O_CREAT, provide an additional third argument specifying the permissions for the new file. See Chapter 10, "Security," Section 10.3, "File System Permissions," for a description of permission bits and how to use them.

For example, the program in Listing B.1 creates a new file with the filename specified on the command line. It uses the O_EXCL flag with open, so if the file already exists, an error occurs. The new file is given read and write permissions for the owner and owning group, and read permissions only for others. (If your umask is set to a nonzero value, the actual permissions may be more restrictive.)

Umasks

When you create a new file with open, some permission bits that you specify may be turned off. This is because your umask is set to a nonzero value. A process's umask specifies bits that are masked out of all newly created files' permissions. The actual permissions used are the bitwise and of the permissions you specify to open and the bitwise complement of the umask.

To change your umask from the shell, use the umask command, and specify the numerical value of the mask, in octal notation. To change the umask for a running process, use the umask call, passing it the desired mask value to use for subsequent open calls.

For example, calling this line

```
umask (S_IRWXO | S_IWGRP);
```

in a program, or invoking this command

```
% umask 027
```

specifies that write permissions for group members and read, write, and execute permissions for others will always be masked out of a new file's permissions.

Listing B.1 *(create-file.c)* **Create a New File**

```
#include <fcntl.h>
#include <stdio.h>
#include <sys/stat.h>
#include <sys/types.h>
#include <unistd.h>

int main (int argc, char* argv[])
{
  /* The path at which to create the new file.  */
  char* path = argv[1];
  /* The permissions for the new file.  */
  mode_t mode = S_IRUSR | S_IWUSR | S_IRGRP | S_IWGRP | S_IROTH;

  /* Create the file.  */
  int fd = open (path, O_WRONLY | O_EXCL | O_CREAT, mode);
  if (fd == -1) {
    /* An error occurred.  Print an error message and bail.  */
    perror ("open");
    return 1;
  }

  return 0;
}
```

Here's the program in action:

```
% ./create-file testfile
% ls -l testfile
-rw-rw-r--  1 samuel   users          0 Feb  1 22:47 testfile
% ./create-file testfile
open: File exists
```

Note that the length of the new file is 0 because the program didn't write any data to it.

B.1.2 Closing File Descriptors

When you're done with a file descriptor, close it with close. In some cases, such as the program in Listing B.1, it's not necessary to call close explicitly because Linux closes all open file descriptors when a process terminates (that is, when the program ends). Of course, once you close a file descriptor, you should no longer use it.

Closing a file descriptor may cause Linux to take a particular action, depending on the nature of the file descriptor. For example, when you close a file descriptor for a network socket, Linux closes the network connection between the two computers communicating through the socket.

Linux limits the number of open file descriptors that a process may have open at a time. Open file descriptors use kernel resources, so it's good to close file descriptors when you're done with them. A typical limit is 1,024 file descriptors per process. You can adjust this limit with the setrlimit system call; see Section 8.5, "getrlimit and setrlimit: Resource Limits," for more information.

B.1.3 Writing Data

Write data to a file descriptor using the `write` call. Provide the file descriptor, a pointer to a buffer of data, and the number of bytes to write. The file descriptor must be open for writing. The data written to the file need not be a character string; `write` copies arbitrary bytes from the buffer to the file descriptor.

The program in Listing B.2 appends the current time to the file specified on the command line. If the file doesn't exist, it is created. This program also uses the `time`, `localtime`, and `asctime` functions to obtain and format the current time; see their respective man pages for more information.

Listing B.2 **(*timestamp.c*) Append a Timestamp to a File**

```c
#include <fcntl.h>
#include <stdio.h>
#include <string.h>
#include <sys/stat.h>
#include <sys/types.h>
#include <time.h>
#include <unistd.h>

/* Return a character string representing the current date and time.  */

char* get_timestamp ()
{
  time_t now = time (NULL);
  return asctime (localtime (&now));
}

int main (int argc, char* argv[])
{
  /* The file to which to append the timestamp.  */
  char* filename = argv[1];
  /* Get the current timestamp.  */
  char* timestamp = get_timestamp ();
  /* Open the file for writing.  If it exists, append to it;
     otherwise, create a new file.  */
  int fd = open (filename, O_WRONLY | O_CREAT | O_APPEND, 0666);
  /* Compute the length of the timestamp string.  */
  size_t length = strlen (timestamp);
  /* Write the timestamp to the file.  */
  write (fd, timestamp, length);
  /* All done.  */
  close (fd);
  return 0;
}
```

Here's how the `timestamp` program works:

```
% ./timestamp tsfile
% cat tsfile
Thu Feb  1 23:25:20 2001
% ./timestamp tsfile
% cat tsfile
Thu Feb  1 23:25:20 2001
Thu Feb  1 23:25:47 2001
```

Note that the first time we invoke `timestamp`, it creates the file `tsfile`, while the second time it appends to it.

The `write` call returns the number of bytes that were actually written, or –1 if an error occurred. For certain kinds of file descriptors, the number of bytes actually written may be less than the number of bytes requested. In this case, it's up to you to call `write` again to write the rest of the data. The function in Listing B.3 demonstrates how you might do this. Note that for some applications, you may have to check for special conditions in the middle of the writing operation. For example, if you're writing to a network socket, you'll have to augment this function to detect whether the network connection was closed in the middle of the write operation, and if it has, to react appropriately.

Listing B.3   *(write-all.c)* **Write All of a Buffer of Data**

```c
/* Write all of COUNT bytes from BUFFER to file descriptor FD.
   Returns -1 on error, or the number of bytes written.  */

ssize_t write_all (int fd, const void* buffer, size_t count)
{
  size_t left_to_write = count;
  while (left_to_write > 0) {
    size_t written = write (fd, buffer, count);
    if (written == -1)
      /* An error occurred; bail.  */
      return -1;
    else
      /* Keep count of how much more we need to write.  */
      left_to_write -= written;
  }
  /* We should have written no more than COUNT bytes!  */
  assert (left_to_write == 0);
  /* The number of bytes written is exactly COUNT.  */
  return count;
}
```

B.1.4 Reading Data

The corresponding call for reading data is read. Like write, it takes a file descriptor, a pointer to a buffer, and a count. The count specifies how many bytes are read from the file descriptor into the buffer. The call to read returns –1 on error or the number of bytes actually read. This may be smaller than the number of bytes requested, for example, if there aren't enough bytes left in the file.

Reading DOS/Windows Text Files

After reading this book, we're positive that you'll choose to write all your programs for GNU/Linux. However, your programs may occasionally need to read text files generated by DOS or Windows programs. It's important to anticipate an important difference in how text files are structured between these two platforms.

In GNU/Linux text files, each line is separated from the next with a newline character. A newline is represented by the character constant '\n', which has ASCII code 10. On Windows, however, lines are separated by a two-character combination: a carriage return character (the character '\r,' which has ASCII code 13), followed by a newline character.

Some GNU/Linux text editors display ^M at the end of each line when showing a Windows text file—this is the carriage return character. Emacs displays Windows text files properly but indicates them by showing (DOS) in the mode line at the bottom of the buffer. Some Windows editors, such as Notepad, display all the text in a GNU/Linux text file on a single line because they expect a carriage return at the end of each line. Other programs for both GNU/Linux and Windows that process text files may report mysterious errors when given as input a text file in the wrong format.

If your program reads text files generated by Windows programs, you'll probably want to replace the sequence '\r\n' with a single newline. Similarly, if your program writes text files that must be read by Windows programs, replace lone newline characters with '\r\n' combinations. You must do this whether you use the low-level I/O calls presented in this appendix or the standard C library I/O functions.

Listing B.4 provides a simple demonstration of read. The program prints a hexadecimal dump of the contents of the file specified on the command line. Each line displays the offset in the file and the next 16 bytes.

Listing B.4   (*hexdump.c*) **Print a Hexadecimal Dump of a File**

```
#include <fcntl.h>
#include <stdio.h>
#include <sys/stat.h>
#include <sys/types.h>
#include <unistd.h>

int main (int argc, char* argv[])
{
  unsigned char buffer[16];
  size_t offset = 0;
  size_t bytes_read;
```

continues

Listing B.4   **Continued**

```
    int i;

    /* Open the file for reading.  */
    int fd = open (argv[1], O_RDONLY);

    /* Read from the file, one chunk at a time.  Continue until read
       "comes up short", that is, reads less than we asked for.
       This indicates that we've hit the end of the file.  */
    do {
      /* Read the next line's worth of bytes.  */
      bytes_read = read (fd, buffer, sizeof (buffer));
      /* Print the offset in the file, followed by the bytes themselves.  */
      printf ("0x%06x : ", offset);
      for (i = 0; i < bytes_read; ++i)
        printf ("%02x ", buffer[i]);
      printf ("\n");
      /* Keep count of our position in the file.  */
      offset += bytes_read;
    }
    while (bytes_read == sizeof (buffer));

    /* All done.  */
    close (fd);
    return 0;
  }
```

Here's hexdump in action. It's shown printing out a dump of its own executable file:

```
% ./hexdump hexdump
0x000000 : 7f 45 4c 46 01 01 01 00 00 00 00 00 00 00 00 00
0x000010 : 02 00 03 00 01 00 00 00 c0 83 04 08 34 00 00 00
0x000020 : e8 23 00 00 00 00 00 00 34 00 20 00 06 00 28 00
0x000030 : 1d 00 1a 00 06 00 00 00 34 00 00 00 34 80 04 08
...
```

Your output may be different, depending on the compiler you used to compile hexdump and the compilation flags you specified.

B.1.5   Moving Around a File

A file descriptor remembers its position in a file. As you read from or write to the file descriptor, its position advances corresponding to the number of bytes you read or write. Sometimes, however, you'll need to move around a file without reading or writing data. For instance, you might want to write over the middle of a file without modifying the beginning, or you might want to jump back to the beginning of a file and reread it without reopening it.

The `lseek` call enables you to reposition a file descriptor in a file. Pass it the file descriptor and two additional arguments specifying the new position.

- If the third argument is `SEEK_SET`, `lseek` interprets the second argument as a position, in bytes, from the start of the file.
- If the third argument is `SEEK_CUR`, `lseek` interprets the second argument as an offset, which may be positive or negative, from the current position.
- If the third argument is `SEEK_END`, `lseek` interprets the second argument as an offset from the end of the file. A positive value indicates a position beyond the end of the file.

The call to `lseek` returns the new position, as an offset from the beginning of the file. The type of the offset is `off_t`. If an error occurs, `lseek` returns –1. You can't use `lseek` with some types of file descriptors, such as socket file descriptors.

If you want to find the position of a file descriptor in a file without changing it, specify a 0 offset from the current position—for example:

```
off_t position = lseek (file_descriptor, 0, SEEK_CUR);
```

Linux enables you to use `lseek` to position a file descriptor beyond the end of the file. Normally, if a file descriptor is positioned at the end of a file and you write to the file descriptor, Linux automatically expands the file to make room for the new data. If you position a file descriptor beyond the end of a file and then write to it, Linux first expands the file to accommodate the "gap" that you created with the `lseek` operation and then writes to the end of it. This gap, however, does not actually occupy space on the disk; instead, Linux just makes a note of how long it is. If you later try to read from the file, it appears to your program that the gap is filled with 0 bytes.

Using this behavior of `lseek`, it's possible to create extremely large files that occupy almost no disk space. The program `lseek-huge` in Listing B.5 does this. It takes as command-line arguments a filename and a target file size, in megabytes. The program opens a new file, advances past the end of the file using `lseek`, and then writes a single 0 byte before closing the file.

Listing B.5   *(lseek-huge.c)* **Create Large Files with** *lseek*

```c
#include <fcntl.h>
#include <stdlib.h>
#include <sys/stat.h>
#include <sys/types.h>
#include <unistd.h>

int main (int argc, char* argv[])
{
  int zero = 0;
  const int megabyte = 1024 * 1024;

  char* filename = argv[1];
```

continues

Listing B.5   **Continued**

```
    size_t length = (size_t) atoi (argv[2]) * megabyte;

    /* Open a new file.  */
    int fd = open (filename, O_WRONLY | O_CREAT | O_EXCL, 0666);
    /* Jump to 1 byte short of where we want the file to end.  */
    lseek (fd, length - 1, SEEK_SET);
    /* Write a single 0 byte.  */
    write (fd, &zero, 1);
    /* All done.  */
    close (fd);

    return 0;
}
```

Using lseek-huge, we'll make a 1GB (1024MB) file. Note the free space on the drive before and after the operation.

```
% df -h .
Filesystem            Size  Used Avail Use% Mounted on
/dev/hda5             2.9G  2.1G  655M  76% /
% ./lseek-huge bigfile 1024
% ls -l bigfile
-rw-r-----   1 samuel    samuel    1073741824 Feb  5 16:29 bigfile
% df -h .
Filesystem            Size  Used Avail Use% Mounted on
/dev/hda5             2.9G  2.1G  655M  76% /
```

No appreciable disk space is consumed, despite the enormous size of bigfile. Still, if we open bigfile and read from it, it appears to be filled with 1GB worth of 0s. For instance, we can examine its contents with the hexdump program of Listing B.4.

```
% ./hexdump bigfile | head -10
0x000000 : 00 00 00 00 00 00 00 00 00 00 00 00 00 00 00 00
0x000010 : 00 00 00 00 00 00 00 00 00 00 00 00 00 00 00 00
0x000020 : 00 00 00 00 00 00 00 00 00 00 00 00 00 00 00 00
0x000030 : 00 00 00 00 00 00 00 00 00 00 00 00 00 00 00 00
0x000040 : 00 00 00 00 00 00 00 00 00 00 00 00 00 00 00 00
0x000050 : 00 00 00 00 00 00 00 00 00 00 00 00 00 00 00 00
...
```

If you run this yourself, you'll probably want to kill it with Ctrl+C, rather than watching it print out 2^{30} 0 bytes.

Note that these magic gaps in files are a special feature of the ext2 file system that's typically used for GNU/Linux disks. If you try to use lseek-huge to create a file on some other type of file system, such as the fat or vfat file systems used to mount DOS and Windows partitions, you'll find that the resulting file does actually occupy the full amount of disk space.

Linux does not permit you to rewind before the start of a file with lseek.

B.2   *stat*

Using open and read, you can extract the contents of a file. But how about other information? For instance, invoking ls -l displays, for the files in the current directory, such information as the file size, the last modification time, permissions, and the owner.

The stat call obtains this information about a file. Call stat with the path to the file you're interested in and a pointer to a variable of type struct stat. If the call to stat is successful, it returns 0 and fills in the fields of the structure with information about that file; otherwise, it returns -1.

These are the most useful fields in struct stat:

- st_mode contains the file's access permissions. File permissions are explained in Section 10.3, "File System Permissions."

- In addition to the access permissions, the st_mode field encodes the type of the file in higher-order bits. See the text immediately following this bulleted list for instructions on decoding this information.

- st_uid and st_gid contain the IDs of the user and group, respectively, to which the file belongs. User and group IDs are described in Section 10.1, "Users and Groups."

- st_size contains the file size, in bytes.

- st_atime contains the time when this file was last accessed (read or written).

- st_mtime contains the time when this file was last modified.

These macros check the value of the st_mode field value to figure out what kind of file you've invoked stat on. A macro evaluates to true if the file is of that type.

S_ISBLK (*mode*)	block device
S_ISCHR (*mode*)	character device
S_ISDIR (*mode*)	directory
S_ISFIFO (*mode*)	fifo (named pipe)
S_ISLNK (*mode*)	symbolic link
S_ISREG (*mode*)	regular file
S_ISSOCK (*mode*)	socket

The st_dev field contains the major and minor device number of the hardware device on which this file resides. Device numbers are discussed in Chapter 6. The major device number is shifted left 8 bits; the minor device number occupies the least significant 8 bits. The st_ino field contains the *inode number* of this file. This locates the file in the file system.

If you call stat on a symbolic link, stat follows the link and you can obtain the information about the file that the link points to, not about the symbolic link itself. This implies that S_ISLNK will never be true for the result of stat. Use the lstat function if you don't want to follow symbolic links; this function obtains information about the link itself rather than the link's target. If you call lstat on a file that isn't a symbolic link, it is equivalent to stat. Calling stat on a broken link (a link that points to a nonexistent or inaccessible target) results in an error, while calling lstat on such a link does not.

If you already have a file open for reading or writing, call fstat instead of stat. This takes a file descriptor as its first argument instead of a path.

Listing B.6 presents a function that allocates a buffer large enough to hold the contents of a file and then reads the file into the buffer. The function uses fstat to determine the size of the buffer that it needs to allocate and also to check that the file is indeed a regular file.

Listing B.6   *(read-file.c)* **Read a File into a Buffer**

```
#include <fcntl.h>
#include <stdio.h>
#include <sys/stat.h>
#include <sys/types.h>
#include <unistd.h>

/* Read the contents of FILENAME into a newly allocated buffer.  The
   size of the buffer is stored in *LENGTH.  Returns the buffer, which
   the caller must free.  If FILENAME doesn't correspond to a regular
   file, returns NULL.  */

char* read_file (const char* filename, size_t* length)
{
  int fd;
  struct stat file_info;
  char* buffer;

  /* Open the file.  */
  fd = open (filename, O_RDONLY);

  /* Get information about the file.  */
  fstat (fd, &file_info);
  *length = file_info.st_size;
  /* Make sure the file is an ordinary file.  */
  if (!S_ISREG (file_info.st_mode)) {
    /* It's not, so give up.  */
    close (fd);
    return NULL;
  }
```

```
/* Allocate a buffer large enough to hold the file's contents.  */
buffer = (char*) malloc (*length);
/* Read the file into the buffer.  */
read (fd, buffer, *length);

/* Finish up.  */
close (fd);
return buffer;
}
```

B.3 Vector Reads and Writes

The write call takes as arguments a pointer to the start of a buffer of data and the length of that buffer. It writes a contiguous region of memory to the file descriptor. However, a program often will need to write several items of data, each residing at a different part of memory. To use write, the program either will have to copy the items into a single memory region, which obviously makes inefficient use of CPU cycles and memory, or will have to make multiple calls to write.

For some applications, multiple calls to write are inefficient or undesirable. For example, when writing to a network socket, two calls to write may cause two packets to be sent across the network, whereas the same data could be sent in a single packet if a single call to write were possible.

The writev call enables you to write multiple discontiguous regions of memory to a file descriptor in a single operation. This is called a *vector write*. The cost of using writev is that you must set up a data structure specifying the start and length of each region of memory. This data structure is an array of struct iovec elements. Each element specifies one region of memory to write; the fields iov_base and iov_len specify the address of the start of the region and the length of the region, respectively. If you know ahead of time how many regions you'll need, you can simply declare a struct iovec array variable; if the number of regions can vary, you must allocate the array dynamically.

Call writev passing a file descriptor to write to, the struct iovec array, and the number of elements in the array. The return value is the total number of bytes written.

The program in Listing B.7 writes its command-line arguments to a file using a single writev call. The first argument is the name of the file; the second and subsequent arguments are written to the file of that name, one on each line. The program allocates an array of struct iovec elements that is twice as long as the number of arguments it is writing—for each argument it writes the text of the argument itself as well as a new line character. Because we don't know the number of arguments in advance, the array is allocated using malloc.

Listing B.7   (*write-args.c*) **Write the Argument List to a File with writev**

```c
#include <fcntl.h>
#include <stdlib.h>
#include <sys/stat.h>
#include <sys/types.h>
#include <sys/uio.h>
#include <unistd.h>

int main (int argc, char* argv[])
{
  int fd;
  struct iovec* vec;
  struct iovec* vec_next;
  int i;
  /* We'll need a "buffer" containing a newline character.  Use an
     ordinary char variable for this.  */
  char newline = '\n';
  /* The first command-line argument is the output filename.  */
  char* filename = argv[1];
  /* Skip past the first two elements of the argument list.  Element
     0 is the name of this program, and element 1 is the output
     filename.  */
  argc -= 2;
  argv += 2;

  /* Allocate an array of iovec elements.  We'll need two for each
     element of the argument list, one for the text itself, and one for
     a newline.  */
  vec = (struct iovec*) malloc (2 * argc * sizeof (struct iovec));

  /* Loop over the argument list, building the iovec entries.  */
  vec_next = vec;
  for (i = 0; i < argc; ++i) {
    /* The first element is the text of the argument itself.  */
    vec_next->iov_base = argv[i];
    vec_next->iov_len = strlen (argv[i]);
    ++vec_next;
    /* The second element is a single newline character.  It's okay for
       multiple elements of the struct iovec array to point to the
       same region of memory.  */
    vec_next->iov_base = &newline;
    vec_next->iov_len = 1;
    ++vec_next;
  }

  /* Write the arguments to a file.  */
  fd = open (filename, O_WRONLY | O_CREAT);
  writev (fd, vec, 2 * argc);
```

```
    close (fd);

    free (vec);
    return 0;
}
```

Here's an example of running `write-args`.

```
% ./write-args outputfile "first arg" "second arg" "third arg"
% cat outputfile
first arg
second arg
third arg
```

Linux provides a corresponding function `readv` that reads in a single operation into multiple discontiguous regions of memory. Similar to `writev`, an array of `struct iovec` elements specifies the memory regions into which the data will be read from the file descriptor.

B.4 Relation to Standard C Library I/O Functions

We mentioned earlier that the standard C library I/O functions are implemented on top of these low-level I/O functions. Sometimes, though, it's handy to use standard library functions with file descriptors, or to use low-level I/O functions on a standard library `FILE*` stream. GNU/Linux enables you to do both.

If you've opened a file using `fopen`, you can obtain the underlying file descriptor using the `fileno` function. This takes a `FILE*` argument and returns the file descriptor. For example, to open a file with the standard library `fopen` call but write to it with `writev`, you could use this code:

```
FILE* stream = fopen (filename, "w");
int file_descriptor = fileno (stream);
writev (file_descriptor, vector, vector_length);
```

Note that `stream` and `file_descriptor` correspond to the same opened file. If you call this line, you may no longer write to `file_descriptor`:

```
fclose (stream);
```

Similarly, if you call this line, you may no longer write to `stream`:

```
close (file_descriptor);
```

To go the other way, from a file descriptor to a stream, use the `fdopen` function. This constructs a `FILE*` stream pointer corresponding to a file descriptor. The `fdopen` function takes a file descriptor argument and a string argument specifying the mode in which to create the stream. The syntax of the mode argument is the same as that of the second argument to fopen, and it must be compatible with the file descriptor. For example, specify a mode of r for a read file descriptor or w for a write file descriptor. As with fileno, the stream and file descriptor refer to the same open file, so if you close one, you may not subsequently use the other.

B.5   Other File Operations

A few other operations on files and directories come in handy:

- getcwd obtains the current working directory. It takes two arguments, a char buffer and the length of the buffer. It copies the path of the current working directory into the buffer.

- chdir changes the current working directory to the path provided as its argument.

- mkdir creates a new directory. Its first argument is the path of the new directory. Its second argument is the access permissions to use for the new file. The interpretation of the permissions are the same as that of the third argument to open and are modified by the process's umask.

- rmdir deletes a directory. Its argument is the directory's path.

- unlink deletes a file. Its argument is the path to the file. This call can also be used to delete other file system objects, such as named pipes (see Section 5.4.5, "FIFOs") or devices (see Chapter 6).

  Actually, unlink doesn't necessarily delete the file's contents. As its name implies, it unlinks the file from the directory containing it. The file is no longer listed in that directory, but if any process holds an open file descriptor to the file, the file's contents are not removed from the disk. Only when no process has an open file descriptor are the file's contents deleted. So, if one process opens a file for reading or writing and then a second process unlinks the file and creates a new file with the same name, the first process sees the old contents of the file rather than the new contents (unless it closes the file and reopens it).

- rename renames or moves a file. Its two arguments are the old path and the new path for the file. If the paths are in different directories, rename moves the file, as long as both are on the same file system. You can use rename to move directories or other file system objects as well.

B.6   Reading Directory Contents

GNU/Linux provides functions for reading the contents of directories. Although these aren't directly related to the low-level I/O functions described in this appendix, we present them here anyway because they're often useful in application programs.

To read the contents of a directory, follow these steps:

1. Call `opendir`, passing the path of the directory that you want to examine. The call to `opendir` returns a `DIR*` handle, which you'll use to access the directory contents. If an error occurs, the call returns NULL.

2. Call `readdir` repeatedly, passing the `DIR*` handle that you obtained from `opendir`. Each time you call `readdir`, it returns a pointer to a `struct dirent` instance corresponding to the next directory entry. When you reach the end of the directory's contents, `readdir` returns NULL.

   The `struct dirent` that you get back from `readdir` has a field d_name, which contains the name of the directory entry.

3. Call `closedir`, passing the `DIR*` handle, to end the directory listing operation.

Include `<sys/types.h>` and `<dirent.h>` if you use these functions in your program.

Note that if you need the contents of the directory arranged in a particular order, you'll have to sort them yourself.

The program in Listing B.8 prints out the contents of a directory. The directory may be specified on the command line, but if it is not specified, the program uses the current working directory. For each entry in the directory, it displays the type of the entry and its path. The `get_file_type` function uses `lstat` to determine the type of a file system entry.

Listing B.8   (*listdir.c*) **Print a Directory Listing**

```
#include <assert.h>
#include <dirent.h>
#include <stdio.h>
#include <string.h>
#include <sys/stat.h>
#include <sys/types.h>
#include <unistd.h>

/* Return a string that describes the type of the file system entry PATH.  */

const char* get_file_type (const char* path)
{
  struct stat st;
  lstat (path, &st);
  if (S_ISLNK (st.st_mode))
    return "symbolic link";
  else if (S_ISDIR (st.st_mode))
    return "directory";
  else if (S_ISCHR (st.st_mode))
    return "character device";
  else if (S_ISBLK (st.st_mode))
    return "block device";
```

continues

Listing B.8   **Continued**

```
    else if (S_ISFIFO (st.st_mode))
      return "fifo";
    else if (S_ISSOCK (st.st_mode))
      return "socket";
    else if (S_ISREG (st.st_mode))
      return "regular file";
    else
      /* Unexpected.  Each entry should be one of the types above.  */
      assert (0);
}

int main (int argc, char* argv[])
{
  char* dir_path;
  DIR* dir;
  struct dirent* entry;
  char entry_path[PATH_MAX + 1];
  size_t path_len;

  if (argc >= 2)
    /* If a directory was specified on the command line, use it.  */
    dir_path = argv[1];
  else
    /* Otherwise, use the current directory.  */
    dir_path = ".";
  /* Copy the directory path into entry_path.  */
  strncpy (entry_path, dir_path, sizeof (entry_path));
  path_len = strlen (dir_path);
  /* If the directory path doesn't end with a slash, append a slash.  */
  if (entry_path[path_len - 1] != '/') {
    entry_path[path_len] = '/';
    entry_path[path_len + 1] = '\0';
    ++path_len;
  }

  /* Start the listing operation of the directory specified on the
     command line.  */
  dir = opendir (dir_path);
  /* Loop over all directory entries.  */
  while ((entry = readdir (dir)) != NULL) {
    const char* type;
    /* Build the path to the directory entry by appending the entry
       name to the path name.  */
    strncpy (entry_path + path_len, entry->d_name,
             sizeof (entry_path) - path_len);
    /* Determine the type of the entry.  */
    type = get_file_type (entry_path);
    /* Print the type and path of the entry.  */
    printf ("%-18s: %s\n", type, entry_path);
  }
```

```
    /* All done.  */
    closedir (dir);
    return 0;
}
```

Here are the first few lines of output from listing the /dev directory. (Your output might differ somewhat.)

```
% ./listdir /dev
directory         : /dev/.
directory         : /dev/..
socket            : /dev/log
character device  : /dev/null
regular file      : /dev/MAKEDEV
fifo              : /dev/initctl
character device  : /dev/agpgart
...
```

To verify this, you can use the ls command on the same directory. Specify the -U flag to instruct ls not to sort the entries, and specify the -a flag to cause the current directory (.) and the parent directory (..) to be included.

```
% ls -lUa /dev
total 124
drwxr-xr-x    7 root     root        36864 Feb  1 15:14 .
drwxr-xr-x   22 root     root         4096 Oct 11 16:39 ..
srw-rw-rw-    1 root     root            0 Dec 18 01:31 log
crw-rw-rw-    1 root     root         1,  3 May  5  1998 null
-rwxr-xr-x    1 root     root        26689 Mar  2  2000 MAKEDEV
prw-------    1 root     root            0 Dec 11 18:37 initctl
crw-rw-r--    1 root     root        10, 175 Feb  3  2000 agpgart
...
```

The first character of each line in the output of ls indicates the type of the entry.

C

Table of Signals

TABLE C.1 LISTS SOME OF THE LINUX SIGNALS YOU'RE MOST LIKELY to encounter or use. Note that some signals have multiple interpretations, depending on where they occur.

The names of the signals listed here are defined as preprocessor macros. To use them in your program, include `<signal.h>`. The actual definitions are in `/usr/include/sys/signum.h`, which is included as part of `<signal.h>`.

For a full list of Linux signals, including a short description of each and the default behavior when the signal is delivered, consult the `signal` man page in Section 7 by invoking the following:

```
% man 7 signal
```

Table C.1 **Linux Signals**

Name	Description
SIGHUP	Linux sends a process this signal when it becomes disconnected from a terminal. Many Linux programs use SIGHUP for an unrelated purpose: to indicate to a running program that it should reread its configuration files.

continues

Table C.1   **Continued**

Name	Description
SIGINT	Linux sends a process this signal when the user tries to end it by pressing Ctrl+C.
SIGILL	A process gets this signal when it attempts to execute an illegal instruction. This could indicate that the program's stack is corrupted.
SIGABRT	The abort function causes the process to receive this signal.
SIGFPE	The process has executed an invalid floating-point math instruction. Depending on how the CPU is configured, an invalid floating-point operation may return a special non-number value such as inf (infinity) or NaN (not a number) instead of raising SIGFPE.
SIGKILL	This signal ends a process immediately and cannot be handled.
SIGUSR1	This signal is reserved for application use.
SIGUSR2	This signal is reserved for application use.
SIGSEGV	The program attempted an invalid memory access. The access may be to an address that is invalid in the process's virtual memory space, or the access may be forbidden by the target memory's permissions. Dereferencing a "wild pointer" can cause a SIGSEGV.
SIGPIPE	The program has attempted to access a broken data stream, such as a socket connection that has been closed by the other party.
SIGALRM	The alarm system call schedules the delivery of this signal at a later time. See Section 8.13, "setitimer: Setting Interval Timers," in Chapter 8, "Linux System Calls," for information about setitimer, a generalized version of alarm.
SIGTERM	This signal requests that a process terminate. This is the default signal sent by the kill command.
SIGCHLD	Linux sends a process this signal when a child process exits. See Section 3.4.4, "Cleaning Up Children Asynchronously," in Chapter 3, "Processes."
SIGXCPU	Linux sends a process this signal when it exceeds the limit of CPU time that it can consume. See Section 8.5, "getrlimit and setrlimit: Resource Limits," in Chapter 8 for information on CPU time limits.
SIGVTALRM	The setitimer schedules the delivery of this signal at a future time. See Section 8.13, "setitimer: Setting Interval Timers."

D

Online Resources

$\mathbf{T}$HIS APPENDIX LISTS SOME PLACES TO VISIT ON THE INTERNET to learn more about programming for the GNU/Linux system.

D.1 General Information

- `http://www.advancedlinuxprogramming.com` is this book's home on the Internet. Here, you can download the full text of this book and program source code, find links to other online resources, and get more information about programming GNU/Linux. The same information can also be found at `http://www.newriders.com`.

- `http://www.linuxdoc.org` is the home of the Linux Documentation Project. This site is a repository for a wealth of documentation, FAQ lists, HOWTOs, and other documentation about GNU/Linux systems and software.

D.2   Information About GNU/Linux Software

- `http://www.gnu.org` is the home of the GNU Project. From this site, you can download a staggering array of sophisticated free software applications. Among them is the GNU C library, which is part of every GNU/Linux system and contains many of the functions described in this book. The GNU Project site also provides information about how you can contribute to the development of the GNU/Linux system by writing code or documentation, by using free software, and by spreading the free software message.

- `http://www.kernel.org` is the primary site for distribution of the Linux kernel source code. For the trickiest and most technically detailed questions about how Linux works, the source code is the best place to look. See also the `Documentation` directory for explanation of the kernel internals.

- `http://www.linuxhq.com` also distributes Linux kernel sources, patches, and related information.

- `http://gcc.gnu.org` is the home of the GNU Compiler Collection (GCC). GCC is the primary compiler used on GNU/Linux systems, and it includes compilers for C, C++, Objective C, Java, Chill, and Fortran.

- `http://www.gnome.org` and `http://www.kde.org` are the homes of the two most popular GNU/Linux windowing environments, Gnome and KDE. If you plan to write an application with a graphical user interface, you should familiarize yourself with either or both.

D.3   Other Sites

- `http://developer.intel.com` provides information about Intel processor architectures, including the x86 (IA32) architecture. If you are developing for x86 Linux and you use inline assembly instructions, the technical manuals available here will be very useful.

- `http://www.amd.com/devconn/` provides similar information about AMD's line of microprocessors and its special features.

- `http://freshmeat.net` is an index of open source software, generally for GNU/Linux. This site is one of the best places to stay abreast of the newest releases of GNU/Linux software, from core system components to more obscure, specialized applications.

- `http://www.linuxsecurity.com` contains information, techniques, and links to software related to GNU/Linux security. The site is of interest to users, system administrators, and developers.

E

Open Publication License
Version 1.0

I. Requirements on Both Unmodified and Modified Versions

The Open Publication works may be reproduced and distributed in whole or in part, in any medium, physical or electronic, provided that the terms of this license are adhered to and that this license or an incorporation of it by reference (with any options elected by the author(s) and/or publisher) is displayed in the reproduction.

Proper form for an incorporation by reference is as follows:

Copyright© <year> by <author's name or designee>. This material may be distributed only subject to the terms and conditions set forth in the Open Publication License, vX.Y or later (the latest version is presently available at http://www.opencontent.org/openpub/).

The reference must be immediately followed with any options elected by the author(s) or publisher of the document (see Section VI, "License Options").

Commercial redistribution of Open Publication-licensed material is permitted.

Any publication in standard (paper) book form shall require the citation of the original publisher and author. The publisher and author's names shall appear on all outer surfaces of the book. On all outer surfaces of the book, the original publisher's name shall be as large as the title of the work and cited as possessive with respect to the title.

II. Copyright

The copyright to each Open Publication is owned by its author(s) or designee.

III. Scope of License

The following license terms apply to all Open Publication works, unless otherwise explicitly stated in the document.

Mere aggregation of Open Publication works or a portion of an Open Publication work with other works or programs on the same media shall not cause this license to apply to those other works. The aggregate work shall contain a notice specifying the inclusion of the Open Publication material and appropriate copyright notice.

- **Severability.** If any part of this license is found to be unenforceable in any jurisdiction, the remaining portions of the license remain in force.

- **No warranty.** Open Publication works are licensed and provided "as is" without warranty of any kind, express or implied, including, but not limited to, the implied warranties of merchantability and fitness for a particular purpose or a warranty of noninfringement.

IV. Requirements on Modified Works

All modified versions of documents covered by this license, including translations, anthologies, compilations, and partial documents, must meet the following requirements:

1. The modified version must be labeled as such.

2. The person making the modifications must be identified, and the modifications must be dated.

3. Acknowledgement of the original author and publisher, if applicable, must be retained according to normal academic citation practices.

4. The location of the original unmodified document must be identified.

5. The original author's (or authors') name(s) may not be used to assert or imply endorsement of the resulting document without the original author's (or authors') permission.

V. Good-Practice Recommendations

In addition to the requirements of this license, it is requested from and strongly recommended of redistributors that:

1. If you are distributing Open Publication works on hard copy or CD-ROM, you provide email notification to the authors of your intent to redistribute at least 30 days before your manuscript or media freeze, to give the authors time to provide updated documents. This notification should describe modifications, if any, made to the document.

2. All substantive modifications (including deletions) be either clearly marked up in the document or else described in an attachment to the document.

3. Finally, although it is not mandatory under this license, it is considered good form to offer a free copy of any hard copy and CD-ROM expression of an Open Publication-licensed work to its author(s).

VI. License Options

The author(s) or publisher of an Open Publication-licensed document may elect certain options by appending language to the reference to or copy of the license. These options are considered part of the license instance and must be included with the license (or its incorporation by reference) in derived works.

A. To prohibit distribution of substantively modified versions without the explicit permission of the author(s). "Substantive modification" is defined as a change to the semantic content of the document and excludes mere changes in format or typographical corrections.

   To accomplish this, add the phrase "Distribution of substantively modified versions of this document is prohibited without the explicit permission of the copyright holder" to the license reference or copy.

B. To prohibit any publication of this work or derivative works in whole or in part in standard (paper) book form for commercial purposes is prohibited unless prior permission is obtained from the copyright holder.

   To accomplish this, add the phrase "Distribution of the work or derivative of the work in any standard (paper) book form is prohibited unless prior permission is obtained from the copyright holder" to the license reference or copy.

Open Publication Policy Appendix

(This is not considered part of the license.)

   Open Publication works are available in source format via the Open Publication home page at http://works.opencontent.org/.

   Open Publication authors who want to include their own license on Open Publication works may do so, as long as their terms are not more restrictive than the Open Publication license.

   If you have questions about the Open Publication License, please contact David Wiley, or the Open Publication Authors' List at opal@opencontent.org, via email.

   To subscribe to the Open Publication Authors' List, send email to opal-request@opencontent.org with the word "subscribe" in the body.

To post to the Open Publication Authors' List, send email to `opal@opencontent.org`, or simply reply to a previous post.

To unsubscribe from the Open Publication Authors' List, send email to `opal-request@opencontent.org` with the word "unsubscribe" in the body.

GNU General Public License[1]

Preamble

The licenses for most software are designed to take away your freedom to share and change it. By contrast, the GNU General Public License is intended to guarantee your freedom to share and change free software—to make sure the software is free for all its users. This General Public License applies to most of the Free Software Foundation's software and to any other program whose authors commit to using it. (Some other Free Software Foundation software is covered by the GNU Library General Public License instead.) You can apply it to your programs, too.

When we speak of free software, we are referring to freedom, not price. Our General Public Licenses are designed to make sure that you have the freedom to distribute copies of free software (and charge for this service if you wish), that you receive source code or can get it if you want it, that you can change the software or use pieces of it in new free programs; and that you know you can do these things.

1. This license can also be found online at http://www.gnu.org/copyleft/gpl.html.

To protect your rights, we need to make restrictions that forbid anyone to deny you these rights or to ask you to surrender the rights. These restrictions translate to certain responsibilities for you if you distribute copies of the software, or if you modify it.

For example, if you distribute copies of such a program, whether gratis or for a fee, you must give the recipients all the rights that you have. You must make sure that they, too, receive or can get the source code. And you must show them these terms so they know their rights.

We protect your rights with two steps: (1) copyright the software, and (2) offer you this license which gives you legal permission to copy, distribute and/or modify the software.

Also, for each author's protection and ours, we want to make certain that everyone understands that there is no warranty for this free software. If the software is modified by someone else and passed on, we want its recipients to know that what they have is not the original, so that any problems introduced by others will not reflect on the original authors' reputations.

Finally, any free program is threatened constantly by software patents. We wish to avoid the danger that redistributors of a free program will individually obtain patent licenses, in effect making the program proprietary. To prevent this, we have made it clear that any patent must be licensed for everyone's free use or not licensed at all.

The precise terms and conditions for copying, distribution and modification follow.

Terms and Conditions for Copying, Distribution and Modification

0. This License applies to any program or other work which contains a notice placed by the copyright holder saying it may be distributed under the terms of this General Public License. The "Program," below, refers to any such program or work, and a "work based on the Program" means either the Program or any derivative work under copyright law: that is to say, a work containing the Program or a portion of it, either verbatim or with modifications and/or translated into another language. (Hereinafter, translation is included without limitation in the term "modification.") Each licensee is addressed as "you."

    Activities other than copying, distribution and modification are not covered by this License; they are outside its scope. The act of running the Program is not restricted, and the output from the Program is covered only if its contents constitute a work based on the Program (independent of having been made by running the Program). Whether that is true depends on what the Program does.

1. You may copy and distribute verbatim copies of the Program's source code as you receive it, in any medium, provided that you conspicuously and appropriately publish on each copy an appropriate copyright notice and disclaimer of warranty; keep intact all the notices that refer to this License and to the absence

of any warranty; and give any other recipients of the Program a copy of this License along with the Program.

You may charge a fee for the physical act of transferring a copy, and you may at your option offer warranty protection in exchange for a fee.

2. You may modify your copy or copies of the Program or any portion of it, thus forming a work based on the Program, and copy and distribute such modifications or work under the terms of Section 1 above, provided that you also meet all of these conditions:

   - a) You must cause the modified files to carry prominent notices stating that you changed the files and the date of any change.

   - b) You must cause any work that you distribute or publish, that in whole or in part contains or is derived from the Program or any part thereof, to be licensed as a whole at no charge to all third parties under the terms of this License.

   - c) If the modified program normally reads commands interactively when run, you must cause it, when started running for such interactive use in the most ordinary way, to print or display an announcement including an appropriate copyright notice and a notice that there is no warranty (or else, saying that you provide a warranty) and that users may redistribute the program under these conditions, and telling the user how to view a copy of this License. (Exception: if the Program itself is interactive but does not normally print such an announcement, your work based on the Program is not required to print an announcement.)

These requirements apply to the modified work as a whole. If identifiable sections of that work are not derived from the Program, and can be reasonably considered independent and separate works in themselves, then this License, and its terms, do not apply to those sections when you distribute them as separate works. But when you distribute the same sections as part of a whole which is a work based on the Program, the distribution of the whole must be on the terms of this License, whose permissions for other licensees extend to the entire whole, and thus to each and every part regardless of who wrote it.

Thus, it is not the intent of this section to claim rights or contest your rights to work written entirely by you; rather, the intent is to exercise the right to control the distribution of derivative or collective works based on the Program.

In addition, mere aggregation of another work not based on the Program with the Program (or with a work based on the Program) on a volume of a storage or distribution medium does not bring the other work under the scope of this License.

3. You may copy and distribute the Program (or a work based on it, under Section 2) in object code or executable form under the terms of Sections 1 and 2 above provided that you also do one of the following:

- a) Accompany it with the complete corresponding machine-readable source code, which must be distributed under the terms of Sections 1 and 2 above on a medium customarily used for software interchange; or,

- b) Accompany it with a written offer, valid for at least three years, to give any third party, for a charge no more than your cost of physically performing source distribution, a complete machine-readable copy of the corresponding source code, to be distributed under the terms of Sections 1 and 2 above on a medium customarily used for software interchange; or,

- c) Accompany it with the information you received as to the offer to distribute corresponding source code. (This alternative is allowed only for noncommercial distribution and only if you received the program in object code or executable form with such an offer, in accord with Subsection b above.)

The source code for a work means the preferred form of the work for making modifications to it. For an executable work, complete source code means all the source code for all modules it contains, plus any associated interface definition files, plus the scripts used to control compilation and installation of the executable. However, as a special exception, the source code distributed need not include anything that is normally distributed (in either source or binary form) with the major components (compiler, kernel, and so on) of the operating system on which the executable runs, unless that component itself accompanies the executable.

If distribution of executable or object code is made by offering access to copy from a designated place, then offering equivalent access to copy the source code from the same place counts as distribution of the source code, even though third parties are not compelled to copy the source along with the object code.

4. You may not copy, modify, sublicense, or distribute the Program except as expressly provided under this License. Any attempt otherwise to copy, modify, sublicense or distribute the Program is void, and will automatically terminate your rights under this License. However, parties who have received copies, or rights, from you under this License will not have their licenses terminated so long as such parties remain in full compliance.

5. You are not required to accept this License, since you have not signed it. However, nothing else grants you permission to modify or distribute the Program or its derivative works. These actions are prohibited by law if you do not accept this License. Therefore, by modifying or distributing the Program (or any work based on the Program), you indicate your acceptance of this License to do so, and all its terms and conditions for copying, distributing or modifying the Program or works based on it.

6. Each time you redistribute the Program (or any work based on the Program), the recipient automatically receives a license from the original licensor to copy, distribute or modify the Program subject to these terms and conditions. You may not impose any further restrictions on the recipients' exercise of the rights granted herein. You are not responsible for enforcing compliance by third parties to this License.

7. If, as a consequence of a court judgment or allegation of patent infringement or for any other reason (not limited to patent issues), conditions are imposed on you (whether by court order, agreement or otherwise) that contradict the conditions of this License, they do not excuse you from the conditions of this License. If you cannot distribute so as to satisfy simultaneously your obligations under this License and any other pertinent obligations, then as a consequence you may not distribute the Program at all. For example, if a patent license would not permit royalty-free redistribution of the Program by all those who receive copies directly or indirectly through you, then the only way you could satisfy both it and this License would be to refrain entirely from distribution of the Program.

If any portion of this section is held invalid or unenforceable under any particular circumstance, the balance of the section is intended to apply and the section as a whole is intended to apply in other circumstances.

It is not the purpose of this section to induce you to infringe any patents or other property right claims or to contest validity of any such claims; this section has the sole purpose of protecting the integrity of the free software distribution system, which is implemented by public license practices. Many people have made generous contributions to the wide range of software distributed through that system in reliance on consistent application of that system; it is up to the author/donor to decide if he or she is willing to distribute software through any other system and a licensee cannot impose that choice.

This section is intended to make thoroughly clear what is believed to be a consequence of the rest of this License.

8. If the distribution and/or use of the Program is restricted in certain countries either by patents or by copyrighted interfaces, the original copyright holder who places the Program under this License may add an explicit geographical distribution limitation excluding those countries, so that distribution is permitted only in or among countries not thus excluded. In such case, this License incorporates the limitation as if written in the body of this License.

9. The Free Software Foundation may publish revised and/or new versions of the General Public License from time to time. Such new versions will be similar in spirit to the present version, but may differ in detail to address new problems or concerns.

Each version is given a distinguishing version number. If the Program specifies a version number of this License which applies to it and "any later version", you have the option of following the terms and conditions either of that version or of any later version published by the Free Software Foundation. If the Program does not specify a version number of this License, you may choose any version ever published by the Free Software Foundation.

10. If you wish to incorporate parts of the Program into other free programs whose distribution conditions are different, write to the author to ask for permission. For software which is copyrighted by the Free Software Foundation, write to the Free Software Foundation; we sometimes make exceptions for this. Our decision will be guided by the two goals of preserving the free status of all derivatives of our free software and of promoting the sharing and reuse of software generally.

No Warranty

11. BECAUSE THE PROGRAM IS LICENSED FREE OF CHARGE, THERE IS NO WARRANTY FOR THE PROGRAM, TO THE EXTENT PERMITTED BY APPLICABLE LAW. EXCEPT WHEN OTHERWISE STATED IN WRITING THE COPYRIGHT HOLDERS AND/OR OTHER PARTIES PROVIDE THE PROGRAM "AS IS" WITHOUT WARRANTY OF ANY KIND, EITHER EXPRESSED OR IMPLIED, INCLUDING, BUT NOT LIMITED TO, THE IMPLIED WARRANTIES OF MERCHANTABILITY AND FITNESS FOR A PARTICULAR PURPOSE. THE ENTIRE RISK AS TO THE QUALITY AND PERFORMANCE OF THE PROGRAM IS WITH YOU. SHOULD THE PROGRAM PROVE DEFECTIVE, YOU ASSUME THE COST OF ALL NECESSARY SERVICING, REPAIR OR CORRECTION.

12. IN NO EVENT UNLESS REQUIRED BY APPLICABLE LAW OR AGREED TO IN WRITING WILL ANY COPYRIGHT HOLDER, OR ANY OTHER PARTY WHO MAY MODIFY AND/OR REDISTRIBUTE THE PROGRAM AS PERMITTED ABOVE, BE LIABLE TO YOU FOR DAMAGES, INCLUDING ANY GENERAL, SPECIAL, INCIDENTAL OR CONSEQUENTIAL DAMAGES ARISING OUT OF THE USE OR INABILITY TO USE THE PROGRAM (INCLUDING BUT NOT LIMITED TO LOSS OF DATA OR DATA BEING RENDERED INACCURATE OR LOSSES SUSTAINED BY YOU OR THIRD PARTIES OR A FAILURE OF THE PROGRAM TO OPERATE WITH ANY OTHER PROGRAMS), EVEN IF SUCH HOLDER OR OTHER PARTY HAS BEEN ADVISED OF THE POSSIBILITY OF SUCH DAMAGES.

End of Terms and Conditions

How to Apply These Terms to Your New Programs

If you develop a new program, and you want it to be of the greatest possible use to the public, the best way to achieve this is to make it free software which everyone can redistribute and change under these terms.

To do so, attach the following notices to the program. It is safest to attach them to the start of each source file to most effectively convey the exclusion of warranty; and each file should have at least the "copyright" line and a pointer to where the full notice is found.

one line to give the program's name and an idea of what it does.

Copyright © yyyy name of author

This program is free software; you can redistribute it and/or modify it under the terms of the GNU General Public License as published by the Free Software Foundation; either version 2 of the License, or (at your option) any later version.

This program is distributed in the hope that it will be useful, but WITHOUT ANY WARRANTY; without even the implied warranty of MERCHANTABILITY or FITNESS FOR A PARTICULAR PURPOSE. See the GNU General Public License for more details.

You should have received a copy of the GNU General Public License along with this program; if not, write to the Free Software Foundation, Inc., 59 Temple Place–Suite 330, Boston, MA 02111-1307, USA.

Also add information on how to contact you by electronic and paper mail.

If the program is interactive, make it output a short notice like this when it starts in an interactive mode:

Gnomovision version 69, Copyright © year name of author

Gnomovision comes with ABSOLUTELY NO WARRANTY; for details type 'show w'. This is free software, and you are welcome to redistribute it under certain conditions; type 'show c' for details.

The hypothetical commands 'show w' and 'show c' should show the appropriate parts of the General Public License. Of course, the commands you use may be called something other than 'show w' and 'show c'; they could even be mouse-clicks or menu items—whatever suits your program.

You should also get your employer (if you work as a programmer) or your school, if any, to sign a "copyright disclaimer" for the program, if necessary. Here is a sample; alter the names:

Yoyodyne, Inc., hereby disclaims all copyright interest in the program 'Gnomovision' (which makes passes at compilers) written by James Hacker.

signature of Ty Coon, 1 April 1989

Ty Coon, President of Vice

This General Public License does not permit incorporating your program into proprietary programs. If your program is a subroutine library, you may consider it more useful to permit linking proprietary applications with the library. If this is what you want to do, use the GNU Library General Public License instead of this License.

FSF & GNU inquiries & questions to gnu@gnu.org.

Comments on these web pages to webmasters@www.gnu.org, send other questions to gnu@gnu.org.

Copyright notice above.

Free Software Foundation, Inc., 59 Temple Place–Suite 330, Boston, MA 02111, USA

Updated: 31 Jul 2000 jonas

Index

A

abort function, terminating processes, 55

accept function, 119

access speed, shared memory, 96–97

access system call, 169–170

accessing
character devices, 134–135
devices by opening files, 133
FIFOs, 115–116
terminals, 135

active processes, viewing, 46–47

addresses
Internet-domain sockets, 123
sockets, 117

alarm system call, 185

allocation. *See also* memory allocation; resource allocation
semaphores (processes), 101
shared memory, 97-98

app.c (program with library functions), listing 2.8, 37

ar command, 37

archives (static libraries), 37–38
versus shared libraries, 41–42

argc parameter (main function), 18–19

arglist.c (argc and argv parameters), listing 2.1, 18–19

argument list, 18–19
command-line options, 19
getopt_long function, 20-23
processes, 152-154

arguments, thread
defined, 62
passing data, 64–65

argv parameter (main function), 18–19

asm statement (assembly code), 189–190
GCC conversion of, 191
maintenance and portability, 196
optimization, 196
syntax, 191–192
assembler instructions, 192
clobbered registers, 194

input operands, 193
output operands, 192-193
versus C code, performance, 194–196
when to use, 190

assembler instructions, asm syntax, 192

assembly code, 189–190
asm syntax, 191–192
assembler instructions, 192
clobbered registers, 194
input operands, 193
output operands, 192-193
GCC conversion of asm, 191
maintenance and portability, 196
optimization, 196
versus C code, performance, 194–196
when to use, 190

assert macro (error checking), 30–31

asynchronously cancelable threads, 70

atomic operations, defined, 79

attachment, shared memory, 98–99

attributes, thread
customized, 68–69
defined, 62

audio, playing sound files, 135

authentication, 208–211

B

better_sleep.c (high-precision sleep), listing 8.8, 182

binary semaphores. *See* semaphores (processes)

bind function, 119

bit position, determining (assembly code versus C code), 194–196

bit-pos-asm.c (bit position with bsrl), listing 9.2, 195

bit-pos-loop.c (bit position with loop), listing 9.1, 194–195

block devices
defined, 130
list of, 133–134
loopback devices, 139–142
warning about, 130

blocking functions, defined, 34

HOW TO CONTACT US

VOICES THAT MATTER

VISIT OUR WEB SITE

WWW.NEWRIDERS.COM

On our Web site, you'll find information about our other books, authors, tables of contents, and book errata. You will also find information about book registration and how to purchase our books, both domestically and internationally.

EMAIL US

Contact us at: **nrfeedback@newriders.com**

- If you have comments or questions about this book
- To report errors that you have found in this book
- If you have a book proposal to submit or are interested in writing for New Riders
- If you are an expert in a computer topic or technology and are interested in being a technical editor who reviews manuscripts for technical accuracy

Contact us at: **nreducation@newriders.com**

- If you are an instructor from an educational institution who wants to preview New Riders books for classroom use. Email should include your name, title, school, department, address, phone number, office days/hours, text in use, and enrollment, along with your request for desk/examination copies and/or additional information.

Contact us at: **nrmedia@newriders.com**

- If you are a member of the media who is interested in reviewing copies of New Riders books. Send your name, mailing address, and email address, along with the name of the publication or Web site you work for.

BULK PURCHASES/CORPORATE SALES

If you are interested in buying 10 or more copies of a title or want to set up an account for your company to purchase directly from the publisher at a substantial discount, contact us at 800-382-3419 or email your contact information to corpsales@pearsontechgroup.com. A sales representative will contact you with more information.

WRITE TO US

New Riders Publishing
201 W. 103rd St.
Indianapolis, IN 46290-1097

CALL/FAX US

Toll-free (800) 571-5840
If outside U.S. (317) 581-3500
Ask for New Riders
FAX: (317) 581-4663

New Riders

ISBN: 073570998X
Available Summer 2001
US $39.99

Embedded Linux

John Lombardo

Embedded Linux provides the reader the information needed to design, develop, and debug an embedded Linux appliance. It explores why Linux is a great choice for an embedded application and what to look for when choosing hardware.

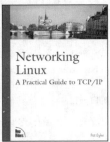

ISBN: 0735710317
400 pages
US $39.99

Networking Linux: A Practical Guide to TCP/IP

Pat Eyler

This book goes beyond the conceptual and shows the necessary know-how to Linux TCP/IP implementation step-by-step. It is ideal for programmers and networking administrators who are in need of a platform-specific guide in order to increase their knowledge and overall efficiency.

ISBN: 0735710643
Available Summer 2001
US $49.99

Berkeley DB

Sleepycat Software

This book is a tutorial on using the Berkeley DB, covering methods, architecture, data applications, memory, and configuring the APIs in Perl, Java, and Tcl, etc. The second part of the book is a reference section of the various Berkeley DB APIs.

ISBN: 0735710201
1152 pages
US $49.99

Inside XML

Steven Holzner

Inside XML is a foundation book that covers both the Microsoft and non-Microsoft approach to XML programming. It covers in detail the hot aspects of XML, such as DTD's vs. XML Schemas, CSS, XSL, XSLT, Xlinks, Xpointers, XHTML, RDF, CDF, parsing XML in Perl and Java, and much more.

ISBN 073570970X
500 pages
US $39.99

PHP Functions Essential Reference

The *PHP Functions Essential Reference* is a simple, clear, and authoritative function reference that clarifies and expands upon PHP's existing documentation. It will help the reader write effective code that makes full use of the rich variety of functions available in PHP.

Solutions from experts you know and trust.

www.informit.com

New Riders has partnered with **InformIT.com** to bring technical information to your desktop. Drawing on New Riders authors and reviewers to provide additional information on topics you're interested in, **InformIT.com** has free, in-depth information you won't find anywhere else.

- **Master the skills you need, when you need them**

- **Call on resources from some of the best minds in the industry**

- **Get answers when you need them, using InformIT's comprehensive library or live experts online**

- **Go above and beyond what you find in New Riders books, extending your knowledge**

As an **InformIT** partner, **New Riders** has shared the wisdom and knowledge of our authors with you online. Visit **InformIT.com** to see what you're missing.

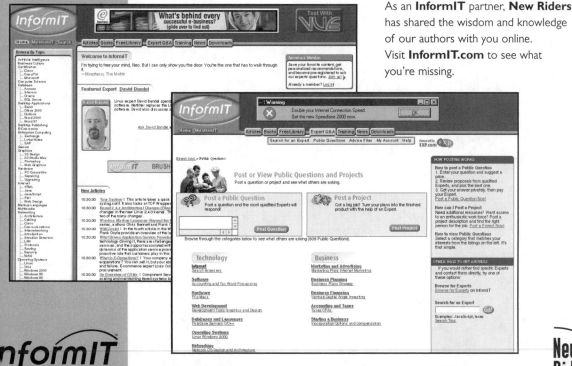

Colophon

The ruins of the Stabian Baths in Pompeii, captured by photographer Mel Curtis, are featured on the cover of this book. Said to be the largest and oldest of the baths, the Stabian baths also offered massages and poetry readings. Residents of Pompeii visited these public baths daily. The baths are named for their location on Stabian Street.

This book was written and edited in LaTeX, and then converted to Microsoft Word by New Riders and laid out in QuarkXPress. The font used for the body text is Bembo and MCPdigital. It was printed on 50# Husky Offset Smooth paper at R.R. Donnelley & Sons in Crawfordsville, Indiana. Prepress consisted of PostScript computer-to-plate technology (filmless process). The cover was printed at Moore Langen Printing in Terre Haute, Indiana, on Carolina, coated on one side.

Vladimir Svirsky
2875 Greenspoint Parkway
Candlewood Suites #344
Hoffman Estates, IL 60195

- -

PACKING SLIP:
Amazon Marketplace Item: Advanced Linux Programming [Paperback] by LLC, CodeSourcery; Mitchell,
Mark L
Listing ID: 0108F591513
SKU:
Quantity: 1

Purchased on: 08-Jan-2005
Shipped by: diana@multimedialibrary.com
Shipping address:

Ship to: Vladimir Svirsky
Address Line 1: 2875 Greenspoint Parkway
Address Line 2: Candlewood Suites #344
City: Hoffman Estates
State/Province/Region: IL
Zip/Postal Code: 60195
Country: United States